THE COMPLETE HOMEMADE DINNER COOKBOOK

100 Easy, and Delicious Recipes for Busy Nights

Fast and Flavorful Dishes to Make Every Evening Special

D1519012

Emma Johnson

Welcome to The Complete Homemade Dinner Cookbook

Life is busy, and finding time to prepare a homemade meal can sometimes feel impossible. Whether you're juggling work, family, or other commitments, cooking dinner may feel like just one more task on an already full to-do list. But what if you could create a satisfying, homemade dinner every night in less time than you think? This cookbook is here to make that possible.

The Complete Homemade Dinner Cookbook was designed with you in mind—to help busy individuals and families quickly prepare healthy, delicious, and memorable meals. With 100 easy-to-follow recipes, this book will show you how to transform your evenings by bringing the warmth and flavor of homemade cooking back into your kitchen, even on the busiest nights.

Benefits of Homemade Dinners

Cooking at home is more than just a way to fill your stomach; it offers a wide range of benefits for your health, budget, and overall well-being. When you cook at home, you control the ingredients, ensuring that your meals are fresh, nutritious, and tailored to your taste preferences. You can skip the added sugars, preservatives, and unhealthy fats often found in takeout or processed foods.

In addition to health benefits, homemade dinners are a fantastic way to save money. With just a few key ingredients, you can create meals that are not only satisfying but also cost-effective, avoiding the high prices of dining out or ordering takeout.

And perhaps most importantly, cooking at home brings families together. Whether it's sharing a meal after a long day or involving your kids in the cooking process, preparing food at home creates opportunities for meaningful connection. Cooking together fosters creativity, teaches valuable skills, and creates lasting memories around the table.

How This Cookbook Works

This cookbook is designed to make homemade dinners both quick and easy. The recipes are simple, practical, and made with accessible ingredients that don't require hours of preparation. You won't find complex techniques here—just clear instructions that get you from start to finish in as little time as possible. Each recipe is carefully crafted to ensure it's flavorful and fulfilling, even on the busiest of nights.

The book is organized into categories that reflect the versatility of homemade meals. You'll find everything from 30-minute meals to one-pan wonders, ensuring there's something for every evening. Whether you're in the mood for a comforting pasta dish, a fresh, healthy salad, or a flavorful international-inspired meal, you'll find ideas that suit all tastes and dietary needs.

Additionally, this book includes helpful time-saving tips, meal prepping ideas, and tricks to streamline your cooking process—so you can spend less time in the kitchen and more time with your loved ones. With step-by-step instructions, along with options for quick substitutions and variations, this cookbook empowers you to prepare meals effortlessly.

The Complete Homemade Dinner Cookbook is about bringing simplicity, flavor, and ease into your kitchen. It's designed for those who want delicious dinners without the stress, so you can feel good about what's on your plate and enjoy more of the moments that matter.

Let's get started—because with the right recipes and a little time, homemade dinner can be both quick and enjoyable!

Warmly,

Emma Johnson

TABLE OF CONTENT

CHAPTER 1:
30-MINUTE MEALS

PRACTICAL TIPS

Cooking quick and delicious meals doesn't mean sacrificing quality, flavor, or nutrition. With the right techniques and planning, you can create satisfying dishes in just 30 minutes, making weeknight dinners effortless and enjoyable. Here are some practical tips to help you get the most out of this chapter:

1. Prepare Ahead of Time:

Plan Your Meals: Choose recipes that align with your ingredients and schedule. Having a plan saves precious time and ensures you have everything you need.

Pre-Chop Ingredients: Prepping vegetables, portioning proteins, or measuring out spices ahead of time can significantly speed up the cooking process. Store them in airtight containers in the fridge for quick access.

2. Master Mise en Place: Gather and measure all your ingredients before starting. This practice helps you stay organized and prevents any delays during cooking.

3. Use Multi-Functional Appliances: Invest in tools like a pressure cooker, air fryer, or food processor. These appliances can cut down cooking time and simplify tasks like chopping, blending, or even cooking.

4. Cook Smart with Shortcuts: Pre-Cooked Ingredients: Use pre-cooked proteins like rotisserie chicken, canned beans, or cooked grains to save time.

Frozen Vegetables: These are a lifesaver for quick meals. They're pre-washed, pre-chopped, and retain their nutritional value.

5. Optimize Cooking Methods: High Heat: Use high heat to sear proteins quickly or to stir-fry vegetables. This locks in flavor while minimizing cooking time.

One-Pot or One-Pan Meals: Reduce cleanup and cooking time by choosing recipes that use a single pot or pan, such as pasta dishes, stir-fries, or skillet meals.

Batch Cooking: Double up on recipes that reheat well, such as soups, stews, or casseroles. Leftovers can be a lifesaver on busy nights.

6. Layer Flavors Effectively: Quick meals rely on bold flavors. Use pantry staples like garlic, onions, citrus, and fresh herbs to enhance taste. Adding spices, sauces, or a splash of vinegar can elevate a dish instantly.

7. Stock Your Pantry and Freezer: Keep essential ingredients on hand, such as olive oil, canned tomatoes, broth, rice, pasta, and frozen proteins or vegetables. These staples can be turned into countless 30-minute meals.

8. Leverage Time-Saving Proteins:

Choose quick-cooking proteins like shrimp, chicken breasts, thinly sliced beef, tofu, or eggs. These can be cooked in minutes without compromising on flavor or texture.

9. Prep While You Cook: Multitask by chopping vegetables or preparing side dishes while your main course is simmering or baking.

10. Embrace Simplicity: Stick to recipes with minimal steps and straightforward techniques. A few high-quality ingredients, combined thoughtfully, can result in a delicious dish without unnecessary complexity.

11. Clean as You Go:

Keep your workspace tidy by cleaning utensils and countertops as you cook. This saves time at the end and keeps you organized throughout the process.

12. Customize for Your Tastes:

Adjust recipes to suit your preferences or dietary needs. Add extra vegetables for more nutrition, swap proteins for what's available, or use gluten-free pasta or grains when needed.

13. Make It Fun:

Cooking 30-minute meals should be an enjoyable process. Play music, experiment with flavors, or involve family members to make it a bonding activity.

LEMON HERB CHICKEN BREAST WITH MIXED GREENS

Yield: 4 servings **Prep**   **Time:** 10 minutes **Cook**   **Time:** 20 minutes **Total**   **Time:** 30 minutes

INGREDIENTS

For the Chicken:

- 4 boneless, skinless chicken breasts
- 3 tbsp olive oil, divided
- 2 tbsp fresh lemon juice
- 2 tsp lemon zest
- 3 garlic cloves, minced
- 1 tsp dried oregano
- 1 tsp dried thyme
- 1 tsp paprika
- ½ tsp salt
- ¼ tsp black pepper

For the Mixed Greens Salad:

- 6 cups mixed greens
- 1 cucumber, thinly sliced
- 1 cup cherry tomatoes, halved
- ¼ red onion, thinly sliced
- 2 tbsp olive oil
- 1 tbsp balsamic vinegar
- 1 tsp Dijon mustard
- Salt and pepper to taste

STEP-BY-STEP INSTRUCTIONS

1. Marinate the Chicken:

- In a small bowl, whisk together 2 tbsp olive oil, lemon juice, lemon zest, garlic, oregano, thyme, paprika, salt, and black pepper.
- Place the chicken breasts in a zip-top bag or shallow dish, pour the marinade over them, and coat evenly. Marinate at room temperature for 10 minutes or refrigerate for up to 1 hour.

2. Cook the Chicken:

- Preheat a large skillet over medium heat and add the remaining 1 tbsp olive oil.
- Remove the chicken from the marinade, shaking off excess liquid, and place it in the skillet.
- Cook for 5–6 minutes on each side until golden brown and the internal temperature reaches 165°F (74°C).
- Remove the chicken from the skillet and let it rest for 5 minutes.

3. Prepare the Salad:

- In a large bowl, combine mixed greens, cucumber, cherry tomatoes, and red onion.
- In a small bowl, whisk together olive oil, balsamic vinegar, Dijon mustard, salt, and pepper to make the dressing. Drizzle over the salad and toss to combine.

4. Serve:

- Slice the chicken breasts and serve them on top of the mixed greens salad. Garnish with extra lemon wedges if desired.

RECIPE VARIATIONS

- **Protein Alternatives:** Substitute chicken breasts with turkey cutlets, boneless pork chops, or tofu for a plant-based option.
- **Vegetable Additions:** Add roasted sweet potatoes, grilled asparagus, or avocado slices to the salad for extra flavor and texture.
- **Culinary Influences:** Incorporate Mediterranean flair with feta cheese and kalamata olives or Asian-inspired flavors by replacing lemon juice with lime juice and adding soy sauce to the marinade.

NUTRITIONAL INFORMATION (PER SERVING)

Calories: 290
Protein: 30g
Carbohydrates: ...6g

Fiber: 2g
Sugars: 3g
Fat: 17g

Saturated Fat: 3g
Cholesterol: 75mg
Sodium: 390mg

QUICK BEEF STIR-FRY WITH BROCCOLI

Yield: 4 servings   **Prep Time:** 10 minutes   **Cook Time:** 15 minutes   **Total Time:** 25 minutes

INGREDIENTS

For the Stir-Fry Sauce:

- 1/3 cup low-sodium soy sauce
- 2 tbsp oyster sauce or hoisin sauce
- 1 tbsp cornstarch
- 1 tbsp rice vinegar or apple cider vinegar
- 1 tbsp honey or brown sugar
- 1 tsp sesame oil
- 2 garlic cloves, minced
- 1 tsp grated fresh ginger

For the Stir-Fry:

- 1 lb beef sirloin or flank steak, thinly sliced against the grain
- 3 cups broccoli florets
- 1 red bell pepper, thinly sliced
- 2 tbsp vegetable oil or avocado oil
- 2 green onions, thinly sliced
- Sesame seeds
- Steamed white or brown rice, for serving

STEP-BY-STEP INSTRUCTIONS

1. Prepare the Sauce:

- In a small bowl, whisk together soy sauce, oyster sauce, cornstarch, rice vinegar, honey, sesame oil, garlic, and ginger. Set aside.

2. Cook the Broccoli:

- Bring a large pot of water to a boil. Add the broccoli florets and blanch for 2 minutes.
- Drain the broccoli and transfer it to a bowl of ice water to retain its vibrant color. Drain and set aside.

3. Sear the Beef:

- Heat 1 tbsp of vegetable oil in a large skillet or wok over high heat.
- Add the sliced beef in a single layer and cook for 1–2 minutes per side until browned but not fully cooked through. Remove the beef and set aside.

4. Stir-Fry the Vegetables:

- In the same skillet, add the remaining 1 tbsp of oil. Add the broccoli and red bell pepper (if using) and stir-fry for 2–3 minutes until crisp-tender.

5. Combine and Cook:

- Return the beef to the skillet. Pour in the sauce and toss everything together.
- Cook for an additional 2–3 minutes, stirring frequently, until the sauce thickens and coats the beef and vegetables.

6. Serve:

- Spoon the stir-fry over steamed rice. Garnish with green onions and sesame seeds, if desired.

Recipe Variations

- **Protein Alternatives:** Use chicken breast, pork tenderloin, shrimp, or tofu instead of beef.
- **Vegetable Additions:** Add snap peas, carrots, or zucchini for more variety. Use locally sourced vegetables for the freshest flavor.
- **Culinary Influences:** Add chili flakes for a spicy kick or replace soy sauce with tamari for a gluten-free option. Incorporate Thai flavors by adding a splash of coconut milk and lime juice.

NUTRITIONAL INFORMATION (PER SERVING)

Calories: 340	Fiber: 3g	Saturated Fat: 4g
Protein: 28g	Sugars: 6g	Cholesterol: 65mg
Carbohydrates: ...14g	Fat: 19g	Sodium: 740mg

SPAGHETTI CARBONARA SIMPLIFIED

Yield: 4 servings   **Prep Time:** 10 minutes   **Cook Time:** 15 minutes   **Total Time:** 25 minutes

INGREDIENTS

- 12 oz spaghetti (use locally made pasta if available)
- 4 oz pancetta or thick-cut bacon, diced
- 2 large eggs
- 2 large egg yolks
- ¾ cup grated Parmesan cheese (plus extra for garnish)
- 2 tbsp olive oil
- 1 garlic clove, smashed (optional for added flavor)
- 1 tsp freshly ground black pepper
- Salt, to taste
- 2 tbsp fresh parsley, chopped (optional garnish)

STEP-BY-STEP INSTRUCTIONS

1. Cook the Spaghetti:

- Bring a large pot of salted water to a boil. Add the spaghetti and cook until al dente according to package instructions.
- Reserve 1 cup of pasta water, then drain the spaghetti and set aside.

2. Prepare the Pancetta:

- While the pasta cooks, heat olive oil in a large skillet over medium heat.
- Add the pancetta or bacon and cook until crisp, stirring occasionally (about 4–5 minutes).
- If using, add the garlic clove to the skillet for an extra layer of flavor, then discard before proceeding. Remove the skillet from heat but leave the pancetta in the pan.

3. Make the Sauce:

- In a bowl, whisk together the eggs, egg yolks, Parmesan cheese, and black pepper until smooth.

4. Combine the Pasta and Sauce:

- Add the cooked spaghetti to the skillet with the pancetta. Toss to coat the pasta in the rendered fat.

- Gradually pour the egg mixture over the pasta, tossing quickly to prevent the eggs from scrambling. The residual heat from the pasta will cook the sauce to a creamy consistency.
- If the sauce is too thick, add reserved pasta water a little at a time until the desired consistency is reached.

5. Season and Serve:

- Taste and adjust with additional salt and pepper, if needed.
- Plate the pasta, sprinkle with fresh parsley and extra Parmesan, and serve immediately.

RECIPE VARIATIONS

- **Meat Alternatives:** Swap pancetta for prosciutto, smoked ham, or turkey bacon for a lighter twist.
- **Vegetarian Option:** Replace pancetta with sautéed mushrooms or roasted zucchini for a plant-based version.
- **Global Influences:** Add a pinch of chili flakes for heat or substitute Parmesan with Pecorino Romano for a sharper flavor.
- **Seasonal Additions:** Incorporate fresh peas or asparagus during spring for added freshness.

NUTRITIONAL INFORMATION (PER SERVING)

Calories: 480	Fiber: 3g	Saturated Fat: 7g
Protein: 19g	Sugars:............... 2g	Cholesterol: 190mg
Carbohydrates: ...52g	Fat: 20g	Sodium: 600mg

SHRIMP TACOS WITH AVOCADO SALSA

Yield: 4 servings   **Prep Time:** 10 minutes   **Cook Time:** 10 minutes   **Total Time:** 20 minutes

INGREDIENTS

For the Shrimp:

- 1 lb shrimp (peeled and deveined, tail removed)
- 1 tbsp olive oil
- 1 tsp chili powder
- 1 tsp smoked paprika
- ½ tsp ground cumin
- ½ tsp garlic powder
- ¼ tsp cayenne pepper (optional, for heat)
- ½ tsp salt
- ¼ tsp black pepper

For the Avocado Salsa:

- 2 ripe avocados, diced
- 1 cup cherry tomatoes, halved (use locally grown tomatoes if in season)
- ½ small red onion, finely diced
- 1 small jalapeño, seeded and finely chopped (optional)
- 2 tbsp fresh lime juice (about 1 lime)
- 2 tbsp fresh cilantro, chopped
- Salt and pepper to taste

For Assembly:

- 8 small corn or flour tortillas
- 2 cups shredded cabbage (red or green)
- ½ cup sour cream or Greek yogurt
- 1 tsp hot sauce (optional)
- Lime wedges for serving

STEP-BY-STEP INSTRUCTIONS

1. Prepare the Shrimp: In a bowl, toss the shrimp with olive oil, chili powder, smoked paprika, cumin, garlic powder, cayenne pepper (if using), salt, and black pepper until well coated.

2. Cook the Shrimp: Heat a large skillet over medium-high heat. Add the shrimp and cook for 2–3 minutes per side until they are pink, opaque, and cooked through. Remove from the skillet and set aside.

3. Make the Avocado Salsa:

- In a medium bowl, combine diced avocados, cherry tomatoes, red onion, jalapeño (if using), lime juice, and cilantro.
- Season with salt and pepper to taste. Gently toss to combine.

4. Warm the Tortillas: Heat the tortillas in a dry skillet over medium heat for about 30 seconds per side, or wrap them in foil and warm them in a 350°F (175°C) oven for 5 minutes.

5. Assemble the Tacos:

- Layer shredded cabbage on each tortilla, followed by a few shrimp.
- Top with a generous spoonful of avocado salsa.
- Drizzle with sour cream or Greek yogurt and a dash of hot sauce if desired.

6. Serve: Garnish with lime wedges and serve immediately.

RECIPE VARIATIONS

- **Protein Alternatives:** Swap shrimp with grilled fish, chicken strips, or crispy tofu for a vegetarian version.
- **Topping Options:** Add roasted corn kernels, pickled onions, or queso fresco for extra flavor.
- **Global Twist:** Use sriracha mayo instead of sour cream for an Asian-inspired flair or add mango chunks to the salsa for a tropical vibe.

NUTRITIONAL INFORMATION (PER SERVING)

Calories: 340	Fiber: 6g	Saturated Fat: 4g
Protein: 23g	Sugars: 3g	Cholesterol: 180mg
Carbohydrates: ...25g	Fat: 18g	Sodium: 670mg

VEGGIE-PACKED FRIED RICE

Yield: 4 servings   **Prep Time:** 10 minutes   **Cook Time:** 15 minutes   **Total Time:** 25 minutes

INGREDIENTS

For the Fried Rice:

- 2 cups cooked rice
- 1 tbsp sesame oil
- 1 tbsp vegetable oil
- 1 small onion, diced
- 1 cup carrots, diced
- 1 cup peas
- 1 red bell pepper, diced
- 2 garlic cloves, minced
- 2 large eggs, beaten
- 3 tbsp low-sodium soy sauce
- 1 tbsp rice vinegar
- 1 tsp honey or brown sugar
- 1 tsp ground ginger
- 2 green onions, sliced
- 1 tbsp toasted sesame seeds

STEP-BY-STEP INSTRUCTIONS

1. Prepare the Rice: If using freshly cooked rice, spread it on a baking sheet to cool down and separate the grains. Day-old rice works best, as it's drier and less sticky.

2. Cook the Vegetables:

Heat sesame oil and vegetable oil in a large skillet or wok over medium-high heat.

Add diced onion, carrots, and bell pepper. Stir-fry for 3–4 minutes until the vegetables are tender but still crisp.

Add the garlic and peas, and cook for another 2–3 minutes. Stir in the ginger, allowing the aroma to bloom.

3. Scramble the Eggs: Push the vegetables to the side of the skillet. Add the beaten eggs to the empty side and scramble until fully cooked, then mix with the vegetables.

4. Combine the Rice: Add the cooked rice to the skillet, breaking up any clumps. Stir everything together until the rice is evenly combined with the vegetables and eggs.

5. Add Flavoring: Drizzle the soy sauce, rice vinegar, and honey (if using) over the rice mixture. Stir well to coat all the ingredients. Taste and adjust seasoning as needed, adding more soy sauce or a pinch of salt if desired.

6. Serve: Garnish the fried rice with sliced green onions and sesame seeds. Serve hot, either as a main dish or as a side with your favorite protein.

RECIPE VARIATIONS

- **Protein Options:** Add cooked chicken, shrimp, tofu, or even ground beef for a heartier dish.

- **Vegetable Alternatives:** Use seasonal vegetables like zucchini, corn, or mushrooms for added flavor and nutrition. Try kale or spinach in place of peas for a different twist.

- **International Influences:** For a Thai-inspired version, add a bit of lime juice and fresh basil, or make a spicy version by stirring in some chili flakes or sriracha.

NUTRITIONAL INFORMATION (PER SERVING)

Calories: 280	Fiber: 5g	Saturated Fat: 1g
Protein: 8g	Sugars: 7g	Cholesterol: 120mg
Carbohydrates: ...42g	Fat: 10g	Sodium: 500mg

GARLIC BUTTER SALMON WITH GREEN BEANS

Yield: 4 servings **Prep Time:** 10 minutes **Cook Time:** 15–20 minutes **Total Time:** 25–30 minutes

INGREDIENTS

For the Garlic Butter Salmon:

- 4 salmon fillets (approximately 6 oz each)
- 4 tbsp unsalted butter, melted
- 4 garlic cloves, minced
- 1 tbsp fresh lemon juice
- 1 tsp dried thyme or 1 tbsp fresh thyme
- Salt and freshly ground black pepper
- 1 tbsp fresh parsley, chopped

For the Green Beans:

- 1 lb fresh green beans, trimmed
- 1 tbsp olive oil
- 2 garlic cloves, minced
- Salt and freshly ground black pepper to taste
- 1 tbsp lemon zest
- 1 tbsp toasted almonds

STEP-BY-STEP INSTRUCTIONS

1. Preheat the Oven: Preheat your oven to 400°F (200°C).

2. Prepare the Salmon:

- In a small bowl, mix the melted butter, minced garlic, lemon juice, thyme, salt, and pepper.
- Place the salmon fillets on a baking sheet lined with parchment paper or foil.
- Brush the garlic butter mixture generously over the top of each salmon fillet, making sure to coat them well.

3. Roast the Salmon: Place the salmon in the preheated oven and bake for 12–15 minutes, depending on the thickness of the fillets, until the salmon is cooked through and flakes easily with a fork. For crispier edges, broil the salmon for the last 2 minutes.

4. Prepare the Green Beans:

- While the salmon is roasting, heat olive oil in a large skillet over medium heat.
- Add the minced garlic and sauté for 30 seconds until fragrant.
- Add the trimmed green beans to the skillet and sauté for 4–5 minutes until tender but still slightly crisp.

Stir occasionally.

- Season with salt, pepper, and lemon zest. Toss to combine.
- Optional: For added texture, sprinkle with toasted almonds just before serving.

5. Serve: Plate the garlic butter salmon with a generous portion of the sautéed green beans on the side. Garnish the salmon with fresh parsley if desired. Serve immediately with extra lemon wedges on the side for squeezing.

RECIPE VARIATIONS

- **Protein Alternatives:** Swap the salmon for other fish like cod, tilapia, or trout, or use chicken breasts for a non-seafood version.
- **Vegetable Variations:** Swap green beans for asparagus, Brussels sprouts, or zucchini, depending on what's in season. Roasted root vegetables like carrots or sweet potatoes also pair beautifully with the garlic butter.
- **Flavor Twist:** Add a pinch of red pepper flakes to the green beans for a subtle heat, or drizzle balsamic glaze over the salmon for a tangy contrast.

NUTRITIONAL INFORMATION (PER SERVING)

Calories: 380	Fiber: 3g	Saturated Fat: 7g
Protein: 28g	Sugars: 4g	Cholesterol: 85mg
Carbohydrates: ...10g	Fat: 28g	Sodium: 350mg

CLASSIC CAPRESE SANDWICH

Yield: 2 servings   **Prep Time:** 10 minutes   **Cook Time:** 5 minutes   **Total Time:** 15 minutes

INGREDIENTS

For the Sandwich:

- 4 slices of fresh Italian bread or ciabatta
- 2 medium tomatoes, sliced
- 4 oz fresh mozzarella cheese, sliced
- 2 tbsp fresh basil leaves

- 2 tbsp extra virgin olive oil
- 1 tbsp balsamic vinegar
- Salt and freshly ground black pepper to taste

STEP-BY-STEP INSTRUCTIONS

1. Prepare the Ingredients:

- Wash and slice the tomatoes.
- Slice the mozzarella into thick, even pieces.
- Tear or roughly chop the fresh basil leaves.
- Toast the bread (optional): If you prefer a warm, crispy sandwich, toast the slices of bread lightly in a toaster or on a skillet over medium heat until golden brown.

2. Assemble the Sandwich:

- Lay the toasted or fresh slices of bread on a flat surface.
- On the bottom slice, layer the fresh mozzarella, tomato slices, and basil leaves.
- Drizzle with extra virgin olive oil and balsamic vinegar. Season with salt and pepper to taste.

3. Serve:

- Place the second slice of bread on top.
- Cut the sandwich in half diagonally for a beautiful presentation.

RECIPE VARIATIONS

- **Protein Additions:** For a heartier sandwich, add a few slices of prosciutto, grilled chicken, or turkey.
- **Vegetable Variations:** For extra crunch and flavor, add slices of cucumber, roasted red peppers, or arugula.
- **Different Cheese:** While mozzarella is traditional, you can experiment with burrata for an extra creamy texture or goat cheese for a tangy twist.
- **Global Twist:** For an Italian-American fusion, spread pesto on the bread before adding the other ingredients for a fresh, herbal flavor. Or, swap the balsamic vinegar for a drizzle of honey and chili flakes for a sweet and spicy combo.

NUTRITIONAL INFORMATION (PER SERVING)

Calories: 350	Fiber: 4g	Saturated Fat: 7g
Protein: 14g	Sugars: 6g	Cholesterol: 30mg
Carbohydrates: ...38g	Fat: 18g	Sodium: 420mg

CREAMY TOMATO BASIL SOUP

Yield: 4 servings   **Prep Time:** 10 minutes   **Cook Time:** 20 minutes   **Total Time:** 30 minutes

INGREDIENTS

For the Soup:

- 2 tbsp olive oil
- 1 medium onion, diced
- 3 garlic cloves, minced
- 2 cans (14.5 oz each) diced tomatoes
- 1 cup vegetable broth (or chicken)

- 1/2 cup heavy cream
- 1/4 cup fresh basil, chopped
- 1 tsp dried oregano
- Salt and freshly ground black pepper to taste
- 1 tbsp sugar
- 1 tbsp balsamic vinegar

For Garnish: Fresh basil leaves, Shaved Parmesan cheese

STEP-BY-STEP INSTRUCTIONS

1. Sauté the Aromatics:

- In a large pot, heat the olive oil over medium heat.
- Add the diced onion and sauté for about 5 minutes, or until it becomes soft and translucent.
- Add the minced garlic and cook for another minute, until fragrant.

2. Add Tomatoes and Broth:

- Add the diced tomatoes (or fresh tomatoes) to the pot. If using canned, include the juice.
- Stir in the vegetable broth and bring the mixture to a simmer.
- Let it cook for 10 minutes, allowing the tomatoes to break down and the flavors to meld.

3. Blend the Soup:

- Once the tomatoes are softened, use an immersion blender directly in the pot to blend the soup until smooth. Alternatively, you can carefully transfer the soup in batches to a blender. If you prefer a chunkier texture, blend only partially.

4. Add Cream and Basil:

- Lower the heat to medium-low and stir in the heavy cream.
- Add the chopped fresh basil, dried oregano (if using), salt, pepper, and optional sugar. Stir well. Taste and adjust seasoning as needed. If you like a touch of sweetness to balance the acidity of the tomatoes, add the sugar.

5. Simmer:

- Let the soup simmer for an additional 5-7 minutes to allow the flavors to develop. If desired, add the balsamic vinegar for an added layer of complexity.

6. Serve:

- Ladle the creamy tomato basil soup into bowls. Garnish with a few fresh basil leaves and shaved Parmesan, if using. Serve with crusty bread or a grilled cheese sandwich for a comforting meal.

RECIPE VARIATIONS

- **Protein Addition:** Stir in shredded rotisserie chicken or ground turkey for a heartier soup.
- **Dairy-Free Option:** Use coconut milk or almond milk instead of heavy cream for a dairy-free version.
- **Vegetable Twist:** Add roasted red peppers or carrots for extra flavor and color.
- **Spicy Kick:** Add a pinch of red pepper flakes or a dash of hot sauce for a spicy variation.
- **Global Influence:** Incorporate curry powder or smoked paprika for a twist on traditional flavors.

NUTRITIONAL INFORMATION (PER SERVING)

Calories: 250	Fiber: 4g	Saturated Fat: 8g
Protein: 4g	Sugars: 9g	Cholesterol: 40mg
Carbohydrates: ...18g	Fat: 19g	Sodium: 520mg

BBQ CHICKEN QUESADILLAS

Yield: 4 servings   **Prep Time:** 10 minutes   **Cook Time:** 15 minutes   **Total Time:** 25 minutes

INGREDIENTS

For the Quesadillas:

- 2 medium chicken breasts
- 1 tbsp olive oil
- 1/2 cup BBQ sauce
- 1 cup shredded cheddar cheese
- 1 cup shredded mozzarella cheese
- 4 large flour tortillas

- 1/4 cup red onion, thinly sliced
- 1/2 cup corn kernels
- 1/2 cup bell peppers, diced
- 1/4 cup fresh cilantro, chopped
- Salt and freshly ground black pepper to taste

For Optional Garnishes: Sour cream or Greek yogurt, Salsa, Fresh avocado slices

STEP-BY-STEP INSTRUCTIONS

1. Prepare the Chicken:

- Heat 1 tablespoon of olive oil in a large skillet over medium heat.
- Season both sides of the chicken breasts with salt and pepper.
- Add the chicken to the skillet and cook for 6-7 minutes per side or until the chicken is cooked through (internal temperature should reach 165°F).
- Remove the chicken from the skillet, let it rest for a few minutes, and then shred it using two forks.

2. Mix with BBQ Sauce:

- In a bowl, toss the shredded chicken with 1/2 cup of BBQ sauce until the chicken is evenly coated. Set aside.

3. Assemble the Quesadillas:

- Heat a large skillet or griddle over medium heat.
- Place a tortilla in the skillet and sprinkle with a small amount of mozzarella and cheddar cheese on one half.
- Add a generous portion of the BBQ chicken mixture, followed by some red onion slices, corn kernels, diced bell peppers, and fresh cilantro.
- Top with more cheese and fold the tortilla in half.

4. Cook the Quesadillas:

- Cook the quesadilla for 2-3 minutes on one side, or until the cheese begins to melt and the bottom is golden brown.
- Flip the quesadilla and cook for another 2-3 minutes, pressing gently to ensure the cheese melts completely and the tortilla crisps up.
- Remove from the skillet and slice into wedges.

5. Serve:

- Serve the quesadillas hot with a side of sour cream or Greek yogurt, salsa, and fresh avocado slices for added richness and flavor.

RECIPE VARIATIONS

- **Protein Options:** Use ground turkey, beef, or pork in place of chicken for a different flavor. You could also make it vegetarian by adding more vegetables like zucchini, mushrooms, or black beans.
- **Cheese Variations:** Swap the mozzarella and cheddar for a mix of pepper jack and Monterey Jack for a spicier kick.
- **Vegetable Additions:** Incorporate sautéed spinach, roasted sweet potatoes, or even jalapeños for extra flavor.
- **Global Twist:** Use a smoky chipotle BBQ sauce or add a bit of chipotle chili powder for a Mexican-inspired flair. For an Asian twist, swap the BBQ sauce with teriyaki or hoisin sauce and add slaw or pickled vegetables inside the quesadilla.

NUTRITIONAL INFORMATION (PER SERVING)

Calories: 450	Fiber: 3g	Saturated Fat: 9g
Protein: 30g	Sugars: 10g	Cholesterol: 70mg
Carbohydrates: ...40g	Fat: 22g	Sodium: 890mg

THAI PEANUT NOODLES

Yield: 4 servings   **Prep Time:** 10 minutes   **Cook Time:** 15 minutes   **Total Time:** 25 minutes

INGREDIENTS

For the Noodles:

- 8 oz rice noodles (or spaghetti)
- 1 tbsp sesame oil
- 1 tbsp olive oil
- 1 medium red bell pepper, julienned
- 1 medium carrot, julienned
- 1 cup broccoli florets
- 1/2 cup green onions, sliced
- 1/4 cup cilantro leaves, chopped
- 1/4 cup crushed peanuts (for garnish)

For the Peanut Sauce:

- 1/4 cup peanut butter
- 2 tbsp soy sauce or tamari
- 1 tbsp rice vinegar
- 1 tbsp honey or maple syrup
- 1 tsp fresh ginger, grated
- 1 garlic clove, minced
- 1 tsp lime juice
- 1-2 tbsp water
- 1/2 tsp chili flakes

STEP-BY-STEP INSTRUCTIONS

1. Cook the Noodles:

- Cook the rice noodles according to the package instructions (typically boiling for 4-5 minutes). Drain and rinse with cold water to stop the cooking process. Set aside.
- If using spaghetti, cook until al dente and rinse under cold water to prevent sticking.

2. Prepare the Peanut Sauce:

- In a small bowl, whisk together the peanut butter, soy sauce, rice vinegar, honey (or maple syrup), lime juice, minced garlic, and grated ginger.
- Gradually add water, one tablespoon at a time, until the sauce reaches a creamy and pourable consistency.
- Stir in chili flakes for a bit of heat, if desired.

3. Cook the Vegetables:

- In a large skillet or wok, heat the sesame oil and olive oil over medium heat.
- Add the julienned red bell pepper, carrot, and broccoli florets. Stir-fry for about 5-7 minutes, until the vegetables are tender-crisp and vibrant.

4. Combine Noodles and Sauce:

- Add the cooked noodles to the skillet with the vegetables.
- Pour the peanut sauce over the noodles and toss well to coat everything evenly. Continue cooking for another 2-3 minutes until the noodles are heated through.

5. Serve:

- Divide the noodles and vegetables among serving plates.
- Garnish with sliced green onions, fresh cilantro, and crushed peanuts. Serve with a wedge of lime on the side for extra freshness.

RECIPE VARIATIONS

- **Protein Additions:**

Chicken: Sauté bite-sized pieces of chicken breast or thigh in sesame oil before adding the vegetables.

Tofu: For a vegetarian option, pan-fry firm tofu cubes until golden brown and add them to the noodles.

Shrimp: Cook shrimp in sesame oil for 2-3 minutes per side, then toss with the noodles and sauce.

- **Vegetable Variations:** Swap the broccoli with snow peas, zucchini, or spinach for a different flavor and texture.

Add sliced mushrooms or bok choy for a more earthy, umami flavor.

- **Noodle Options:** You can substitute rice noodles with soba noodles, udon, or even spaghetti for a fusion twist.
- **Global Twist:** Add a spoonful of curry paste for a Thai-inspired curry peanut noodle variation.

For an Indonesian-style noodle dish, stir in some coconut milk to the sauce.

NUTRITIONAL INFORMATION (PER SERVING)

Calories: 380	Fiber: 6g	Saturated Fat: 3g
Protein: 12g	Sugars: 8g	Cholesterol: 0mg
Carbohydrates: ...45g	Fat: 18g	Sodium: 550mg

CHAPTER 2:
ONE-POT AND ONE-PAN WONDERS

PRACTICAL TIPS

Cooking with just one pot or pan is the ultimate way to save time and effort while still creating hearty, flavorful meals. These recipes are perfect for busy days or when you want to minimize cleanup without sacrificing taste or variety. Here are some tips to make the most of your one-pot and one-pan cooking adventures:

1. Choose the Right Equipment:

- **Nonstick Skillet or Cast-Iron Pan:** Great for stir-fries, skillet pastas, and pan-seared dishes.
- **Dutch Oven:** Ideal for soups, stews, and casseroles because it distributes heat evenly.
- **Sheet Pan:** Perfect for roasting vegetables, proteins, or even full meals like sheet pan dinners.
- **Slow Cooker or Instant Pot:** These are excellent for set-it-and-forget-it meals that require minimal hands-on time.

2. Layer Ingredients for Maximum Flavor:

- Start by sautéing aromatics like onions, garlic, or ginger to build a flavor base.
- Add proteins and vegetables in stages, depending on their cooking times, so everything finishes perfectly cooked.

3. Use Versatile Ingredients:

- Incorporate items that cook quickly and absorb flavors well, such as chicken thighs, shrimp, tofu, or canned beans.
- Opt for seasonal produce, like zucchini in summer or squash in fall, to keep recipes fresh and vibrant.

4. Master the Art of Deglazing:

- After sautéing, add a splash of broth, wine, or water to the pan to scrape up flavorful browned bits (fond) from the bottom. This adds depth to your dish.

5. Balance Liquid Levels:

- Avoid adding too much liquid at once, as it can dilute the flavors. You can always add more broth or water as needed during cooking.

6. Make It a Complete Meal:

- Include a mix of protein, vegetables, and a starch (like rice, pasta, or potatoes) in your dish for a balanced and satisfying one-pot or one-pan dinner.

7. Use the Oven Wisely:

- Many one-pan recipes finish beautifully in the oven, allowing flavors to meld and surfaces to caramelize. A stovetop-to-oven pan (like cast iron) makes this transition seamless.

8. Customize to Your Taste:

- Adjust seasoning and ingredients to suit your family's preferences. Swap proteins, change up the spices, or add extra veggies for more nutrients.

9. Embrace Prepped Ingredients:

- Save time by using pre-cut vegetables, rotisserie chicken, or canned goods like diced tomatoes and beans.

10. Cook in Batches:

- For larger families or meal prep, double your recipe. Many one-pot dishes store and reheat well, making them ideal for leftovers.

11. Don't Overcrowd the Pan:

- When roasting or stir-frying, leave space between ingredients to ensure they cook evenly and develop a nice sear.

12. Let Simmer for Perfection:

- Once all ingredients are combined, let your dish simmer gently. This helps flavors meld beautifully and allows proteins to become tender.

13. Enhance with Toppings:

- Finish with fresh herbs, grated cheese, toasted nuts, or a drizzle of olive oil to add brightness and texture.

14. Clean as You Cook:

- Since you're only using one pot or pan, keep the rest of your workspace tidy by cleaning utensils or chopping boards as you go.

15. Experiment with Global Flavors:

- One-pot meals are versatile and adapt easily to different cuisines. Try:
  - **Italian:** A skillet lasagna or creamy risotto.
  - **Mexican:** A one-pan enchilada bake or taco rice skillet.
  - **Asian:** Stir-fried noodles or Thai-inspired curries.
  - **Mediterranean:** One-pot chicken with olives, lemon, and rice.

CONCLUSION:

One-pot and one-pan cooking is all about simplifying your kitchen routine while delivering maximum flavor and nutrition. These dishes allow you to focus on enjoying the cooking process without worrying about a mountain of dishes afterward. With the right techniques and creativity, you can turn one pot or pan into endless possibilities for satisfying homemade meals.

ONE-PAN CHICKEN PARMESAN PASTA

Yield: 4 servings　　　**Prep Time:** 10 minutes　　　**Cook Time:** 25 minutes　　　**Total Time:** 35 minutes

INGREDIENTS

For the Chicken Parmesan:
- 2 boneless, skinless chicken breasts
- 1 cup all-purpose flour
- 2 large eggs, beaten
- 1 1/2 cups seasoned breadcrumbs
- 1/2 cup grated Parmesan cheese
- 1 tbsp Italian seasoning
- Salt and pepper, to taste
- 2 tbsp olive oil

For the Pasta & Sauce:
- 12 oz penne or rigatoni pasta
- 1 tbsp olive oil
- 3 cloves garlic, minced
- 1 can (14.5 oz) crushed tomatoes
- 1/2 cup tomato sauce
- 1/2 cup chicken broth
- 1 tsp dried basil
- 1/2 tsp red pepper flakes
- 1 cup shredded mozzarella cheese
- 1/4 cup fresh basil leaves, chopped
- Salt and pepper, to taste

STEP-BY-STEP INSTRUCTIONS

1. Prepare the Chicken:
- Preheat the oven to 375°F (190°C).
- Season the chicken breasts with salt, pepper, and Italian seasoning on both sides.
- In three shallow dishes, place the flour in one, beaten eggs in another, and a mixture of breadcrumbs and grated Parmesan in the third.
- Dredge each chicken breast in flour, dip into the beaten eggs, and then coat with the breadcrumb-Parmesan mixture, pressing down gently to ensure even coating.

2. Brown the Chicken:
- Heat 2 tablespoons of olive oil in a large oven-safe skillet over medium-high heat.
- Add the chicken breasts and cook for 3-4 minutes per side, until golden brown. The chicken doesn't need to be fully cooked yet, as it will finish in the oven.
- Remove the chicken from the skillet and set aside.

3. Make the Pasta Sauce:
- In the same skillet, add 1 tablespoon of olive oil and minced garlic. Cook for 1 minute, until fragrant.
- Add the crushed tomatoes, tomato sauce, chicken broth, dried basil, and red pepper flakes (if using). Stir to combine.
- Season with salt and pepper to taste. Bring the sauce to a simmer and cook for about 5 minutes to let the flavors meld.

4. Combine Chicken, Pasta, and Sauce:
- Add the uncooked pasta to the skillet with the sauce. Stir to combine and ensure the pasta is coated in the sauce.
- Place the chicken breasts on top of the pasta in the skillet.
- Sprinkle the mozzarella cheese evenly over the chicken and pasta.

5. Bake:
- Transfer the skillet to the preheated oven and bake for 15-20 minutes, or until the chicken reaches an internal temperature of 165°F (75°C) and the cheese is melted and bubbly.

6. Serve:
- Remove the skillet from the oven and let it cool for a few minutes.
- Garnish with freshly chopped basil leaves before serving.

RECIPE VARIATIONS
- Different Proteins:
  - **Turkey or Pork:** Swap the chicken for turkey or pork cutlets for a leaner alternative.
  - **Vegetarian Option:** Use eggplant slices or large portobello mushrooms as a substitute for the chicken to create a vegetarian version.
- Pasta Options:
  - Use any short pasta, like ziti, fusilli, or farfalle, depending on what's available. You could also opt for a gluten-free pasta.
- Veggie Additions:
  - Add sautéed spinach, zucchini, or bell peppers to the sauce for extra vegetables and flavor.
  - Toss in some olives or artichoke hearts for a Mediterranean twist.

NUTRITIONAL INFORMATION (PER SERVING)

Calories: 530	Carbohydrates: ...46g	Sugars: 8g	Saturated Fat: 6g
Protein: 40g	Fiber: 3g	Fat: 22g	Cholesterol: 105mg
			Sodium: 650mg

BEEF AND LENTIL CHILI

Yield: 6 servings   **Prep Time:** 10 minutes   **Cook Time:** 45 minutes   **Total Time:** 55 minutes

INGREDIENTS
For the Chili:
- 1 lb (450g) ground beef
- 1 medium onion, chopped
- 2 cloves garlic, minced
- 1 cup dried lentils, rinsed
- 1 can (14.5 oz) diced tomatoes
- 1 can (8 oz) tomato paste
- 1 can (15 oz) kidney beans, drained and rinsed
- 1 can (15 oz) black beans, drained and rinsed
- 1 1/2 cups beef broth
- 1 tbsp olive oil
- 1 tbsp chili powder
- 1 tsp ground cumin
- 1 tsp smoked paprika
- 1/2 tsp ground cinnamon
- 1/2 tsp dried oregano
- 1/4 tsp ground cayenne pepper
- Salt and pepper, to taste

For Topping (Optional):
- Fresh cilantro leaves, chopped
- Sour cream or plain Greek yogurt
- Shredded cheese
- Lime wedges

STEP-BY-STEP INSTRUCTIONS

1. Brown the Beef:
- In a large pot or Dutch oven, heat 1 tablespoon of olive oil over medium heat.
- Add the ground beef and cook, breaking it apart with a spoon, until browned and fully cooked, about 5-7 minutes.
- Drain any excess fat and set the beef aside on a plate.

2. Sauté the Vegetables:
- In the same pot, add the chopped onion and garlic. Sauté for 2-3 minutes, until softened and fragrant.
- Stir in the chili powder, cumin, paprika, cinnamon, oregano, and cayenne pepper (if using). Cook for an additional 1 minute, allowing the spices to bloom.

3. Add the Tomatoes, Beans, and Broth:
- Stir in the diced tomatoes (with juices), tomato paste, kidney beans, black beans, and beef broth.
- Bring the mixture to a simmer over medium-high heat.

4. Simmer the Chili:
- Add the lentils to the pot, stirring to combine. Reduce the heat to low and cover the pot.
- Let the chili simmer for 35-40 minutes, stirring occasionally, until the lentils are tender and the flavors have melded together. If the chili gets too thick, add a little more broth or water to reach your desired consistency.

5. Season to Taste:
- Once the lentils are cooked through, taste the chili and adjust the seasoning with salt, pepper, and more chili powder or cayenne if you want extra heat.

6. Serve:
- Ladle the chili into bowls and top with fresh cilantro, a dollop of sour cream or Greek yogurt, shredded cheese, and a squeeze of lime juice if desired. Serve hot with crusty bread or cornbread on the side for added comfort.

RECIPE VARIATIONS
- **Different Meats:**
  ◊ **Ground turkey or chicken:** Use ground turkey or chicken for a leaner version of this chili. You can also use ground pork for a slightly different flavor profile.
- **Vegetarian Version:** Omit the ground beef and double the lentils or use additional beans like pinto or chickpeas. Add more veggies such as bell peppers, zucchini, or carrots for extra heartiness.
- **Spice Adjustments:** If you prefer a milder chili, reduce or omit the cayenne pepper and use a mild chili powder. For a spicier version, increase the cayenne or add a chopped jalapeño during the sautéing process.
- **Regional Influences:** Add a touch of cocoa powder or dark chocolate for a mole-inspired twist, or stir in a splash of apple cider vinegar or a bit of honey for a touch of tangy-sweet balance.

NUTRITIONAL INFORMATION (PER SERVING)

			Saturated Fat: 4g
Calories: 380	Carbohydrates: ...40g	Sugars: 6g	Cholesterol: 55mg
Protein: 30g	Fiber: 12g	Fat: 12g	Sodium: 650mg

SHEET PAN SAUSAGE AND VEGGIES

Yield: 4 servings   **Prep Time:** 15 minutes   **Cook Time:** 25 minutes   **Total Time:** 40 minutes

INGREDIENTS
Base Ingredients:
- 4 (4 oz each) Italian sausage links (mild or spicy)
- 2 cups baby potatoes, halved
- 1 cup cherry tomatoes
- 1 cup zucchini, sliced into half-moons
- 1 cup bell peppers, sliced
- 1 medium red onion, cut into wedges

Seasoning Mix:
- 3 tbsp olive oil
- 1 tsp smoked paprika
- 1 tsp garlic powder
- 1/2 tsp dried thyme
- 1/2 tsp dried oregano
- 1/4 tsp red pepper flakes
- Salt and black pepper, to taste

Optional Garnish:
- Fresh parsley, chopped
- Grated Parmesan cheese

STEP-BY-STEP INSTRUCTIONS

1. Preheat the Oven:
- Preheat your oven to 425°F (220°C). Line a large baking sheet with parchment paper or foil for easy cleanup.

2. Prep the Veggies:
- Place the halved baby potatoes, cherry tomatoes, zucchini, bell peppers, and red onion in a large mixing bowl.

3. Season the Veggies:
- Drizzle the olive oil over the vegetables. Add smoked paprika, garlic powder, thyme, oregano, red pepper flakes (if using), salt, and black pepper. Toss well to coat evenly.

4. Arrange on the Sheet Pan:
- Spread the seasoned vegetables onto the prepared baking sheet in a single layer. Place the sausage links on top of the vegetables.

5. Bake:
- Bake in the preheated oven for 20–25 minutes, flipping the sausage halfway through. Cook until the sausages are browned and the vegetables are tender.

6. Broil (Optional):
- For extra caramelization, broil on high for 2–3 minutes, keeping an eye on the veggies and sausage to prevent burning.

7. Serve:
- Remove from the oven and let cool slightly. Garnish with fresh parsley and Parmesan cheese if desired. Serve warm with crusty bread or a side salad.

VARIATIONS AND ADAPTATIONS
Different Proteins:
- Use chicken sausage, turkey sausage, or even plant-based sausage for dietary preferences.

Vegetable Swaps:
- Replace zucchini with asparagus, broccoli, or green beans. Use sweet potatoes or butternut squash in place of baby potatoes for a fall-inspired twist.

Global Flavor Twist:
- For a Mediterranean flavor, add olives and sprinkle with feta cheese.
- For a Cajun-style dish, use Andouille sausage and Cajun seasoning instead of Italian sausage and herbs.

Grain Addition:
- Serve over a bed of quinoa, couscous, or rice for a heartier meal.

NUTRITIONAL INFORMATION (PER SERVING)

Calories:............. 400	Fiber: 5g	Saturated Fat: 7g
Protein: 18g	Sugar: 7g	Cholesterol: 50mg
Carbohydrates: ...28g	Fat: 24g	Sodium: 850mg

CREAMY MUSHROOM RISOTTO

Yield: 4 servings   **Prep Time:** 15 minutes   **Cook Time:** 30 minutes   **Total Time:** 45 minutes

INGREDIENTS

Base Ingredients:

- 1 tbsp olive oil
- 2 tbsp unsalted butter
- 1 medium yellow onion, finely chopped
- 3 cloves garlic, minced
- 1 cup Arborio rice
- 1/2 cup dry white wine
- 4 cups vegetable or chicken broth, warmed
- 2 cups mushrooms, sliced
- 1/4 cup grated Parmesan cheese
- 1/4 cup heavy cream or mascarpone cheese

Seasonings:

- Salt and black pepper, to taste
- 1/2 tsp dried thyme or 1 tsp fresh thyme leaves
- 1/4 cup fresh parsley, chopped

STEP-BY-STEP INSTRUCTIONS

1. Warm the Broth:

- Heat the broth in a small saucepan over low heat. Keep it warm throughout the cooking process.

2. Sauté the Mushrooms:

- Heat 1 tablespoon of olive oil and 1 tablespoon of butter in a large skillet over medium heat.
- Add the mushrooms, a pinch of salt, and thyme. Cook until the mushrooms are golden and tender, about 5–7 minutes. Remove from the skillet and set aside.

3. Sauté Aromatics and Rice:

- In the same skillet, melt the remaining 1 tablespoon of butter. Add the chopped onion and cook until translucent, about 3–4 minutes.
- Add the garlic and cook for 1 minute until fragrant.
- Stir in the Arborio rice, ensuring each grain is coated with butter. Cook for 2–3 minutes until the edges of the rice are translucent.

4. Deglaze and Begin Cooking the Risotto:

- Pour in the white wine (if using) and stir until mostly absorbed.
- Add one ladleful (about 1/2 cup) of warm broth to the rice and stir frequently. Once the liquid is mostly absorbed, add another ladleful. Continue this process, stirring often, until the rice is creamy and tender, about 20–25 minutes.

5. Add Mushrooms and Finish:

- Stir the cooked mushrooms back into the skillet along with the Parmesan cheese. For extra creaminess, fold in heavy cream or mascarpone. Adjust seasoning with salt and pepper as needed.

6. Serve:

- Garnish with chopped parsley and an extra sprinkle of Parmesan cheese. Serve warm.

VARIATIONS AND ADAPTATIONS

Add Protein:

- Include cooked chicken, shrimp, or pancetta for a heartier dish.

Vegetarian Twist:

- Add roasted butternut squash or asparagus for additional seasonal vegetables.

Global Influence:

- Use coconut milk and a touch of curry powder for a Thai-inspired risotto.
- Replace Parmesan with Manchego and add saffron for a Spanish touch.

Gluten-Free Option:

- Ensure the broth and wine used are gluten-free.

NUTRITIONAL INFORMATION (PER SERVING)

Calories: 370	Fiber: 2g	Saturated Fat: 6g
Protein: 8g	Sugar: 4g	Cholesterol: 20mg
Carbohydrates: ...45g	Fat: 15g	Sodium: 650mg

ROASTED SALMON AND ASPARAGUS

Yield: 4 servings   **Prep Time:** 10 minutes   **Cook Time:** 20 minutes   **Total Time:** 30 minutes

INGREDIENTS
Main Ingredients:
- 4 (6-ounce) salmon fillets
- 1 bunch asparagus (about 1 pound), ends trimmed
- 2 tbsp olive oil
- 2 cloves garlic, minced
- 1 lemon, sliced into rounds
- 1 tbsp fresh lemon juice
- 1 tsp Dijon mustard
- 1 tsp honey
- 1 tsp dried Italian seasoning or fresh thyme
- Salt and black pepper, to taste

Optional Garnish:
- Fresh parsley or dill, chopped
- Lemon wedges for serving

STEP-BY-STEP INSTRUCTIONS

1. Preheat the Oven:
- Preheat the oven to 400°F (200°C). Line a large baking sheet with parchment paper or foil for easy clean-up.

2. Prepare the Marinade:
- In a small bowl, whisk together 1 tablespoon of olive oil, lemon juice, Dijon mustard, honey, garlic, and Italian seasoning.

3. Season the Salmon:
- Place the salmon fillets on the prepared baking sheet, skin-side down.
- Brush the marinade over the salmon fillets evenly. Season with salt and black pepper.

4. Prepare the Asparagus:
- Place the trimmed asparagus spears next to the salmon on the baking sheet.
- Drizzle with the remaining 1 tablespoon of olive oil and season with salt and pepper. Toss gently to coat. Arrange lemon slices over the salmon and asparagus.

5. Roast the Salmon and Asparagus:
- Transfer the baking sheet to the oven and roast for 12–15 minutes, or until the salmon is cooked through and flakes easily with a fork. The asparagus should be tender-crisp.

6. Broil for a Crispy Finish (Optional):
- For a golden finish, switch the oven to broil mode and broil for 1–2 minutes. Keep a close eye to avoid burning.

7. Serve:
- Garnish the dish with fresh parsley or dill, if desired. Serve with lemon wedges for an extra burst of citrus.

VARIATIONS AND ADAPTATIONS
Protein Swaps:
- Replace salmon with cod, trout, or halibut for similar cooking methods. For a non-fish option, try boneless chicken thighs (adjust cooking time to 25–30 minutes).

Vegetable Options:
- Substitute asparagus with green beans, zucchini, or Brussels sprouts.

Global Flavors:
- Add a sprinkle of sesame seeds and soy sauce for an Asian twist.
- Use smoked paprika and cumin for a Spanish-inspired dish.

Pairings:
- Serve with a side of roasted potatoes, quinoa, or a fresh mixed greens salad for a complete meal.

NUTRITIONAL INFORMATION (PER SERVING)

Calories: 360	Fiber: 2g	Saturated Fat: 3g
Protein: 35g	Sugar: 2g	Cholesterol: 80mg
Carbohydrates: ...5g	Fat: 20g	Sodium: 300mg

CHICKEN ALFREDO CASSEROLE

Yield: 6 servings   **Prep Time:** 15 minutes   **Cook Time:** 30 minutes   **Total Time:** 45 minutes

INGREDIENTS

For the Casserole:
- 12 oz (3 cups) uncooked penne pasta
- 2 tbsp olive oil or butter
- 2 cups cooked chicken breast, shredded or diced
- 1 tbsp garlic, minced
- 1 small onion, finely chopped
- 1½ cups broccoli florets
- 2 cups Alfredo sauce
- 1 cup milk (whole or 2%)
- 1½ cups shredded mozzarella cheese, divided
- ½ cup grated Parmesan cheese
- 1 tsp dried Italian seasoning
- ½ tsp black pepper
- ¼ tsp salt

Optional Garnishes:
- Fresh parsley, chopped
- Red pepper flakes for heat

STEP-BY-STEP INSTRUCTIONS

1. Preheat and Prep:
- Preheat your oven to 375°F (190°C). Lightly grease a 9x13-inch baking dish with olive oil or cooking spray.

2. Cook the Pasta:
- Bring a large pot of salted water to a boil. Cook the penne pasta until al dente according to package instructions. Drain and set aside.

3. Sauté the Vegetables:
- Heat the olive oil or butter in a large skillet over medium heat. Add the minced garlic and onion, sautéing until fragrant, about 2 minutes.
- Add the broccoli florets and cook for another 3–4 minutes until tender-crisp.

4. Combine the Sauce:
- Stir in the cooked chicken, Alfredo sauce, and milk. Mix well to combine. Season with Italian seasoning, black pepper, and salt. Simmer for 2 minutes.

5. Assemble the Casserole:
- Add the cooked pasta to the skillet and toss to coat evenly in the sauce. Transfer the mixture to the prepared baking dish.
- Sprinkle 1 cup of mozzarella cheese and all of the Parmesan cheese over the top.

6. Bake the Casserole:
- Cover the dish with foil and bake for 20 minutes. Remove the foil, sprinkle the remaining ½ cup of mozzarella cheese on top, and bake for an additional 10 minutes, or until the cheese is melted and bubbly.

7. Serve and Enjoy:
- Remove from the oven and let the casserole rest for 5 minutes before serving. Garnish with fresh parsley and a pinch of red pepper flakes, if desired.

VARIATIONS AND ADAPTATIONS

Protein Swaps:
- Substitute chicken with cooked turkey, diced ham, or shrimp.

Vegetable Additions:
- Add sautéed mushrooms, spinach, or cherry tomatoes for extra flavor and nutrition.

Global Inspirations:
- **Mediterranean Twist:** Add sun-dried tomatoes, artichoke hearts, and feta cheese.
- **Mexican-Style Alfredo:** Use a queso-based sauce, add diced green chilies, and top with Monterey Jack cheese.

NUTRITIONAL INFORMATION (PER SERVING)

Calories: 490	Fiber: 3g	Saturated Fat: 9g
Protein: 33g	Sugar: 4g	Cholesterol: 90mg
Carbohydrates: ...42g	Fat: 19g	Sodium: 730mg

VEGETARIAN BAKED ZITI

Yield: 6 servings   **Prep Time:** 15 minutes   **Cook Time:** 30 minutes   **Total Time:** 45 minutes

INGREDIENTS
For the Ziti:
- 12 oz (3 cups) ziti or penne pasta
- 1 tbsp olive oil
- 1 small onion, finely chopped
- 2 garlic cloves, minced
- 1 medium zucchini, diced
- 1 cup baby spinach, chopped
- 1½ cups marinara sauce
- 1½ cups ricotta cheese
- 1 cup shredded mozzarella cheese, divided
- ½ cup grated Parmesan cheese
- 1 tsp dried basil
- 1 tsp dried oregano
- ½ tsp red pepper flakes
- Salt and black pepper to taste

Optional Garnishes:
- Fresh basil leaves, chopped
- Additional Parmesan cheese

STEP-BY-STEP INSTRUCTIONS

1. Preheat the Oven:
- Preheat your oven to 375°F (190°C). Grease a 9x13-inch baking dish lightly with olive oil.

2. Cook the Pasta:
- Bring a large pot of salted water to a boil. Cook the ziti until just al dente according to package instructions. Drain and set aside.

3. Sauté the Vegetables:
- Heat the olive oil in a large skillet over medium heat. Add the chopped onion and garlic, sautéing for 2–3 minutes until fragrant.
- Add the zucchini and cook for another 3–4 minutes until softened. Stir in the spinach and cook until wilted. Season with salt, pepper, and red pepper flakes (if using).

4. Prepare the Ricotta Mixture:
- In a large mixing bowl, combine ricotta cheese, ½ cup of mozzarella cheese, Parmesan cheese, dried basil, and dried oregano. Mix well and set aside.

5. Assemble the Ziti:
- In the same bowl as the ricotta mixture, add the cooked pasta, sautéed vegetables, and marinara sauce. Stir gently to coat everything evenly.

6. Layer the Dish:
- Spread half of the pasta mixture in the prepared baking dish. Dollop with half of the ricotta mixture, then layer the remaining pasta mixture on top. Spread the remaining ricotta mixture evenly over the top and sprinkle with the remaining mozzarella cheese.

7. Bake:
- Cover the dish with foil and bake for 20 minutes. Remove the foil and bake for another 10 minutes, or until the cheese is melted and bubbling.

8. Serve:
- Remove from the oven and let rest for 5 minutes. Garnish with fresh basil and additional Parmesan if desired.

VARIATIONS AND ADAPTATIONS
Add Protein:
- Include plant-based sausage crumbles or chickpeas for a heartier version.

Switch Vegetables:
- Substitute zucchini with eggplant or mushrooms, or add roasted bell peppers for a sweeter flavor.

Global Inspirations:
- **Greek Style:** Replace ricotta with crumbled feta, add kalamata olives and oregano.
- **Mexican Twist:** Use salsa instead of marinara, add black beans, and top with Monterey Jack cheese.

NUTRITIONAL INFORMATION (PER SERVING)

Calories: 420	Fiber: 5g	Saturated Fat: 8g
Protein: 20g	Sugar: 7g	Cholesterol: 40mg
Carbohydrates: ...48g	Fat: 16g	Sodium: 720mg

ONE-POT MEDITERRANEAN COUSCOUS

Yield: 4 servings   **Prep Time:** 10 minutes   **Cook Time:** 20 minutes   **Total Time:** 30 minutes

INGREDIENTS

For the Couscous:

- 1 tbsp olive oil
- 1 small red onion, finely chopped
- 2 garlic cloves, minced
- 1 small zucchini, diced
- 1 small red bell pepper, diced
- 1 cup cherry tomatoes, halved
- 1 tsp dried oregano
- ½ tsp smoked paprika
- ½ tsp ground cumin
- ½ tsp red pepper flakes
- 1 cup pearl (Israeli) couscous
- 1¾ cups vegetable broth
- ½ cup canned chickpeas, drained and rinsed
- ½ cup crumbled feta cheese
- 2 tbsp chopped fresh parsley
- Juice of ½ a lemon

Optional Garnishes:

- Fresh basil leaves
- Toasted pine nuts

STEP-BY-STEP INSTRUCTIONS

1. Prepare Your Ingredients:

- Chop all vegetables, rinse the chickpeas, and measure out the spices, broth, and couscous.

2. Sauté the Aromatics:

- Heat olive oil in a large pot or deep skillet over medium heat. Add the onion and sauté for 2–3 minutes until softened. Stir in the garlic and cook for another 30 seconds.

3. Cook the Vegetables:

- Add the zucchini, red bell pepper, and cherry tomatoes. Cook for 4–5 minutes until the vegetables begin to soften. Season with oregano, smoked paprika, cumin, red pepper flakes (if using), salt, and pepper.

4. Toast the Couscous:

- Stir in the couscous, coating it with the vegetable mixture and allowing it to toast for 1–2 minutes.

5. Add Broth and Simmer:

- Pour in the vegetable broth and bring the mixture to a boil. Reduce the heat to low, cover, and simmer for 8–10 minutes, or until the couscous is tender and has absorbed most of the liquid.

6. Add Chickpeas:

- Stir in the chickpeas and cook for 2 more minutes to warm them through.

7. Finish with Feta and Lemon:

- Remove the pot from heat. Stir in crumbled feta cheese, parsley, and a squeeze of lemon juice for brightness.

8. Serve:

- Spoon the couscous into bowls and garnish with fresh basil and toasted pine nuts if desired.

VARIATIONS AND ADAPTATIONS

Add Protein:

- **Chicken:** Sauté diced chicken breast in olive oil before cooking the vegetables.

- **Seafood:** Add shrimp in the last 5 minutes of simmering.

Switch the Vegetables:

- Use seasonal favorites like eggplant, spinach, or artichoke hearts.

Global Inspirations:

- **Indian Style:** Replace oregano and paprika with garam masala and turmeric. Top with a dollop of yogurt.

- **Italian Twist:** Swap smoked paprika for basil and oregano, and sprinkle with Parmesan instead of feta.

NUTRITIONAL INFORMATION (PER SERVING)

Calories: 320	Fiber: 6g	Saturated Fat: 3g
Protein: 11g	Sugar: 6g	Cholesterol: 12mg
Carbohydrates: ...41g	Fat: 11g	Sodium: 450mg

TURKEY AND SWEET POTATO HASH

Yield: 4 servings   **Prep Time:** 10 minutes   **Cook Time:** 25 minutes   **Total Time:** 35 minutes

INGREDIENTS

- **2 tbsp olive oil**, divided
- **1 lb ground turkey** (or substitute with ground chicken)
- **1 medium onion**, diced
- **2 cloves garlic**, minced
- **2 medium sweet potatoes**, peeled and diced into ½-inch cubes
- **1 red bell pepper**, diced
- **1 cup kale or spinach**, chopped
- **1 tsp smoked paprika**
- **1 tsp ground cumin**
- **½ tsp dried thyme**
- **½ tsp chili powder**
- **Salt and pepper to taste**
- **2 tbsp fresh parsley**, chopped
- **4 eggs**

STEP-BY-STEP INSTRUCTIONS

1. Prepare Ingredients:
- Dice the vegetables and peel and cube the sweet potatoes. Set aside.

2. Cook the Turkey:
- Heat 1 tablespoon of olive oil in a large skillet over medium heat. Add the ground turkey and season lightly with salt and pepper. Cook for 6–8 minutes, breaking it up with a spoon, until browned and fully cooked. Remove from the skillet and set aside.

3. Sauté Aromatics:
- In the same skillet, add the remaining tablespoon of olive oil. Add the diced onion and sauté for 2–3 minutes until translucent. Stir in the garlic and cook for an additional minute.

4. Cook the Sweet Potatoes:
- Add the sweet potatoes to the skillet and cook for 10–12 minutes, stirring occasionally, until they are tender and lightly browned. If the pan becomes dry, add a splash of water or broth to help them soften.

5. Add Vegetables and Spices:
- Stir in the red bell pepper and cook for another 3–4 minutes until softened. Add the smoked paprika, cumin, thyme, chili powder (if using), and additional salt and pepper.

6. Combine and Heat Through:
- Return the cooked turkey to the skillet and mix it with the vegetables. Stir in the kale or spinach, if using, and cook for 1–2 minutes until wilted.

7. Optional Fried Eggs:
- In a separate small pan, fry the eggs to your desired doneness. Serve each portion of hash with a fried egg on top for added richness.

8. Garnish and Serve:
- Sprinkle with chopped parsley before serving. Enjoy warm!

VARIATIONS AND ADAPTATIONS

Protein Alternatives:
- **Vegetarian:** Substitute turkey with black beans or lentils.
- **Beef or Pork:** Use ground beef or sausage for a heartier flavor.

Vegetable Swaps:
- Replace sweet potatoes with Yukon gold or red potatoes.
- Use seasonal vegetables such as zucchini, mushrooms, or butternut squash.

Global Flavors:
- **Mexican-Inspired:** Add black beans, corn, and a dash of cayenne; top with avocado and salsa.
- **Mediterranean:** Incorporate sun-dried tomatoes, feta, and oregano.

NUTRITIONAL INFORMATION (PER SERVING)

Calories: 320	Fiber: 4g	Saturated Fat: 2g	Sodium: 300mg
Protein: 25g	Sugar: 6g	Cholesterol: 140mg	
Carbohydrates: ...25g	Fat: 12g	(with egg)	

CHAPTER 3: COMFORT CLASSICS MADE QUICK

PRACTICAL TIPS

This chapter is all about bringing the warmth of beloved comfort dishes to your table without the long preparation time. With these practical tips, you can create hearty, nostalgic meals that fit perfectly into a busy lifestyle, all while maintaining the homemade coziness you love.

1. Keep It Simple, But Satisfying:
- Focus on recipes with fewer steps or fewer than 10 ingredients to save time while still delivering maximum flavor.

2. Leverage Pantry and Freezer Staples:
- Items like canned tomatoes, frozen vegetables, and dried pasta are key for many quick comfort classics. Stock up on these essentials to make dinner preparation seamless.

3. Use Pre-Cooked Proteins for Speed:
- Rotisserie chicken, pre-cooked sausage, or canned beans can be lifesavers for recipes like casseroles, soups, or skillet meals.

4. One-Pot Wonders Are Your Ally:
- Many comfort dishes, such as creamy pasta, soups, or stews, can be prepared in one pot, saving both time and cleanup.

5. Enhance with Simple Garnishes:
- Add fresh herbs, grated cheese, or a drizzle of olive oil to make your quick meals feel extra special and homey.

6. Don't Skip on Flavor:
- Use ingredients like garlic, onion, or broth to quickly build rich, comforting flavors. Deglaze your pan with wine or a splash of vinegar for extra depth.

7. Quick Baking Hacks:
- For recipes like pot pies or casseroles, opt for store-bought puff pastry or biscuit dough. These shortcuts reduce prep time while maintaining the homemade feel.

8. Repurpose Leftovers:
Transform leftovers into new dishes! For example:
- ◊ Use mashed potatoes as a topping for shepherd's pie.
- ◊ Turn roast chicken into creamy chicken and rice soup.

9. Layering for Better Results:
- Dishes like lasagna or layered casseroles can still be quick if you use no-boil noodles or pre-cooked fillings. Layer strategically for even cooking.

10. Balance Richness with Fresh Ingredients:
- Comfort foods are often rich, so brighten them with fresh elements like a squeeze of lemon, fresh herbs, or a crisp side salad.

11. Time-Saving Tools:
- Use tools like pressure cookers, slow cookers, or air fryers to prepare hearty meals faster. A cast-iron skillet is also excellent for stove-to-oven dishes like cornbread or frittatas.

12. Incorporate Global Comfort Foods:
- Expand your comfort food repertoire with quick favorites from other cuisines:
  - ◊ **Italian:** 20-minute risotto or creamy carbonara.
  - ◊ **Mexican:** Easy enchiladas or quesadillas.
  - ◊ **Asian:** Stir-fried noodles or miso soup.

13. Batch Cooking for Later:
- Make double portions of comfort foods like chili or casseroles and freeze extras for busy nights.

14. Set the Mood:
- Comfort food is about more than taste—it's about atmosphere. Serve these meals with warm lighting, cozy table settings, or family-style plating to enhance the experience.

CONCLUSION:

Comfort classics are the ultimate way to bring joy and warmth to your dinner table, and this chapter makes it easier than ever to enjoy them even on busy nights. With a focus on simplicity and speed, these recipes and tips allow you to savor the flavors of home while keeping preparation stress-free. Perfect for nourishing both body and soul, these dishes prove that even quick meals can feel like a big, warm hug.

CHICKEN POT PIE IN A SKILLET

Yield: 4 servings   **Prep Time:** 15 minutes   **Cook Time:** 30 minutes   **Total Time:** 45 minutes

INGREDIENTS

- **2 tbsp olive oil** or butter
- **1 lb boneless, skinless chicken thighs**, diced into bite-sized pieces (or substitute with chicken breast)
- **1 medium onion**, diced
- **2 medium carrots**, peeled and diced
- **1 stalk celery**, diced
- **1 cup frozen peas**
- **2 cups diced potatoes**
- **2 tbsp all-purpose flour**
- **1 ½ cups chicken broth**, low-sodium
- **½ cup whole milk** or heavy cream
- **½ tsp dried thyme**
- **½ tsp dried rosemary**
- **Salt and black pepper to taste**
- **1 sheet puff pastry**, thawed (or use refrigerated pie crust)
- **1 egg**, beaten (for egg wash)

STEP-BY-STEP INSTRUCTIONS

1. Preheat the Oven:
- Preheat your oven to 400°F (200°C).

2. Cook the Chicken:
- Heat the olive oil in an oven-safe skillet (10–12 inches) over medium heat. Add the diced chicken, season with salt and pepper, and cook for 6–8 minutes, stirring occasionally, until browned and fully cooked. Remove the chicken from the skillet and set aside.

3. Sauté Vegetables:
- In the same skillet, add the onion, carrots, celery, and potatoes. Cook for 5–7 minutes, stirring occasionally, until the vegetables begin to soften.

4. Make the Sauce:
- Sprinkle the flour over the vegetables and stir well to coat. Cook for 1–2 minutes to remove the raw flour taste. Gradually add the chicken broth, stirring constantly to avoid lumps. Stir in the milk, thyme, and rosemary. Bring the mixture to a simmer and cook for 5 minutes, until the sauce thickens slightly.

5. Combine and Assemble:
- Return the cooked chicken to the skillet and stir in the frozen peas. Taste and adjust the seasoning with salt and pepper.

6. Top with Puff Pastry:
- Lay the puff pastry over the skillet, trimming any overhang. Tuck the edges slightly inside the skillet and make a few small slits in the pastry to allow steam to escape. Brush the beaten egg over the pastry for a golden finish.

7. Bake:
- Place the skillet in the preheated oven and bake for 15–20 minutes, or until the puff pastry is golden brown and crispy.

8. Serve:
- Let the skillet rest for 5 minutes before serving. Spoon the pot pie into bowls and enjoy the comforting flavors.

VARIATIONS AND ADAPTATIONS

Meat Alternatives:
- Beef Pot Pie: Substitute chicken with ground beef or leftover roast beef.
- Vegetarian: Omit chicken and add mushrooms, zucchini, or chickpeas for protein.

Cultural Influences:
- **Indian-Inspired:** Add curry powder and a touch of coconut milk.
- **French-Inspired:** Use white wine in place of some of the broth, and add leeks.

Crust Options:
- Use biscuits or mashed potatoes instead of puff pastry for a different twist.

NUTRITIONAL INFORMATION (PER SERVING)

Calories: 460	Fiber: 5g	Saturated Fat: 8g
Protein: 27g	Sugar: 4g	Cholesterol: 90mg
Carbohydrates: ...35g	Fat: 23g	Sodium: 430mg

EASY BEEF STROGANOFF

Yield: 4 servings   **Prep Time:** 15 minutes   **Cook Time:** 25 minutes   **Total Time:** 40 minutes

INGREDIENTS

- **1 lb beef sirloin or tenderloin**, cut into thin strips (or use ground beef for a quicker version)
- **2 tbsp olive oil** (or butter)
- **1 small onion**, finely chopped
- **2 cloves garlic**, minced
- **1 cup mushrooms**, sliced
- **1 cup beef broth**
- **¾ cup sour cream**
- **1 tbsp Dijon mustard**
- **1 tsp Worcestershire sauce**
- **1 tbsp all-purpose flour**
- **2 tbsp butter**
- **Salt and black pepper**, to taste
- **8 oz egg noodles**
- **Fresh parsley**, chopped

STEP-BY-STEP INSTRUCTIONS

1. Cook the Noodles:
- Start by cooking the egg noodles according to the package instructions. Drain and set aside, reserving about ½ cup of pasta water.

2. Brown the Beef:
- In a large skillet or sauté pan, heat 1 tablespoon of olive oil over medium-high heat. Add the sliced beef in batches (to avoid overcrowding the pan) and sear until browned on both sides, about 2-3 minutes per side. Remove the beef from the skillet and set aside.

3. Sauté the Vegetables:
- In the same skillet, add another tablespoon of olive oil (or butter) and sauté the chopped onion for 2-3 minutes until softened. Add the garlic and mushrooms and cook for an additional 4-5 minutes, stirring occasionally, until the mushrooms release their moisture and become tender.

4. Make the Sauce:
- Sprinkle the flour over the cooked onions and mushrooms, and stir to coat the vegetables. Cook for 1-2 minutes, allowing the flour to absorb the juices and create a roux. Gradually pour in the beef broth while stirring constantly to prevent lumps. Stir in the Dijon mustard and Worcestershire sauce. Bring the mixture to a simmer, allowing it to thicken slightly, about 4-5 minutes.

5. Add the Beef and Sour Cream:
- Return the browned beef to the skillet, along with any juices that have accumulated. Stir in the sour cream and cook for 2-3 minutes until the beef is heated through and the sauce is creamy. If the sauce is too thick, add a little reserved pasta water to reach your desired consistency.

6. Combine with Noodles:
- Add the cooked noodles to the skillet, tossing them gently to coat in the sauce. Season with salt and black pepper to taste. Cook for another 1-2 minutes, allowing the flavors to meld together.

7. Serve:
- Remove from heat and garnish with freshly chopped parsley if desired. Serve immediately and enjoy your comforting homemade beef stroganoff.

VARIATIONS AND ADAPTATIONS

Meat Alternatives:
- **Chicken Stroganoff:** Use boneless, skinless chicken breasts or thighs, cut into strips.
- **Pork Stroganoff:** Swap the beef for pork tenderloin or ground pork.
- **Vegetarian:** Use mushrooms, tofu, or tempeh as a substitute for meat, and use vegetable broth instead of beef broth.

Flavor Variations:
- **Greek-Inspired:** Add a little feta cheese and olives for a Mediterranean twist.
- **Spicy:** Stir in a pinch of red pepper flakes or a small chopped chili pepper for some heat.
- **Herb Variations:** Add fresh thyme, tarragon, or rosemary for a more aromatic flavor profile.

Serving Suggestions:
- Serve over mashed potatoes, rice, or cauliflower rice for a low-carb version.
- Add a side salad with a tangy vinaigrette to balance out the richness of the stroganoff.

NUTRITIONAL INFORMATION (PER SERVING)

Calories: 550	Carbohydrates: ...45g	Sugar: 5g	Saturated Fat: 12g
Protein: 32g	Fiber: 3g	Fat: 26g	Cholesterol: 90mg
			Sodium: 620mg

QUICK LASAGNA ROLL-UPS

Yield: 4 servings   **Prep Time:** 15 minutes   **Cook Time:** 30 minutes   **Total Time:** 45 minutes

INGREDIENTS

- **8-10 lasagna noodles** (whole wheat)
- **1 lb ground beef** (or ground turkey)
- **1 tbsp olive oil** (for sautéing)
- **1 small onion**, finely chopped
- **2 cloves garlic**, minced
- **1 cup ricotta cheese** (or cottage cheese)
- **1½ cups shredded mozzarella cheese**
- **1 cup grated Parmesan cheese**
- **2 cups marinara sauce**
- **1 tbsp dried basil**
- **1 tsp dried oregano**
- **Salt and black pepper**, to taste
- **1 egg** (helps bind the filling)
- **Fresh basil**, chopped (for garnish)

STEP-BY-STEP INSTRUCTIONS

1. Prepare the Lasagna Noodles:

- Cook the lasagna noodles according to package instructions. Drain and set aside, making sure to lay them flat to avoid sticking.

2. Cook the Meat Filling:

- In a large skillet, heat olive oil over medium heat. Add the chopped onion and garlic, cooking until the onion is softened, about 3-4 minutes.
- Add the ground beef (or turkey) to the skillet, breaking it apart with a spoon as it cooks. Season with salt, black pepper, basil, and oregano. Cook until the meat is browned and fully cooked, about 7-8 minutes. Drain excess fat if necessary, then stir in 1 cup of marinara sauce. Simmer for another 2-3 minutes and set aside.

3. Prepare the Cheese Mixture:

- In a medium bowl, mix the ricotta cheese, 1 cup of mozzarella cheese, Parmesan cheese, and egg. Stir until fully combined and smooth. Season with a pinch of salt and pepper.

4. Assemble the Roll-Ups:

- Preheat your oven to 375°F (190°C).
- Spread a thin layer of marinara sauce on the bottom of a 9x13-inch baking dish.
- Lay the cooked lasagna noodles flat on a clean surface. Spoon 2-3 tablespoons of the ricotta mixture onto each noodle, spreading it evenly. Then, spoon 2-3 tablespoons of the meat sauce on top of the cheese mixture. Carefully roll each noodle up tightly into a cylinder.
- Place each roll-up seam-side down in the baking dish, lined up next to each other.

5. Bake the Lasagna Roll-Ups:

- Pour the remaining marinara sauce over the top of the roll-ups. Sprinkle the remaining mozzarella cheese on top, followed by a sprinkle of Parmesan.
- Cover with aluminum foil and bake for 20 minutes. Remove the foil and bake for an additional 5-10 minutes until the cheese is melted and bubbly.

6. Serve and Enjoy:

- Remove from the oven and let the roll-ups sit for a few minutes before serving. Garnish with freshly chopped basil if desired.

VARIATIONS AND ADAPTATIONS

Vegetarian Option:

- Replace the ground meat with sautéed vegetables such as spinach, mushrooms, zucchini, or a mixture of roasted seasonal vegetables. You can add a bit of ricotta or cottage cheese to enhance the filling.

Dairy-Free Option:

- Use dairy-free ricotta cheese and mozzarella (such as cashew-based or coconut-based versions). Replace the Parmesan with a dairy-free alternative or omit it entirely.

Meat Substitutes:

- Try using ground turkey, chicken, or even Italian sausage for a variation in flavor.
- For a more traditional taste, use a mixture of beef and pork, typical for lasagna recipes.

Spicy Version:

- Add a pinch of red pepper flakes to the meat sauce for a bit of heat.

Different Sauces:

- Use a white sauce (béchamel) instead of marinara for a creamy twist. You could also make a pesto lasagna roll-up using a basil pesto sauce and fresh mozzarella.

NUTRITIONAL INFORMATION (PER SERVING)

Calories: 450   Carbohydrates: ...35g   Sugar: ....7g   Saturated Fat: 10g
Protein: ....28g   Fiber: ....3g   Fat: 24g   Cholesterol: 80mg
Sodium: 600mg

CHEESY SHEPHERD'S PIE

Yield: 6 servings   **Prep Time:** 20 minutes   **Cook Time:** 40 minutes   **Total Time:** 1 hour

INGREDIENTS

- **2 lbs potatoes**
- **1 lb ground beef**
- **1 tbsp olive oil** (or butter)
- **1 small onion**, finely chopped
- **2 cloves garlic**, minced
- **2 medium carrots**, peeled and diced
- **1 cup frozen peas** (or fresh peas when)
- **1 cup beef broth** (or vegetable)
- **2 tbsp tomato paste**
- **1 tsp Worcestershire sauce**
- **1 tsp dried thyme**
- **1 tsp dried rosemary**
- **Salt and pepper**, to taste
- **1/4 cup whole milk**
- **1/2 cup shredded cheddar cheese**
- **2 tbsp butter** (for mashed potatoes)

STEP-BY-STEP INSTRUCTIONS

1. Prepare the Potatoes:

- Peel and dice the potatoes into even-sized chunks. Place them in a large pot and cover with water. Bring to a boil and cook until the potatoes are fork-tender, about 15-20 minutes.
- Drain the potatoes, then return them to the pot. Mash with butter, milk, salt, and pepper until smooth and creamy. Set aside.

2. COOK THE MEAT AND VEGGIES:

- While the potatoes are boiling, heat olive oil (or butter) in a large skillet over medium heat. Add the chopped onion and garlic, cooking until softened, about 3-4 minutes.
- Add the ground beef (or other meat) to the skillet, breaking it apart with a spoon. Cook until browned and fully cooked, about 7-8 minutes. Drain excess fat if needed.
- Stir in the diced carrots and cook for 5-7 minutes, until they begin to soften.
- Add the tomato paste, Worcestershire sauce, thyme, rosemary, salt, and pepper. Stir to combine.
- Pour in the beef broth, scraping up any browned bits from the skillet. Simmer the mixture for about 5-7 minutes until the sauce thickens slightly.
- Stir in the frozen peas (or fresh peas if in season) and cook for another 2 minutes. Remove from heat.

3. Assemble the Shepherd's Pie:

- Preheat the oven to 375°F (190°C).
- Spread the meat and vegetable mixture evenly in the bottom of a baking dish (9x9 or 9x13-inch dish depending on your preference).
- Spoon the mashed potatoes over the top, spreading them out evenly with a spatula. If you like a golden top, you can lightly score the top with a fork for a textured finish.
- Sprinkle shredded cheddar cheese (if using) on top of the mashed potatoes for extra cheesiness.

4. Bake the Shepherd's Pie:

- Place the baking dish in the preheated oven and bake for 20-25 minutes, until the top is golden and the filling is bubbly.
- If you want a crispier top, you can broil for an additional 1-2 minutes at the end (watch carefully to avoid burning).

5. Serve and Enjoy:

- Let the shepherd's pie cool for 5-10 minutes before serving. This allows the filling to set and makes it easier to slice.

VARIATIONS AND ADAPTATIONS

- **Vegetarian Shepherd's Pie:** Substitute the ground meat with lentils or mushrooms (such as cremini or portobello) for a plant-based option. Add extra vegetables like zucchini or bell peppers for more flavor and texture.
- **Different Meat Options:** If you prefer a leaner version, use ground turkey or chicken instead of beef. Lamb is the traditional choice for shepherd's pie, and it adds a rich, distinct flavor.
- **Spicy Version:** Add a teaspoon of smoked paprika or chili flakes to the meat mixture for a bit of heat. You can also include diced chili peppers in the vegetable mix.
- **Cheese Lovers:** Add shredded mozzarella, Gruyère, or a blend of cheeses to the mashed potatoes for an even cheesier topping.
- **Greek-Inspired Shepherd's Pie:** Substitute some of the beef broth with red wine, add a pinch of cinnamon, and top the potatoes with crumbled feta cheese and a sprinkle of oregano for a Mediterranean twist.

NUTRITIONAL INFORMATION (PER SERVING)

Calories: 480
Protein: 30g
Carbohydrates: ...42g
Fiber: 5g
Sugar: 6g
Fat: 22g
Saturated Fat: 8g
Cholesterol: 60mg
Sodium: 580mg

CRISPY FRIED CHICKEN TENDERS

Yield: 4 servings   **Prep Time:** 15 minutes   **Cook Time:** 15 minutes   **Total Time:** 30 minutes

INGREDIENTS
- 1 lb chicken tenders
- 1 cup all-purpose flour
- 1 tsp garlic powder
- 1 tsp onion powder
- 1 tsp paprika
- 1/2 tsp salt
- 1/4 tsp black pepper
- 1/4 tsp cayenne pepper (optional)
- 2 large eggs
- 2 tbsp milk
- 1 1/2 cups panko breadcrumbs
- 1/2 cup buttermilk (optional)
- Vegetable oil or canola oil (for frying)

STEP-BY-STEP INSTRUCTIONS

1. Prepare the Chicken:
- Pat the chicken tenders dry with paper towels to ensure they fry up crispy.
- If you prefer, you can soak the chicken tenders in buttermilk for 30 minutes to enhance the flavor and tenderness, but this step is optional.

2. Set Up the Breading Station:
- In a shallow bowl, mix the flour, garlic powder, onion powder, paprika, salt, pepper, and cayenne pepper (if using).
- In another shallow bowl, whisk together the eggs and milk.
- In a third shallow bowl, place the panko breadcrumbs.

3. Dredge the Chicken:
- Coat each chicken tender first in the flour mixture, pressing gently to adhere.
- Dip it into the egg wash, making sure it's fully coated.
- Finally, coat the chicken in the panko breadcrumbs, pressing down lightly to ensure the breadcrumbs stick well. Repeat with all the tenders.

4. Heat the Oil:
- In a large skillet, pour enough oil to cover the bottom, about 1/4 inch deep. Heat the oil over medium-high heat until it reaches 350°F (175°C).
- You can check if the oil is hot enough by dropping a small piece of bread in. If it browns in about 60 seconds, the oil is ready.

5. Fry the Chicken Tenders:
- Carefully place the breaded chicken tenders into the hot oil. Avoid overcrowding the pan to ensure they cook evenly.
- Fry the tenders for 3-4 minutes per side, or until golden brown and crispy. Use tongs to flip them gently.
- Remove the cooked chicken tenders and place them on a paper towel-lined plate to drain excess oil.

6. Serve:
- Serve the crispy fried chicken tenders hot with your favorite dipping sauce, such as honey mustard, ranch, or BBQ sauce.

VARIATIONS AND ADAPTATIONS
- **Spicy Chicken Tenders:** Add more cayenne pepper to the breading mixture for a spicier kick, or incorporate some hot sauce into the egg wash for additional heat.
- **Gluten-Free Option:** Swap the all-purpose flour and panko breadcrumbs for gluten-free alternatives. You can use gluten-free flour and gluten-free breadcrumbs, or even crushed gluten-free crackers for a crispier coating.
- **Baked Version:** To reduce the amount of oil used, bake the breaded chicken tenders instead of frying. Preheat the oven to 400°F (200°C) and bake the tenders on a baking sheet lined with parchment paper for about 20-25 minutes, flipping halfway through, until golden and cooked through.
- **Herb-Infused Tenders:** Add finely chopped fresh herbs, such as thyme, parsley, or rosemary, to the breadcrumb mixture for a fresh and aromatic twist.
- **Panko and Parmesan Version:** Mix grated Parmesan cheese into the panko breadcrumbs for an extra cheesy and crispy texture.

NUTRITIONAL INFORMATION (PER SERVING)

Calories: 380
Protein: 35g
Carbohydrates: ...30g

Fiber: 2g
Sugar: 1g
Fat: 15g

Saturated Fat: 2g
Cholesterol: 120mg
Sodium: 700mg

LOADED BAKED POTATOES

Yield: 4 servings   **Prep Time:** 10 minutes   **Cook Time:** 60 minutes   **Total Time:** 1 hour 10 minutes

INGREDIENTS
- 4 large russet potatoes
- 2 tbsp olive oil
- 1/2 tsp salt
- 1/4 tsp black pepper
- 1/2 cup sour cream
- 1 cup shredded cheddar cheese
- 1/2 cup cooked bacon bits (optional)
- 1/4 cup green onions
- 1/4 cup butter
- 1/2 cup broccoli florets (steamed)
- 1/2 tsp garlic powder (for flavor)
- 1/4 tsp paprika (for color)

STEP-BY-STEP INSTRUCTIONS

1. Preheat the Oven and Prepare Potatoes:
- Preheat your oven to **400°F (200°C)**.
- Wash the russet potatoes thoroughly and scrub them to remove any dirt. Pat them dry with a paper towel.
- Pierce each potato a few times with a fork to allow steam to escape during baking.

2. Season the Potatoes:
- Rub the potatoes with **olive oil**, then sprinkle them with **salt** and **black pepper** to enhance flavor.
- Place the potatoes directly on the oven rack or on a baking sheet lined with parchment paper. Bake for about **45-60 minutes**, or until the potatoes are tender when pierced with a fork.

3. Prepare Toppings While Potatoes Bake:
- **Cook bacon** (if using) in a skillet over medium heat until crispy, then chop into small bits. Set aside.
- **Steam the broccoli florets** in a pot or microwave until tender, about 5-7 minutes. Set aside.
- Chop the **green onions** into small pieces for garnish.
- Shred the **cheddar cheese** and set it aside.

4. Assemble the Loaded Potatoes:
- Once the potatoes are done, remove them from the oven. Let them cool for a few minutes until they are easy to handle.
- Slice each potato open lengthwise and gently fluff the insides with a fork.
- **Add butter** and **sour cream** to the potato, then season with **garlic powder**, **paprika**, and more salt and pepper to taste. Mash the insides a bit to create a creamy base.

5. Add Toppings:
- **Top each potato** with a generous portion of **shredded cheddar cheese, crispy bacon bits**, and **steamed broccoli florets**.
- If desired, add a dollop of extra **sour cream** and garnish with **chopped green onions**.

6. Serve:
- Serve the loaded baked potatoes immediately while they're hot and enjoy as a hearty, comforting meal.
- Optionally, serve with a side salad or steamed veggies for a complete meal.

Variations and Adaptations
- **Vegetarian Version:** Skip the bacon and substitute with crispy **tempeh** or **vegetarian bacon** for a plant-based protein option. You can also add sautéed mushrooms for extra umami flavor.
- **Mexican-Inspired Loaded Potatoes:** Top with **guacamole**, **salsa**, and a sprinkle of **cilantro**. Swap cheddar cheese for **queso fresco** or **pepper jack** for a spicier kick.
- **BBQ Chicken Loaded Potatoes:** Instead of bacon, top the potatoes with **shredded cooked chicken** tossed in **BBQ sauce**. Add extra **cilantro** and **red onion** for a delicious twist.
- **Greek-Inspired Loaded Potatoes:** Use **feta cheese** instead of cheddar, and top with **kalamata olives**, **cucumbers**, and a drizzle of **tzatziki sauce** for a Mediterranean touch.

NUTRITIONAL INFORMATION (PER SERVING)

Calories: 450	Fiber: 7g	Saturated Fat: 9g
Protein: 16g	Sugar: 4g	Cholesterol: 40mg
Carbohydrates: ...49g	Fat: 22g	Sodium: 800mg

SLOPPY JOES WITH A TWIST

Yield: 4 servings   **Prep Time:** 15 minutes   **Cook Time:** 20 minutes   **Total Time:** 35 minutes

INGREDIENTS

- **1 lb ground turkey** (or beef)
- **1 tablespoon olive oil**
- **1 small onion**, finely chopped
- **1/2 bell pepper**, finely chopped
- **2 cloves garlic**, minced
- **1 cup tomato sauce**
- **1/4 cup ketchup**
- **1 tablespoon Worcestershire sauce**
- **1 tablespoon Dijon mustard**
- **1 tablespoon apple cider vinegar**
- **1 tablespoon honey** or **maple syrup**
- **1/2 teaspoon smoked paprika**
- **1/4 teaspoon chili powder**
- **1/2 teaspoon dried oregano**
- **Salt and pepper**, to taste
- **4 whole wheat burger buns**
- **Fresh greens** (spinach, arugula)
- **Pickles or sliced cucumbers**

STEP-BY-STEP INSTRUCTIONS

1. Cook the Ground Meat:
- Heat **1 tablespoon olive oil** in a large skillet over medium heat.
- Add **ground turkey** (or beef) to the skillet, breaking it apart with a wooden spoon. Cook for **5-7 minutes** until browned and fully cooked. Drain any excess fat, if necessary.

2. Sauté Vegetables:
- Add the **chopped onion**, **bell pepper**, and **minced garlic** to the skillet. Cook for an additional **3-4 minutes**, stirring occasionally, until the vegetables have softened and become fragrant.

3. Prepare the Sloppy Joe Sauce:
- Stir in the **tomato sauce, ketchup, Worcestershire sauce, Dijon mustard, apple cider vinegar**, and **honey**.
- Add the **smoked paprika, chili powder, oregano**, and season with **salt** and **pepper** to taste.
- Bring the mixture to a simmer over medium-low heat and let it cook for **10 minutes**, stirring occasionally. The sauce should thicken, and the flavors will meld together.

4. Assemble the Sloppy Joes:
- While the sauce is simmering, lightly toast the burger buns in a separate pan or in the oven.
- Spoon the hearty Sloppy Joe mixture onto the bottom halves of the buns.
- Top with fresh greens or **pickles** for added crunch and flavor, if desired. Place the top halves of the buns on top.

5. Serve and Enjoy:
- Serve the **Sloppy Joes with a Twist** hot, with your favorite side dishes such as roasted vegetables, a salad, or sweet potato fries.

VARIATIONS AND ADAPTATIONS

- **Vegetarian Version:** Replace the ground meat with **lentils** or **black beans** for a plant-based option. You can also use **crumbled tempeh** for a hearty texture.
- **Spicy Sloppy Joes:** Add **jalapeños** or **serrano peppers** to the mix for extra heat. You can also include a splash of **hot sauce** or **chipotle in adobo** for smokiness and spice.
- **Tex-Mex Inspired Sloppy Joes:** Replace the smoked paprika with **cumin** and **chili powder** and add a splash of **lime juice**. Top with **avocado slices, shredded cheddar**, and **cilantro** for a Southwest flair.
- **BBQ Sloppy Joes:** Swap the ketchup with **BBQ sauce** and add a touch of **liquid smoke**. Top with **coleslaw** for a tangy, crunchy addition.

NUTRITIONAL INFORMATION (PER SERVING)

Calories: 400	Fiber: 6g	Saturated Fat: 2g
Protein: 30g	Sugar: 14g	Cholesterol: 60mg
Carbohydrates: ...40g	Fat: 12g	Sodium: 700mg

CREAMY MASHED POTATO BOWLS

Yield: 4 servings   **Prep Time:** 15 minutes   **Cook Time:** 25 minutes   **Total Time:** 40 minutes

INGREDIENTS

- **2 lbs russet potatoes**
- **1/2 cup whole milk**
- **1/4 cup unsalted butter**
- **1/2 cup sour cream**
- **1/2 teaspoon garlic powder**
- **Salt and pepper**, to taste
- **1 tablespoon fresh parsley**, chopped

For the Toppings:
- **1 lb cooked chicken breast or rotisserie chicken**, shredded (or ground turkey, beef)
- **1 cup corn kernels**
- **1 cup steamed broccoli**
- **1/2 cup shredded cheese** (cheddar or mozzarella)
- **1/4 cup crumbled bacon**

STEP-BY-STEP INSTRUCTIONS

1. Cook the Potatoes:
- Peel and cut the **russet potatoes** into chunks.
- Place them in a large pot and cover with water.
- Bring to a boil and cook for **12-15 minutes**, or until the potatoes are fork-tender. Drain the potatoes and return them to the pot.

2. Make the Mashed Potatoes:
- Add the **butter, milk**, and **sour cream** (if using) to the pot with the potatoes.
- Use a potato masher or hand mixer to mash the potatoes until smooth and creamy.
- Season with **garlic powder, salt**, and **pepper** to taste.

3. Prepare the Toppings:
- While the potatoes are cooking, **cook the chicken** (either roast or use leftover rotisserie chicken, shred it into bite-sized pieces).
- Steam the **broccoli** by placing it in a steam basket over boiling water for about **5 minutes**.
- If using **corn**, sauté it in a skillet with a little butter or olive oil for **5-7 minutes** until tender.

4. Assemble the Mashed Potato Bowls:
- Scoop a generous portion of the creamy mashed potatoes into each bowl.
- Top each serving with shredded **chicken**, steamed broccoli, **corn**, and a sprinkle of **shredded cheese**.
- Optionally, add **crumbled bacon** for extra flavor and crunch.
- Garnish with freshly chopped **parsley**.

5. Serve and Enjoy:
- Serve the mashed potato bowls hot for a comforting and filling meal. These bowls are perfect as a complete meal, combining creamy mashed potatoes with a variety of healthy toppings.

VARIATIONS AND ADAPTATIONS

- **Vegetarian Version:** Replace the chicken with **sautéed mushrooms** or **tofu** for a plant-based alternative. You can also add **roasted chickpeas** or **lentils** for protein.
- **Southwest-Inspired:** Use **black beans, avocado slices**, and a drizzle of **salsa** or **chipotle sauce** instead of the chicken, and top with a sprinkle of **cilantro** for a Mexican-inspired bowl.
- **Bacon and Ranch Version:** Top with **crispy bacon** and a drizzle of **ranch dressing** for a hearty, savory twist.
- **Spicy Version:** Add some **jalapeños** and drizzle with **sriracha sauce** for a kick of heat.
- **Greek-Inspired:** Use **grilled chicken** and top with **cucumber slices, feta cheese**, and a dollop of **tzatziki sauce**.

NUTRITIONAL INFORMATION (PER SERVING)

Calories: 520	Fiber: 6g	Saturated Fat: 8g
Protein: 32g	Sugar: 6g	Cholesterol: 60mg
Carbohydrates: ...54g	Fat: 19g	Sodium: 740mg

SOUTHERN-STYLE SHRIMP AND GRITS

Yield: 4 servings   **Prep Time:** 15 minutes   **Cook Time:** 25 minutes   **Total Time:** 40 minutes

INGREDIENTS

For the Shrimp:
- **1 lb large shrimp**, peeled and deveined
- **2 tablespoons olive oil**
- **2 tablespoons unsalted butter**
- **2 cloves garlic**, minced
- **1/2 teaspoon smoked paprika**
- **1/4 teaspoon cayenne pepper**
- **Salt and black pepper**, to taste
- **1 tablespoon fresh lemon juice**
- **2 tablespoons fresh parsley**, chopped

For the Grits:
- **1 cup stone-ground grits**
- **4 cups water** (or half water, half milk)
- **1/2 cup shredded sharp cheddar cheese**
- **1/4 cup heavy cream**
- **2 tablespoons unsalted butter**
- **Salt and black pepper**, to taste

STEP-BY-STEP INSTRUCTIONS

1. Cook the Grits:

- In a medium saucepan, bring **4 cups of water** to a boil. Add a pinch of **salt** to the water.

- Gradually stir in the **stone-ground grits** and reduce the heat to low.

- Stir frequently and cook for **20-25 minutes**, or until the grits are tender and have absorbed most of the liquid. Add more water if needed during cooking.

- Once cooked, stir in the **butter**, **cheese**, and **heavy cream** (if using) to make the grits creamy and smooth. Season with **salt** and **pepper** to taste. Set aside, covered, to keep warm.

2. Prepare the Shrimp:

- While the grits are cooking, heat a large skillet over medium-high heat and add **olive oil** and **butter**.

- Once the butter is melted, add the **garlic** and cook for about **30 seconds**, until fragrant.

- Add the **shrimp** to the skillet and season with **smoked paprika**, **cayenne pepper** (if using), **salt**, and **pepper**. Cook for about **2-3 minutes per side** until the shrimp are pink and opaque.

- Once cooked, drizzle with **lemon juice** and sprinkle with **fresh parsley**.

3. Assemble the Dish:

- Spoon the creamy grits into bowls and top with the cooked shrimp.

- Garnish with additional parsley, if desired, and serve with lemon wedges on the side.

VARIATIONS AND ADAPTATIONS

- **Vegetarian Version:** Substitute the shrimp with **sautéed mushrooms** or **tofu** for a plant-based version of this dish. You can also use **smoked paprika** and **garlic** to add depth of flavor.

- **Spicy Version:** For extra heat, increase the **cayenne pepper** or add **chopped jalapeños** to the shrimp as they cook. You can also drizzle the dish with **hot sauce** for a tangy kick.

- **Southern-Style with Bacon:** Add **crispy bacon crumbles** on top of the grits and shrimp for extra flavor and a crunch. Bacon is often used in traditional Southern recipes for added smokiness.

- **Non-Shrimp Seafood Version:** Replace shrimp with **scallops**, **catfish fillets**, or **white fish** for a different seafood twist.

- **Cheese Variations:** You can experiment with other cheeses like **parmesan** or **cream cheese** to vary the flavor of the grits.

NUTRITIONAL INFORMATION (PER SERVING)

Calories: 500	Fiber: 2g	Saturated Fat: 9g
Protein: 35g	Sugar: 2g	Cholesterol: 210mg
Carbohydrates: ...44g	Fat: 24g	Sodium: 920mg

HEARTY CHICKEN NOODLE SOUP

Yield: 6 servings   **Prep Time:** 15 minutes   **Cook Time:** 40 minutes   **Total Time:** 55 minutes

INGREDIENTS
For the Soup:
- **2 tablespoons olive oil**
- **1 medium onion**, diced
- **2 medium carrots**, peeled and sliced
- **2 celery stalks**, sliced
- **3 cloves garlic**, minced
- **6 cups chicken broth** (homemade)

- **2 cups cooked chicken**, shredded
- **1 1/2 cups egg noodles** (or any pasta)
- **1 teaspoon dried thyme**
- **1/2 teaspoon dried rosemary**
- **1 bay leaf**
- **Salt and black pepper**, to taste
- **1 tablespoon fresh parsley**, chopped
- **1 tablespoon lemon juice**

STEP-BY-STEP INSTRUCTIONS

1. Sauté the Vegetables:
- In a large soup pot, heat the **olive oil** over medium heat.
- Add the **onion**, **carrots**, and **celery** to the pot. Sauté for about **5 minutes** until the vegetables start to soften.
- Add the **garlic** and cook for another **30 seconds** until fragrant.

2. Add the Broth and Seasonings:
- Pour in the **chicken broth** and bring the mixture to a boil.
- Add the **dried thyme**, **dried rosemary**, and **bay leaf**. Stir to combine.
- Season with **salt** and **pepper** to taste.
- Reduce the heat and let the soup simmer uncovered for **10-15 minutes** so the flavors can meld together.

3. Add the Chicken and Noodles:
- Stir in the **shredded chicken** and **egg noodles**.
- Continue to simmer for an additional **8-10 minutes**, or until the noodles are tender and cooked through.

4. Finish the Soup:
Remove the bay leaf from the soup.

- Stir in the fresh parsley and lemon juice (optional) to brighten up the flavors.

5. Serve:
- Ladle the soup into bowls, ensuring each bowl gets a good portion of noodles, chicken, and vegetables.
- Garnish with extra fresh parsley if desired.

VARIATIONS AND ADAPTATIONS
- **Vegetarian Version:** For a vegetarian version, replace the **chicken broth** with **vegetable broth** and omit the **shredded chicken**. Add extra vegetables like **zucchini**, **potatoes**, or **spinach** for a hearty and filling alternative.
- **Different Meats:** You can swap out the chicken for **turkey** or **beef** for a different flavor profile. Ground turkey or cooked sausage can be a great option for added richness.
- **Gluten-Free Version:** For a gluten-free version, use **gluten-free noodles** or substitute with **rice** or **quinoa** for a hearty alternative.
- **Asian-Inspired Version:** For a twist, you can use **rice noodles** and add **ginger**, **soy sauce**, and **scallions** to the broth, creating a more Asian-inspired flavor.
- **Spicy Version:** Add a dash of **hot sauce** or **chili flakes** for some heat. You can also incorporate **jalapeños** or **fresh chilies** for extra spice.

NUTRITIONAL INFORMATION (PER SERVING)

Calories: 280	Fiber: 3g	Saturated Fat: 1g
Protein: 22g	Sugar: 6g	Cholesterol: 50mg
Carbohydrates: ...32g	Fat: 8g	Sodium: 900mg

CHAPTER 4: LIGHT AND HEALTHY DINNERS

PRACTICAL TIPS

This chapter is all about creating meals that are nutritious, satisfying, and easy to prepare. Perfect for busy weeknights, these recipes focus on fresh, wholesome ingredients and balanced flavors, proving that healthy eating can be both simple and delicious. Follow these tips to make the most of your light and healthy dinners!

1. Prioritize Fresh and Seasonal Ingredients:
♦ Use locally sourced, in-season vegetables and fruits to maximize flavor and nutrition. Seasonal ingredients not only taste better but are often more affordable.

2. Opt for Lean Proteins:
♦ Incorporate proteins like chicken breast, turkey, fish, tofu, or legumes. They cook quickly and keep meals light yet satisfying.

3. Use Healthy Cooking Methods:
♦ Favor techniques like steaming, grilling, roasting, or stir-frying with minimal oil to retain nutrients and avoid unnecessary calories.

4. Build Flavor with Herbs and Spices:
♦ Skip heavy sauces and dressings by using fresh herbs, citrus juice, and a variety of spices to create bold, vibrant flavors. For example:

◊ Add fresh dill and lemon to fish.

◊ Use smoked paprika and cumin for roasted vegetables.

5. Balance Your Plate:
♦ Aim for a balance of lean protein, whole grains, and colorful vegetables. This not only keeps the dish visually appealing but ensures you get a variety of nutrients.

6. Embrace Quick Cooking Grains:
♦ Use fast-cooking grains like quinoa, bulgur, or couscous for a hearty base that's ready in minutes. Precooked brown rice or farro is another time-saver.

7. Portion Control Made Easy:
♦ Serve meals on smaller plates or pre-portion servings to avoid overeating while still feeling satisfied.

8. Lighten Up Dressings and Sauces:
♦ Create healthy dressings using ingredients like Greek yogurt, avocado, or tahini. Flavor with garlic, lemon, or Dijon mustard for an added kick.

9. Use Healthy Fats Wisely:
♦ Add good fats like avocado, olive oil, or nuts in moderation. A drizzle of olive oil or a sprinkle of chopped almonds can elevate the dish without overloading on calories.

10. Batch Prep for Ease:
♦ Chop vegetables, cook grains, or prepare marinades in advance. Having ingredients ready saves time on busy nights and encourages healthy choices.

11. Incorporate Plant-Based Proteins:
♦ Explore the versatility of beans, lentils, and chickpeas. They're packed with fiber and protein, making them ideal for light yet filling dinners.

12. Experiment with Global Flavors:
♦ Keep things exciting by incorporating international cuisines. Examples include:

◊ **Asian:** Stir-fried veggies with tofu and a light sesame-ginger dressing.

◊ **Mediterranean:** Grilled chicken with tabbouleh and a drizzle of tzatziki.

◊ **Mexican:** Lettuce wraps with black beans, avocado, and salsa.

13. Use Broths and Stocks for Depth:
♦ Cooking grains or vegetables in low-sodium broth instead of water enhances flavor without adding unhealthy ingredients.

14. Add a Crunchy Element:
♦ Top salads or bowls with roasted chickpeas, seeds, or slivered almonds for texture and a boost of nutrients.

15. Focus on Hydrating Foods:
♦ Include hydrating vegetables like cucumbers, tomatoes, and leafy greens, which are especially refreshing in lighter meals.

16. Prepare One-Dish Meals:
♦ Recipes like Buddha bowls, sheet pan dinners, or hearty soups combine all the elements of a healthy meal in one dish, minimizing cleanup.

17. Savor the Cooking Process:
♦ Even on busy nights, take a moment to enjoy the process of preparing fresh ingredients. Cooking with intention can make healthy meals more enjoyable.

CONCLUSION:
Light and healthy dinners don't have to be bland or boring. By focusing on fresh ingredients, simple techniques, and vibrant flavors, this chapter empowers you to create meals that nourish your body and delight your taste buds. With these tips and recipes, you'll find it easier than ever to make wholesome, satisfying meals part of your everyday routine!

ZUCCHINI NOODLES WITH PESTO

Yield: 4 servings   **Prep Time:** 10 minutes   **Cook Time:** 10 minutes   **Total Time:** 20 minutes

INGREDIENTS

For the Zucchini Noodles:
- **4 medium zucchini**
- **1 tablespoon olive oil**
- **Salt and pepper**, to taste

For the Pesto Sauce:
- **2 cups fresh basil leaves**
- **1/4 cup pine nuts** (or walnuts)
- **1/4 cup grated Parmesan cheese**
- **2 cloves garlic**, minced
- **1/4 cup olive oil**
- **1 tablespoon lemon juice** (optional)
- **Salt and pepper**, to taste

STEP-BY-STEP INSTRUCTIONS

1. Prepare the Zucchini Noodles:
- Wash the **zucchini** thoroughly and trim off the ends. Using a spiralizer or julienne peeler, create noodles from the zucchini. If you don't have a spiralizer, a regular vegetable peeler can create thin ribbons of zucchini.

- Heat **olive oil** in a large skillet over medium heat.

- Add the zucchini noodles to the skillet and sauté for **3-5 minutes**, tossing frequently, until just tender but still slightly crisp. Season with **salt** and **pepper** to taste. Set aside.

2. Make the Pesto Sauce:
- In a food processor or blender, combine the **basil leaves**, **pine nuts**, **Parmesan cheese**, **garlic**, and **lemon juice** (if using).

- With the processor running, slowly stream in the **olive oil** until the pesto reaches a smooth, creamy consistency. Scrape down the sides of the bowl if necessary. Season with **salt** and **pepper** to taste.

3. Combine and Serve:
- Add the prepared pesto sauce to the zucchini noodles and toss gently to combine, ensuring all the noodles are coated with the pesto.

- Serve immediately, garnishing with extra **Parmesan** and **fresh basil**, if desired.

VARIATIONS AND ADAPTATIONS

- **Vegan Version:** For a dairy-free version, substitute the **Parmesan** cheese with **nutritional yeast** or vegan Parmesan alternatives.

- **Different Vegetables:** Try substituting zucchini with other vegetables like **carrot noodles** or **sweet potato noodles** for a different flavor profile. You can also use a mix of zucchini and **yellow squash** for a colorful variation.

- **Add Protein:** For a more filling meal, you can top the zucchini noodles with **grilled chicken**, **shrimp**, or even **tofu** for a vegetarian option. Grilled **salmon** or **steak** would also pair wonderfully with the pesto.

- **Nutrient Boost:** Add a handful of **spinach** or **kale** to the pesto for a nutrient boost. You can also use **walnuts** or **almonds** instead of pine nuts for a different flavor and texture.

- **Spicy Version:** Add a pinch of **red pepper flakes** or a small diced **jalapeño** to the pesto for a spicy kick.

NUTRITIONAL INFORMATION (PER SERVING)

Calories: 250	Fiber: 3g	Saturated Fat: 3g
Protein: 7g	Sugar: 6g	Cholesterol: 5mg
Carbohydrates: ...15g	Fat: 20g	Sodium: 300mg

GRILLED LEMON CHICKEN SALAD

Yield: 4 servings   **Prep Time:** 15 minutes   **Cook Time:** 10 minutes   **Total Time:** 25 minutes

INGREDIENTS

For the Grilled Lemon Chicken:
- **4 boneless, skinless chicken breasts**
- **1 lemon**, juiced and zest
- **2 tablespoons olive oil**
- **1 teaspoon dried oregano**
- **1 teaspoon garlic powder**
- **Salt and pepper**, to taste

For the Salad:
- **6 cups mixed greens**
- **1 cucumber**, sliced
- **1 cup cherry tomatoes**, halved
- **1/2 red onion**, thinly sliced
- **1/4 cup crumbled feta cheese**
- **1/4 cup Kalamata olives**, pitted
- For the Dressing:
- **1/4 cup extra virgin olive oil**
- **2 tablespoons lemon juice**
- **1 teaspoon Dijon mustard**
- **1 teaspoon honey**
- **Salt and pepper**, to taste

STEP-BY-STEP INSTRUCTIONS

1. Marinate the Chicken:
- In a bowl, combine the **lemon juice, lemon zest, olive oil, oregano, garlic powder, salt,** and **pepper**. Whisk well to combine.
- Add the **chicken breasts** to the marinade, making sure they are fully coated. Cover and refrigerate for **at least 15 minutes**, or up to **2 hours** for a deeper flavor.

2. Grill the Chicken:
- Preheat your grill or grill pan over medium-high heat.
- Once hot, place the marinated chicken breasts on the grill. Cook for **5-7 minutes per side**, or until the chicken reaches an internal temperature of **165°F (75°C)** and the juices run clear.
- Remove the chicken from the grill and let it rest for a few minutes before slicing it into thin strips.

3. Prepare the Salad:
- While the chicken is grilling, prepare the salad. In a large bowl, combine the **mixed greens, cucumber slices, cherry tomatoes, red onion,** and **feta cheese** (if using).
- Add the **Kalamata olives** for extra flavor, if desired.

4. Make the Dressing:
- In a small bowl, whisk together the **extra virgin olive oil, lemon juice, Dijon mustard,** and **honey** (if using).
- Season with **salt** and **pepper** to taste. Whisk until the dressing is smooth and emulsified.

5. Assemble the Salad:
- Drizzle the dressing over the salad and toss gently to combine.
- Top with the grilled, sliced **lemon chicken** and serve immediately.

VARIATIONS AND ADAPTATIONS

- **Different Proteins:** You can replace the chicken with **grilled shrimp**, **tofu** (for a vegetarian option), or even **grilled steak** for a heartier variation.
- **Add More Vegetables:** Try adding roasted **sweet potatoes**, **avocado**, or **grilled zucchini** to give the salad more texture and flavor.
- **Spicy Kick:** Add a sprinkle of **red pepper flakes** to the dressing or top the salad with a few **sliced jalapeños** for some heat.
- **Vegan Option:** Omit the **feta cheese** and use a **vegan dressing** (such as a tahini-lemon dressing) to keep it plant-based.
- **Grilled Vegetables:** For a smoky flavor, consider grilling some vegetables, like **bell peppers**, **eggplant**, or **asparagus**, and adding them to the salad.

NUTRITIONAL INFORMATION (PER SERVING)

Calories: 370	Fiber: 3g	Saturated Fat: 4g
Protein: 38g	Sugar: 5g	Cholesterol: 80mg
Carbohydrates: ...15g	Fat: 22g	Sodium: 700mg

TERIYAKI SALMON BOWLS

Yield: 4 servings   **Prep Time:** 15 minutes   **Cook Time:** 10 minutes   **Total Time:** 25 minutes

INGREDIENTS

For the Teriyaki Salmon:
- **4 skinless salmon fillets** (about 6 oz each)
- **1/4 cup low-sodium soy sauce**
- **2 tablespoons honey**
- **2 tablespoons rice vinegar**
- **1 tablespoon sesame oil**
- **2 teaspoons freshly grated ginger**
- **2 garlic cloves**, minced
- **1 tablespoon cornstarch** (optional)

For the Bowls:
- **2 cups cooked rice**
- **1 cup steamed broccoli**
- **1/2 cup shredded carrots**
- **1/2 cucumber**, thinly sliced
- **1 tablespoon sesame seeds**
- **1 tablespoon chopped green onions**

STEP-BY-STEP INSTRUCTIONS

1. Prepare the Teriyaki Sauce:
- In a small saucepan, combine the **soy sauce, honey, rice vinegar, sesame oil, grated ginger,** and **minced garlic**. Stir well to combine.
- Bring the mixture to a gentle simmer over medium heat. Allow it to cook for about **3-4 minutes**, letting the flavors meld together.
- If you prefer a thicker sauce, mix the **cornstarch** with **1 tablespoon of cold water** to make a slurry, then whisk it into the sauce. Continue simmering for an additional **1-2 minutes** until it thickens.
- Remove from heat and set aside.

2. Cook the Salmon:
- Preheat a non-stick skillet or grill pan over medium-high heat. Lightly oil the pan with a small amount of sesame oil or vegetable oil.
- Season the **salmon fillets** with a pinch of salt and pepper.
- Place the fillets in the pan, skin-side down if they have skin, and cook for about **3-4 minutes** per side, or until the salmon is cooked through and easily flakes with a fork.
- During the last minute of cooking, brush the salmon generously with the **teriyaki sauce** to coat it in the glaze. Flip the fillets to ensure both sides are covered.

3. Assemble the Bowls:
- In each serving bowl, start by adding a base of cooked rice.
- Top the rice with **steamed broccoli, shredded carrots,** and **sliced cucumber**. Arrange them around the bowl for a vibrant presentation.
- Place a salmon fillet on top of the vegetables and rice.
- Drizzle the remaining teriyaki sauce over the salmon.
- Garnish with a sprinkle of **sesame seeds** and **chopped green onions** for an extra burst of flavor and texture.

4. Serve and Enjoy:
- Serve the bowls immediately while warm, and enjoy the fresh, savory flavors of the teriyaki salmon paired with the vibrant vegetables and rice.

VARIATIONS AND ADAPTATIONS
- **Different Proteins:** If you're not a fan of salmon, you can substitute with **grilled chicken, tofu,** or even **shrimp** for a lighter version.
- **Vegetarian Option:** For a vegetarian version, replace the salmon with **tofu** and marinate it in the same teriyaki sauce before pan-frying or baking. This adds a great texture and flavor while keeping it plant-based.
- **Vegetable Variations:** Experiment with different vegetables depending on what's in season. You can add **edamame, sautéed spinach,** or **roasted sweet potatoes** for variety and extra nutrients.
- **Spicy Kick:** If you prefer a little heat, add some **chili flakes** or **sriracha** to the teriyaki sauce, or drizzle some over the finished bowl.

NUTRITIONAL INFORMATION (PER SERVING)

Calories: 430	Fiber: 5g	Saturated Fat: 2g
Protein: 30g	Sugar: 14g	Cholesterol: 70mg
Carbohydrates: ...50g	Fat: 14g	Sodium: 700mg

VEGGIE STIR-FRY WITH TOFU

Yield: 4 servings   **Prep Time:** 15 minutes   **Cook Time:** 15 minutes   **Total Time:** 30 minutes

INGREDIENTS

For the Stir-Fry:
- 1 block (14 oz) firm tofu
- 1 tablespoon sesame oil
- 2 tablespoons soy sauce
- 1 tablespoon rice vinegar
- 1 tablespoon honey
- 1/2 teaspoon fresh grated ginger
- 2 garlic cloves, minced
- 1 medium zucchini, sliced
- 1 red bell pepper, sliced
- 1 cup broccoli florets
- 1/2 cup carrots, julienned
- 1/2 cup snap peas
- 1/4 cup green onions, chopped
- 1 tablespoon toasted sesame seeds

For the Sauce:
- 2 tablespoons soy sauce
- 1 tablespoon hoisin sauce
- 1 tablespoon rice vinegar
- 1 teaspoon sesame oil
- 1/2 teaspoon chili flakes

STEP-BY-STEP INSTRUCTIONS

1. Prepare the Tofu:
- Press the **tofu** to remove excess moisture. Place the block of tofu between two paper towels, then set something heavy (like a can or a cast iron skillet) on top for about **10 minutes**. This helps the tofu become crispy when fried.
- Once pressed, cut the tofu into **1-inch cubes**.

2. Make the Stir-Fry Sauce:
- In a small bowl, whisk together the **soy sauce, hoisin sauce, rice vinegar, sesame oil,** and **chili flakes** (if using). Set aside.

3. Cook the Tofu:
- Heat **1 tablespoon of sesame oil** in a large skillet or wok over medium-high heat.
- Add the tofu cubes and fry, stirring occasionally, until they are golden brown and crispy on all sides, about **5-7 minutes**. Once cooked, remove the tofu from the pan and set aside.

4. Cook the Vegetables:
- In the same skillet or wok, add a bit more **sesame oil** if needed.
- Add the **minced garlic** and **grated ginger**, cooking for **30 seconds** until fragrant.
- Add the **zucchini, red bell pepper, broccoli, carrots,** and **snap peas**. Stir-fry for about **5-6 minutes**, or until the vegetables are tender-crisp. If you prefer your vegetables softer, cook a few extra minutes.

5. Combine Tofu and Sauce:
- Add the crispy tofu back to the pan with the vegetables.
- Pour the stir-fry sauce over the tofu and vegetables. Stir well to coat everything evenly.
- Let the mixture cook for another **2-3 minutes**, allowing the sauce to thicken and the tofu to absorb the flavors.

6. Serve:
- Divide the stir-fry into bowls. Garnish with chopped **green onions** and a sprinkle of **toasted sesame seeds** for extra flavor and texture.
- Serve as is or over a bed of steamed **brown rice** or **quinoa** for a more substantial meal.

VARIATIONS AND ADAPTATIONS

- **Protein Variations:** If you're not a fan of tofu, you can swap it for **chicken breast** or **shrimp**. Simply cook the protein until fully cooked through, and then follow the same steps to combine with the vegetables and sauce.

- **Vegetable Variations:** Use any seasonal vegetables you prefer. Try **mushrooms, bok choy, baby corn,** or **green beans** for more variety. Root vegetables like **sweet potatoes** also work well if you prefer a heartier stir-fry.

- **Flavor Boosters:** For a more robust flavor, add a tablespoon of **peanut butter** to the sauce for creaminess or some **curry paste** for extra spice and complexity. You could also try adding **lime juice** or **fish sauce** for a tangy twist.

- **Spicy Version:** If you enjoy heat, increase the amount of **chili flakes**, or add a teaspoon of **Sriracha** sauce to the stir-fry sauce.

NUTRITIONAL INFORMATION (PER SERVING)

Calories: 280	Carbohydrates: ...30g	Sugar: 7g	Saturated Fat: 2g
Protein: 15g	Fiber: 7g	Fat: 14g	Cholesterol: 0mg
			Sodium: 800mg

QUINOA-STUFFED BELL PEPPERS

Yield: 4 servings   **Prep Time:** 15 minutes   **Cook Time:** 35 minutes   **Total Time:** 50 minutes

INGREDIENTS

For the Stuffed Peppers:
- **4 medium bell peppers**
- **1 cup quinoa**, rinsed
- **2 cups vegetable broth**
- **1 tablespoon olive oil**
- **1 small onion**, finely chopped
- **2 cloves garlic**, minced
- **1 zucchini**, diced
- **1 cup cherry tomatoes**, halved
- **1/2 cup black beans**, drained and rinsed
- **1/4 cup corn kernels**
- **1 teaspoon ground cumin**
- **1/2 teaspoon chili powder**
- **1/4 teaspoon smoked paprika**
- **Salt and pepper**, to taste
- **1/4 cup shredded cheese** (optional)
- **Fresh cilantro**, chopped (optional)

For the Sauce:
- **1/2 cup tomato sauce**
- **1 tablespoon lime juice**
- **1 teaspoon honey or agave syrup**
- **1/2 teaspoon ground cumin**
- **1/4 teaspoon chili flakes**

STEP-BY-STEP INSTRUCTIONS

1. Prepare the Bell Peppers:
- Preheat your oven to **375°F (190°C)**.
- Cut the tops off of the **bell peppers** and remove the seeds and membranes. Set them aside.
- Lightly brush the insides of the peppers with **olive oil** and place them in a baking dish. Set aside.

2. Cook the Quinoa:
- In a medium saucepan, combine the **quinoa** and **vegetable broth**. Bring to a boil, then cover and reduce the heat to low. Let it simmer for **15 minutes**, or until the quinoa is tender and the liquid is absorbed. Fluff the quinoa with a fork and set it aside.

3. Sauté the Vegetables:
- In a large skillet, heat the **olive oil** over medium heat.
- Add the **onion** and cook for **3-4 minutes**, until softened.
- Add the **garlic** and sauté for **30 seconds** until fragrant.
- Stir in the **zucchini, cherry tomatoes**, and **corn**. Cook for **5-7 minutes**, until the vegetables are tender and the tomatoes have softened.
- Add the cooked **quinoa, black beans, cumin, chili powder, smoked paprika**, salt, and pepper. Stir well to combine and cook for another **2 minutes**, allowing the flavors to meld together.

4. Stuff the Bell Peppers:
- Spoon the quinoa-vegetable mixture into the prepared bell peppers, packing them in tightly. If using cheese, sprinkle the **shredded cheese** on top of each stuffed pepper.
- Place the stuffed peppers in the oven and bake for **25 minutes**, or until the peppers are tender and the cheese (if used) is melted and bubbly.

5. Prepare the Sauce:
- While the peppers are baking, whisk together the **tomato sauce, lime juice, honey** (or agave syrup), **cumin**, and **chili flakes** in a small bowl.
- Heat the sauce over low heat for **3-4 minutes** to warm it through.

6. Serve:
- Once the peppers are done baking, remove them from the oven. Drizzle the warm sauce over the stuffed peppers and garnish with fresh **cilantro**.
- Serve the quinoa-stuffed bell peppers warm, as is, or with a side of greens for extra freshness.

VARIATIONS AND ADAPTATIONS

- **Protein Variations:**
  - ◇ For a non-vegetarian version, substitute the **black beans** with **ground turkey** or **chicken breast**. Brown the meat with the onions and garlic before adding the other vegetables.
  - ◇ Alternatively, use **ground beef** or **shrimp** for a different protein option.
- Vegetable Variations:
  - ◇ You can add **spinach, kale**, or **sweet potatoes** for more depth of flavor and nutrition.
  - ◇ Try adding roasted **eggplant, mushrooms**, or **carrots** to the quinoa mix for a richer taste.
- Cuisines Influences:
  - ◇ **Mediterranean Twist:** Swap the cumin and chili powder for **oregano** and **basil**. Use **feta cheese** instead of cheddar, and add **black olives** or **sun-dried tomatoes** to the stuffing.
  - ◇ **Indian-Inspired:** Add **garam masala, turmeric**, and **coriander** to the quinoa mixture, and serve the stuffed peppers with a yogurt-based sauce or chutney.
- Vegan Option:
  - ◇ Omit the cheese or use a plant-based alternative to make the dish fully vegan. You can also add **tofu** or **tempeh** for additional protein.

NUTRITIONAL INFORMATION (PER SERVING): Calories: 280, Protein: 9g, Carbohydrates: 45g, Fiber: 9g Sugar: 6g, Fat: 7g, Saturated Fat: 2g, Cholesterol: 10mg (if cheese is used), Sodium: 350mg

BALSAMIC GLAZED CHICKEN BREASTS

Yield: 4 servings   **Prep Time:** 10 minutes   **Cook Time:** 20 minutes   **Total Time:** 30 minutes

INGREDIENTS

For the Chicken Breasts:
- 4 boneless, skinless chicken breasts
- 2 tablespoons olive oil
- 1 teaspoon garlic powder
- 1 teaspoon onion powder
- **Salt and pepper**, to taste
- 1 tablespoon fresh thyme or 1 teaspoon dried thyme
- 1 tablespoon butter

For the Balsamic Glaze:
- 1/2 cup balsamic vinegar
- 2 tablespoons honey or maple syrup
- 1 tablespoon Dijon mustard
- 1 teaspoon garlic, minced
- 1 teaspoon fresh rosemary (optional)
- **Salt and pepper**, to taste

STEP-BY-STEP INSTRUCTIONS

1. Prepare the Chicken Breasts:
- Season the **chicken breasts** on both sides with **salt, pepper, garlic powder, onion powder**, and **fresh thyme**.
- Heat **olive oil** in a large skillet over medium-high heat. Once the oil is hot, add the chicken breasts and cook for about **5-7 minutes per side**, or until they are golden brown and cooked through (internal temperature should reach 165°F / 75°C). Remove the chicken from the skillet and set aside.

2. Make the Balsamic Glaze:
- In the same skillet, add the **balsamic vinegar, honey** (or maple syrup), **Dijon mustard**, and **minced garlic**. Stir to combine, scraping up any browned bits from the bottom of the pan.
- Bring the mixture to a simmer over medium heat and cook for about **3-5 minutes**, or until it reduces and thickens into a glossy glaze. If desired, add **fresh rosemary** for additional flavor. Taste and adjust seasoning with **salt** and **pepper**.
- Optionally, whisk in **butter** for a richer, silkier glaze.
- **3. Coat the Chicken:**
- Once the glaze has thickened, return the chicken breasts to the skillet and spoon the glaze over the chicken. Allow the chicken to cook in the glaze for an additional **1-2 minutes** so it can soak in the flavors and become caramelized.

4. Serve:
- Remove the chicken from the skillet and plate. Spoon any remaining glaze over the top.
- Garnish with extra **fresh thyme** or **rosemary** if desired.
- Serve with your favorite side dish like roasted vegetables, mashed potatoes, or a fresh salad.

VARIATIONS AND ADAPTATIONS

- **Protein Variations:**
  - ◊ **Chicken Thighs:** For a juicier option, swap chicken breasts for **boneless, skinless chicken thighs**. They will take a bit longer to cook, but they will be extra tender and flavorful.
  - ◊ **Pork Tenderloin:** You can also use **pork tenderloin** for a richer, heartier variation of the dish. The balsamic glaze pairs wonderfully with pork as well.

- **Vegetable Additions:**
  - ◊ Add **roasted vegetables** such as carrots, Brussels sprouts, or sweet potatoes as a side. For a more complete meal, you can even roast the vegetables with the chicken in the oven.
  - ◊ If you prefer a one-pan meal, you can sauté **spinach, zucchini**, or **mushrooms** in the same skillet after removing the chicken and before adding the glaze.

- **Herb Variations:**
  - ◊ Swap **thyme** with **oregano, basil**, or **sage** for different flavor profiles.
  - ◊ If you prefer a stronger flavor, consider adding a teaspoon of **fresh lemon juice** to the balsamic glaze for a citrusy kick.

- **Cuisines Influences:**
  - ◊ **Italian Twist:** Serve the balsamic glazed chicken with a side of **pasta** or **risotto** for a more Mediterranean-inspired meal.
  - ◊ **Asian-Inspired:** Add a tablespoon of **soy sauce** and **sesame oil** to the balsamic glaze for an Asian flair. Serve with a side of **steamed jasmine rice** and stir-fried vegetables.

NUTRITIONAL INFORMATION (PER SERVING)

Calories: 290	Carbohydrates: ...16g	Sugar: 11g	Saturated Fat: 2g
Protein: 36g	Fiber: 1g	Fat: 10g	Cholesterol: 80mg
			Sodium: 220mg

MEDITERRANEAN CHICKPEA SALAD

Yield: 4 servings   **Prep Time:** 15 minutes   **Total Time:** 15 minutes

INGREDIENTS

For the Salad:
- **1 can (15 oz) chickpeas**, drained and rinsed
- **1 medium cucumber**, diced
- **1 pint cherry tomatoes**, halved
- **1/4 red onion**, finely sliced
- **1/2 cup Kalamata olives**, pitted and sliced
- **1/4 cup feta cheese**, crumbled
- **1/4 cup fresh parsley**, chopped
- **1 tablespoon extra virgin olive oil**
- **1 tablespoon lemon juice**
- **1 teaspoon dried oregano**
- **Salt and pepper**, to taste

Optional Protein Additions:
- **Grilled chicken, grilled shrimp, or tofu cubes** for extra protein.

STEP-BY-STEP INSTRUCTIONS

1. Prepare the Salad Ingredients:
- Drain and rinse the **chickpeas** (if using canned). If using dry chickpeas, cook them ahead of time according to package instructions.
- Dice the **cucumber** and halve the **cherry tomatoes**. Thinly slice the **red onion**.
- Slice the **Kalamata olives** and crumble the **feta cheese**.
- Chop the **fresh parsley** for garnish.

2. Assemble the Salad:
- In a large bowl, combine the **chickpeas, cucumber, cherry tomatoes, red onion, Kalamata olives, feta cheese**, and **parsley**.

3. Prepare the Dressing:
- In a small bowl or jar, whisk together the **extra virgin olive oil, lemon juice, dried oregano, salt**, and **pepper** to taste. This creates a simple yet flavorful Mediterranean dressing.

4. Toss and Serve:
- Pour the dressing over the salad and toss gently to combine, ensuring all ingredients are well-coated.
- Taste and adjust seasoning if needed.

5. Optional Protein:
- If adding **grilled chicken, shrimp**, or **tofu**, top the salad with your choice of protein and serve immediately, or pack it for a delicious, on-the-go lunch or dinner.

VARIATIONS AND ADAPTATIONS

- **Grilled Vegetables:** Add **grilled zucchini, eggplant**, or **bell peppers** for extra flavor and seasonal variety. Grilled vegetables pair beautifully with the Mediterranean flavors of this salad.
- **Quinoa:** For a heartier version, add a 1/2 cup of **cooked quinoa** to the salad. This will make it more filling and turn it into a complete meal.
- **Herb Variations:** If you don't have fresh parsley, you can substitute with fresh **basil, mint**, or **oregano** for different flavor profiles.
- **Vegan Option:** Omit the **feta cheese** and use **vegan feta** or another plant-based cheese. For extra richness, you can also add **avocado** or top with **toasted pine nuts**.
- **Meat Alternatives:** For a twist, you can replace the feta with **grilled chicken** or **grilled shrimp**. You could also try **grilled lamb** or **salmon** for a more robust flavor profile.
- **Middle Eastern Twist:** Incorporate **hummus** or **tzatziki sauce** into the salad for an added creaminess and tang.

NUTRITIONAL INFORMATION (PER SERVING)

Calories: 230	Fiber: 6g	Saturated Fat: 2g
Protein: 8g	Sugar: 6g	Cholesterol: 15mg
Carbohydrates: ...22g	Fat: 14g	Sodium: 430mg

SWEET POTATO AND BLACK BEAN TACOS

Yield: 4 servings (2 tacos per serving)   **Prep Time:** 15 minutes   **Cook Time:** 25 minutes   **Total Time:** 40 minutes

INGREDIENTS
For the Tacos:
- **2 medium sweet potatoes,** peeled and diced into 1/2-inch cubes
- **1 can (15 oz) black beans,** drained and rinsed
- **1 tablespoon olive oil**
- **1 teaspoon ground cumin**
- **1 teaspoon chili powder**
- **1/2 teaspoon smoked paprika** (
- **1/4 teaspoon garlic powder**
- **1/4 teaspoon onion powder**
- **Salt and pepper,** to taste
- **8 small corn or flour tortillas**
- **1/4 cup fresh cilantro,** chopped
- **1 avocado,** sliced
- **1/2 cup red cabbage,** thinly sliced
- **1/2 cup crumbled feta cheese** or **cotija cheese**
- **1 tablespoon lime juice**

For the Optional Toppings:
- **Sour cream** or **Greek yogurt**
- **Salsa** or **hot sauce** for extra spice

STEP-BY-STEP INSTRUCTIONS

1. Roast the Sweet Potatoes:
- Preheat the oven to 400°F (200°C).
- In a large bowl, toss the diced **sweet potatoes** with **olive oil, cumin, chili powder, smoked paprika, garlic powder, onion powder, salt,** and **pepper** until evenly coated.
- Spread the seasoned sweet potatoes in a single layer on a baking sheet lined with parchment paper.
- Roast for 20-25 minutes, tossing halfway through, until the sweet potatoes are tender and lightly caramelized.

2. Prepare the Black Beans:
- While the sweet potatoes are roasting, heat a small saucepan over medium heat.
- Add the **black beans** to the pan, and cook for 5-7 minutes, stirring occasionally. You can season them with a pinch of **cumin** and **chili powder** for extra flavor, if desired.
- Once heated, remove from heat and set aside.

3. Warm the Tortillas:
- Heat a dry skillet or griddle over medium heat.
- Warm the **tortillas** for about 30 seconds on each side until soft and pliable. Alternatively, you can wrap them in a damp paper towel and microwave them for 15-20 seconds.

4. Assemble the Tacos:
- To assemble, start with a warm tortilla and add a spoonful of roasted **sweet potatoes** and a spoonful of **black beans.**
- Top with **red cabbage, avocado slices,** and a sprinkle of **cilantro.**
- Add a bit of **feta cheese** or **cotija cheese** (optional), and squeeze some fresh **lime juice** over the top for a burst of brightness.

5. Serve:
- Serve the tacos with **sour cream** or **Greek yogurt,** and your choice of **salsa** or **hot sauce** for added flavor and heat.

VARIATIONS AND ADAPTATIONS
- **Protein Additions:** If you'd like to add more protein to the tacos, you can top them with **grilled chicken, ground turkey,** or **shrimp.** For a plant-based option, **grilled tempeh** or **tofu** would also work well.
- **Vegetable Variations:** Try adding other seasonal vegetables such as **roasted bell peppers, zucchini,** or **corn** for extra flavor and texture. You can also swap the red cabbage for **shredded lettuce** or **spinach.**
- **Spicy Variation:** If you enjoy extra heat, add some **jalapeño slices, chipotle peppers in adobo sauce,** or a dash of **hot sauce** to the filling.
- **Grain-Free Option:** Use **lettuce wraps** instead of tortillas for a grain-free option.
- **Middle Eastern Twist:** For a unique twist, add some **hummus** or **tzatziki** as a topping, and use **pita** bread instead of tortillas.

NUTRITIONAL INFORMATION (PER SERVING)

Calories: 330	Carbohydrates: ...51g	Sugar: 7g	Saturated Fat: 2g
Protein: 9g	Fiber: 13g	Fat: 12g	Cholesterol: 10mg
			Sodium: 420mg

GREEK CHICKEN BOWLS

Yield: 4 servings　　**Prep Time:** 15 minutes　　**Cook Time:** 20 minutes　　**Total Time:** 35 minutes

INGREDIENTS

For the Chicken:
- ♦ **4 boneless, skinless chicken breasts**
- ♦ **1 tablespoon olive oil**
- ♦ **1 teaspoon dried oregano**
- ♦ **1 teaspoon garlic powder**
- ♦ **1/2 teaspoon paprika**
- ♦ **Salt and pepper**, to taste
- ♦ **1 tablespoon lemon juice**

For the Bowls:
- ♦ **2 cups cooked quinoa** (or brown rice)
- ♦ **1 cup cherry tomatoes**, halved
- ♦ **1 cucumber**, diced
- ♦ **1/2 red onion**, thinly sliced
- ♦ **1/2 cup Kalamata olives**, pitted
- ♦ **1/2 cup feta cheese**, crumbled
- ♦ **1/4 cup fresh parsley**, chopped
- ♦ **1/4 cup tzatziki sauce**

For Homemade Tzatziki Sauce (optional):
- ♦ **1/2 cup plain Greek yogurt**
- ♦ **1/2 cucumber**, grated
- ♦ **1 tablespoon olive oil**
- ♦ **1 teaspoon lemon juice**
- ♦ **1 garlic clove**, minced
- ♦ **1 tablespoon fresh dill**, chopped
- ♦ **Salt and pepper**, to taste

STEP-BY-STEP INSTRUCTIONS

1. Marinate and Cook the Chicken:
- ♦ In a small bowl, combine **olive oil, oregano, garlic powder, paprika, lemon juice, salt,** and **pepper**. Rub this mixture all over the **chicken breasts** and let them marinate for 10 minutes.
- ♦ Heat a grill pan or skillet over medium-high heat. Once hot, add the chicken breasts and cook for 6-7 minutes per side, or until the internal temperature reaches 165°F (74°C) and the chicken is golden brown. Remove from heat and let the chicken rest for 5 minutes before slicing it into thin strips.

2. Prepare the Quinoa:
- ♦ While the chicken is cooking, rinse **quinoa** under cold water. In a medium pot, bring **2 cups of water** to a boil, then add the rinsed quinoa. Reduce the heat to low, cover, and cook for 15 minutes or until the water is absorbed. Fluff with a fork and set aside.

3. Make the Tzatziki Sauce (if using homemade):
- ♦ In a small bowl, combine **Greek yogurt, grated cucumber, olive oil, lemon juice, minced garlic, dill,** and a pinch of **salt** and **pepper**. Stir until well combined. Adjust seasoning to taste.

4. Assemble the Greek Chicken Bowls:
- ♦ Divide the **quinoa** evenly between 4 bowls.
- ♦ Arrange slices of **grilled chicken** on top of the quinoa.
- ♦ Add a handful of **cherry tomatoes, cucumber, red onion, Kalamata olives,** and **feta cheese** to each bowl.
- ♦ Drizzle with **tzatziki sauce** and garnish with **fresh parsley**.

5. Serve and Enjoy:
- ♦ Serve the bowls with additional lemon wedges on the side, if desired, and enjoy this fresh and satisfying meal.

VARIATIONS AND ADAPTATIONS
- ♦ **Vegetarian Version:** Replace the chicken with **grilled tofu** or **falafel** for a plant-based option. You can also add roasted **chickpeas** for more protein and crunch.
- ♦ **Grains:** Swap the **quinoa** for **brown rice, bulgur wheat,** or **couscous** for a different base.
- ♦ **Veggie Variations:** Add roasted seasonal vegetables such as **zucchini, eggplant,** or **sweet potatoes** for extra texture and flavor.
- ♦ **Cultural Twist:** Add a drizzle of **hummus** or **harissa** for an additional layer of flavor, or incorporate **pita bread** as a side for a more Mediterranean-style meal.

NUTRITIONAL INFORMATION (PER SERVING)

Calories: 480	Fiber: 6g	Saturated Fat: 6g
Protein: 34g	Sugar: 5g	Cholesterol: 70mg
Carbohydrates: ...42g	Fat: 22g	Sodium: 650mg

SPINACH AND MUSHROOM FRITTATA

Yield: 4 servings   **Prep Time:** 10 minutes   **Cook Time:** 20 minutes   **Total Time:** 30 minutes

INGREDIENTS
- **8 large eggs**
- **1 tablespoon olive oil**
- **1 small onion**, diced
- **2 cups fresh spinach**, roughly chopped
- **1 1/2 cups mushrooms**, sliced
- **1/2 cup milk**
- **1/2 teaspoon garlic powder**
- **Salt and pepper**, to taste
- **1/2 teaspoon dried thyme**
- **1/4 cup grated Parmesan cheese**
- **1/4 cup shredded mozzarella cheese**
- **1 tablespoon fresh parsley**, chopped

STEP-BY-STEP INSTRUCTIONS

1. Prepare the Vegetables:
- Heat **olive oil** in a 10-inch oven-safe skillet over medium heat.
- Add the **diced onion** to the skillet and sauté for about 2-3 minutes, until softened.
- Add the **sliced mushrooms** and cook for another 5 minutes, until the mushrooms are tender and browned.
- Stir in the **chopped spinach** and cook for 2-3 minutes, until wilted. Season with **salt, pepper, garlic powder**, and **dried thyme**. Remove from heat and set aside.

2. Prepare the Egg Mixture:
- In a large bowl, whisk together the **eggs, milk**, and **a pinch of salt and pepper** until well combined. Stir in the **Parmesan cheese** and **mozzarella cheese** (if using).

3. Combine and Cook the Frittata:
- Pour the egg mixture over the cooked vegetables in the skillet, making sure the vegetables are evenly distributed. Let the mixture cook undisturbed over medium heat for about 5 minutes, until the edges begin to set.
- Once the edges are set, transfer the skillet to the oven and broil for 3-4 minutes, or until the top is golden brown and the frittata is fully set in the middle. Be sure to keep an eye on it to prevent burning.

4. Serve and Garnish:
- Remove the skillet from the oven and let the frittata cool for a couple of minutes. Sprinkle with **fresh parsley** for garnish, slice into wedges, and serve warm.

VARIATIONS AND ADAPTATIONS
- **Add Meat:** For a heartier meal, add **cooked bacon, sausage**, or **chicken** to the vegetable mixture.
- **Swap Vegetables:** Experiment with other seasonal veggies such as **zucchini, tomatoes**, or **peppers**. Roasted **butternut squash** or **sweet potatoes** would also be delicious.
- **Dairy-Free:** Omit the **Parmesan** and **mozzarella** or use dairy-free alternatives like nutritional yeast or plant-based cheese.
- **Herb Variations:** Try adding **basil, oregano**, or **rosemary** for a different flavor profile.

NUTRITIONAL INFORMATION (PER SERVING)

Calories: 220	Fiber: 2g	Saturated Fat: 5g
Protein: 16g	Sugar: 3g	Cholesterol: 300mg
Carbohydrates: ...7g	Fat: 16g	Sodium: 330mg

CHAPTER 5:
KID-APPROVED MEALS

PRACTICAL TIPS

Cooking for kids can be a rewarding yet challenging experience. This chapter is filled with recipes designed to satisfy picky eaters while ensuring balanced nutrition. These tips will help you create meals that kids love and parents feel good about serving!

1. Keep It Fun and Interactive:
- Involve kids in the meal preparation process. Let them mix ingredients, choose toppings, or help assemble dishes like mini pizzas or taco bowls.
- Serve meals in playful ways, like using fun-shaped cookie cutters for sandwiches or arranging food into smiley faces.

2. Sneak in the Veggies:
- Puree vegetables like carrots, zucchini, or spinach and mix them into sauces, soups, or casseroles.
- Add grated veggies to favorites like meatballs, burgers, or pasta.

3. Prioritize Finger Foods:
- Kids often enjoy foods they can eat with their hands. Think homemade chicken tenders, veggie sticks with dip, or quesadilla wedges.

4. Opt for Mild Flavors:
- Stick to simple seasoning for younger palates, like garlic, mild paprika, or a pinch of cheese. Gradually introduce new spices and flavors over time.

5. Create Build-Your-Own Options:
- Set up «DIY» meals, such as taco bars, baked potato toppings, or salad stations. Giving kids choices makes them more likely to try something new.

6. Make It Bite-Sized:
- Cut foods into smaller, manageable pieces to make them easier for kids to handle and eat. Mini sliders, fruit skewers, or pasta shapes work well.

7. Balance Familiar with New:
- Pair familiar ingredients with new ones. For example, serve grilled cheese with a side of roasted sweet potato fries or add small pieces of broccoli to mac and cheese.

8. Use Healthy Swaps:
- Swap refined grains for whole grains (e.g., whole wheat pasta, brown rice, or whole-grain tortillas).
- Replace sugary drinks with water infused with fruit or milk alternatives if needed.

9. Go for Bright Colors:
- Create colorful plates using a variety of fruits and vegetables. Kids are often drawn to visually appealing meals.
- Use naturally vibrant ingredients like cherry tomatoes, bell peppers, and blueberries.

10. Pack Nutrients into Sauces and Spreads:
- Blend nuts or seeds into pesto, add yogurt to dressings, or mix hummus into sandwich spreads for extra nutrition.

11. Make Breakfast for Dinner:
- Many kids love breakfast foods any time of day. Try recipes like mini pancakes with fruit, veggie-loaded scrambled eggs, or breakfast burritos.

12. Don't Forget the Classics:
- Reinvent traditional kid-friendly meals with healthier ingredients. For example:
  ◊ **Chicken nuggets:** Bake instead of fry, and use whole-grain breading.
  ◊ **Pizza:** Use whole-wheat crust and load it with colorful veggies.
  ◊ **Spaghetti:** Add finely chopped veggies to the sauce or use whole-grain pasta.

13. Offer Dipping Options:
- Kids love to dip! Serve meals with healthy dips like yogurt-based ranch, guacamole, salsa, or hummus to make vegetables and proteins more appealing.

14. Add a Touch of Sweetness:
- Incorporate naturally sweet ingredients like honey, maple syrup, or fruit to balance flavors in dishes like baked chicken or roasted veggies.

15. Prepare in Advance:
- Batch-cook kid-friendly staples like pasta, roasted chicken, or veggie sticks for quick assembly during busy evenings.

16. Make Meals Predictable Yet Exciting:
- Establish a theme night, such as «Taco Tuesday» or «Pasta Friday,» but switch up the ingredients each week to keep things interesting.

17. Encourage Small Portions:
- Serve smaller portions to avoid overwhelming kids, and let them ask for seconds if they're still hungry.

18. Celebrate Treats in Moderation:
- Include occasional treats in meals, like a small serving of chocolate chips in a yogurt parfait or a sprinkle of shredded cheese on veggies.

19. Be Patient with New Foods:
- Encourage kids to try new foods but don't force them. Offer the same ingredient in different ways over time to build familiarity.

20. Make It a Family Affair:
- Enjoy meals together as a family whenever possible. Modeling healthy eating habits is one of the best ways to inspire kids to eat well.

CONCLUSION:
This chapter is designed to help you navigate the joys and challenges of cooking for kids. By focusing on fun, balanced nutrition, and engaging presentation, you can create meals that kids will love and parents will appreciate. With these tips, you'll be equipped to turn even the pickiest eater into a happy and healthy diner!

MINI CHEESEBURGER SLIDERS

Yield: 12 sliders   **Prep Time:** 15 minutes   **Cook Time:** 10-15 minutes   **Total Time:** 30 minutes

INGREDIENTS
- **1 lb ground beef**
- **1/4 cup finely diced onion**
- **1/4 cup bread crumbs**
- **1 large egg**
- **1 teaspoon garlic powder**
- **Salt and pepper**, to taste
- **12 mini slider buns**
- **6 slices cheddar cheese**

- **Condiments:**
  - ◊ **Ketchup**
  - ◊ **Mustard**
  - ◊ **Pickles**, sliced
  - ◊ **Lettuce**
  - ◊ **Tomato slices**

STEP-BY-STEP INSTRUCTIONS

1. Prepare the Burger Patties:
- In a large bowl, combine **ground beef**, **diced onion**, **bread crumbs**, **egg**, **garlic powder**, and a pinch of **salt** and **pepper**.
- Mix everything together gently, being careful not to overwork the meat. Shape the mixture into 12 small patties, about the size of the slider buns.

2. Cook the Sliders:
- Heat a skillet or grill pan over medium-high heat and lightly grease it with **olive oil**.
- Cook the patties in batches, depending on the size of your skillet. Grill each side for about **3-4 minutes** or until browned and cooked through (internal temperature should reach 160°F for beef).
- A minute before the patties are done, place **half a slice of cheese** on top of each patty to melt. If you prefer more cheese, you can use a whole slice, but cutting them in half fits perfectly for sliders.

3. Toast the Buns:
- While the patties are cooking, slice the **slider buns** in half and lightly toast them on the grill pan or in the oven at **350°F** for about **2-3 minutes** until they're slightly golden and crispy.

4. Assemble the Sliders:
- Once the patties and buns are ready, assemble the sliders by placing each cheese-covered patty on the bottom half of a toasted bun.
- Top with your choice of condiments: a smear of **ketchup** and **mustard**, a few slices of **pickles**, a leaf of **lettuce**, and a slice of **tomato**.
- Place the top bun on each slider and serve immediately.

VARIATIONS AND ADAPTATIONS
- **Chicken Sliders:** Swap out the ground beef for **ground chicken** or **turkey** for a lighter option.
- **Vegetarian Sliders:** Use **black beans**, **chickpeas**, or **lentils** as a base and bind with breadcrumbs, adding your choice of spices and seasonings. You can also use **plant-based patties**.
- **Asian-Inspired Sliders:** Use **ground pork** or **chicken**, and season with **soy sauce**, **ginger**, and **green onions**. Top with **hoisin sauce**, **pickled cucumbers**, and **cilantro**.
- **Mexican Sliders:** Use **ground beef** mixed with **chili powder**, **cumin**, and **garlic**. Add **sliced jalapeños**, **avocado**, and **salsa** for a spicy twist.

NUTRITIONAL INFORMATION (PER SLIDER)

Calories: 220	Fiber: 2g	Saturated Fat: 5g
Protein: 16g	Sugar: 3g	Cholesterol: 40mg
Carbohydrates: ...16g	Fat: 12g	Sodium: 450mg

BAKED CHICKEN NUGGETS

Yield: 4 servings (about 16-18 nuggets)   **Prep Time:** 15 minutes   **Cook Time:** 20-25 minutes   **Total Time:** 40 minutes

- ◆ **Ingredients**
- ◆ **1 lb boneless, skinless chicken breasts**
- ◆ **1 cup panko breadcrumbs**
- ◆ **1/2 cup grated Parmesan cheese**
- ◆ **1 teaspoon garlic powder**
- ◆ **1 teaspoon onion powder**
- ◆ **1 teaspoon paprika**
- ◆ **1/2 teaspoon salt**
- ◆ **1/2 teaspoon pepper**
- ◆ **2 large eggs**
- ◆ **1/2 cup all-purpose flour**
- ◆ **Olive oil spray**

Optional Dipping Sauces:
- ◆ **Honey mustard**
- ◆ **Ketchup**
- ◆ **Ranch dressing**

STEP-BY-STEP INSTRUCTIONS

1. Preheat the Oven:
- ◆ Preheat your oven to **400°F** (200°C). Line a baking sheet with parchment paper or lightly grease it with **olive oil** spray.

2. Prepare the Chicken:
- ◆ Cut the **chicken breasts** into bite-sized cubes, about 1 to 1.5 inches each. For uniform cooking, try to keep the pieces the same size.

3. Set up the Dipping Stations:
- ◆ In a shallow dish, place the **flour**.
- ◆ In another shallow dish, beat the **eggs**.
- ◆ In a third shallow dish, mix the **panko breadcrumbs**, **Parmesan cheese, garlic powder, onion powder, paprika, salt**, and **pepper** until well combined.

4. Coat the Chicken:
- ◆ First, dredge each piece of chicken in the **flour**, shaking off the excess.
- ◆ Next, dip the chicken into the **egg** mixture, allowing any excess to drip off.
- ◆ Finally, coat the chicken in the **panko breadcrumb mixture**, pressing gently to ensure the breadcrumbs stick evenly to each piece.

5. Arrange on Baking Sheet:
- ◆ Place the coated chicken pieces on the prepared baking sheet in a single layer, making sure there is space between each nugget for even cooking.
- ◆ Lightly spray the top of the nuggets with **olive oil** or vegetable oil to promote crisping during baking.

- ◆ **6. Bake the Nuggets:**
- ◆ Bake in the preheated oven for **20-25 minutes**, flipping the nuggets halfway through the cooking time. They should be golden brown and crispy on the outside and fully cooked through inside (internal temperature should reach 165°F).

7. Serve and Enjoy:
- ◆ Serve the baked chicken nuggets immediately with your favorite **dipping sauces** such as **honey mustard, ketchup**, or **ranch dressing**.

VARIATIONS AND ADAPTATIONS

- ◆ **Chicken Thighs:** For juicier nuggets, use **boneless, skinless chicken thighs** instead of breasts. Thighs tend to have more fat, which can add flavor and moisture.

- ◆ **Spicy Chicken Nuggets:** Add **cayenne pepper** or **chili powder** to the breadcrumb mixture for an extra kick. Alternatively, dip the nuggets in a spicy sriracha sauce.

- ◆ **Vegetarian Option:** Substitute the chicken with **tofu** (pressed and cut into cubes) or **cauliflower florets** for a veggie-packed, plant-based version.

- ◆ **Asian-Inspired:** Use **sesame seeds** and **ginger powder** in the breadcrumb mixture. Serve with a dipping sauce made from **soy sauce, rice vinegar**, and **honey**.

- ◆ **Gluten-Free:** Substitute **gluten-free breadcrumbs** and **rice flour** for a completely gluten-free meal.

NUTRITIONAL INFORMATION (PER SERVING, 4 SERVINGS TOTAL)

Calories: 350	Fiber: 2g	Saturated Fat: 3g
Protein: 33g	Sugar: 1g	Cholesterol: 180mg
Carbohydrates: ...28g	Fat: 14g	Sodium: 600mg

CHEESY PASTA BAKE

Yield: 6 servings   **Prep Time:** 15 minutes   **Cook Time:** 30-35 minutes   **Total Time:** 45-50 minutes

INGREDIENTS

- 1 lb (450g) pasta (penne, rigatoni)
- 2 cups shredded mozzarella cheese
- 1 cup grated Parmesan cheese
- 2 cups marinara sauce
- 1 cup ricotta cheese
- 1 tablespoon olive oil
- 2 cloves garlic, minced
- 1 small onion, chopped
- 1 cup cooked chicken breast, shredded
- 1 teaspoon dried Italian seasoning
- 1/2 teaspoon red pepper flakes
- Salt and pepper to taste
- Fresh basil or parsley for garnish

STEP-BY-STEP INSTRUCTIONS

1. Preheat the Oven:
- Preheat your oven to **375°F (190°C)**. Grease a large baking dish (9x13-inch or similar) with a little olive oil or cooking spray.

2. Cook the Pasta:
- Bring a large pot of salted water to a boil. Cook the pasta according to the package instructions, but reduce the cooking time by about 2 minutes so the pasta is slightly undercooked (it will finish cooking in the oven). Drain the pasta and set aside.

3. Prepare the Sauce:
- In a large skillet, heat **1 tablespoon olive oil** over medium heat. Add the **chopped onion** and cook for about **3-4 minutes**, until softened. Add the **minced garlic** and cook for an additional **1 minute** until fragrant.
- Stir in the **marinara sauce, Italian seasoning, red pepper flakes**, and a pinch of **salt** and **pepper**. Bring the sauce to a simmer and cook for 5 minutes to allow the flavors to meld together. If using **shredded chicken**, stir it into the sauce at this point.

4. Combine the Pasta and Sauce:
- In a large mixing bowl, combine the cooked pasta with the marinara sauce mixture. Stir in the **ricotta cheese** and **half of the shredded mozzarella**. Mix until the pasta is evenly coated with the sauce and cheese.

5. Assemble the Pasta Bake:
- Pour the pasta mixture into the prepared baking dish, spreading it out evenly. Top with the remaining **mozzarella cheese** and **Parmesan cheese**.

6. Bake the Pasta:
- Place the baking dish in the preheated oven and bake for **20-25 minutes**, or until the cheese is melted, bubbly, and golden brown on top.

7. Serve and Garnish:
- Let the pasta bake cool for 5 minutes before serving. Garnish with fresh **basil** or **parsley** for a burst of color and freshness.

VARIATIONS AND ADAPTATIONS

- **Vegetarian Version:** Omit the chicken and instead add **sautéed mushrooms, zucchini**, or **spinach** for added flavor and nutrition. You can also include roasted bell peppers or eggplant for a more Mediterranean flair.

- **Meat Lovers Version:** Add crumbled **Italian sausage, ground beef**, or **ground turkey** for a heartier meal. Cook the meat first and stir it into the sauce before combining with the pasta.

- **Spicy Cheesy Pasta Bake:** Stir in some **jalapeños** or use a spicy marinara sauce to kick up the heat. You can also add extra **red pepper flakes** for more spice.

- **Cheese Variations:** Swap out the mozzarella for other cheeses like **cheddar, gouda**, or **fontina** for a different flavor profile. You can even mix in a bit of **blue cheese** for a tangy twist.

NUTRITIONAL INFORMATION (PER SERVING, 6 SERVINGS TOTAL)

Calories: 450	Fiber: 4g	Saturated Fat: 9g	Calcium: ....30% DV
Protein: 28g	Sugar: 8g	Cholesterol: 55mg	Iron: ....10% DV
Carbohydrates: ...43g	Fat: 18g	Sodium: 950mg	

HOMEMADE PIZZA NIGHT

Yield: 2 medium-sized pizzas (8 slices per pizza)

Prep Time: 15 minutes (plus time for dough rising)

Cook Time: 12-15 minutes

INGREDIENTS

For the Pizza Dough:
- 3 cups all-purpose flour (plus extra for dusting)
- 1 packet (2 1/4 teaspoons) active dry yeast
- 1 teaspoon sugar
- 1 teaspoon salt
- 1 tablespoon olive oil
- 1 cup warm water (110°F)

For the Pizza Sauce:
- 1 cup crushed tomatoes
- 1 tablespoon olive oil
- 1 clove garlic, minced
- 1 teaspoon dried oregano
- 1/2 teaspoon dried basil
- A pinch of sugar
- Salt and pepper to taste

Toppings (Choose according to season):
- 1/2 cup shredded mozzarella cheese
- 1/2 cup fresh spinach leaves
- 1 medium-sized tomato, sliced
- 1/4 cup sliced red onion
- 1/4 cup black olives, sliced
- 1/4 cup bell peppers (red or green), diced
- Fresh arugula or parsley, for garnish

Optional Protein Topping:
- 1/4 cup cooked Italian sausage or pepperoni

STEP-BY-STEP INSTRUCTIONS

1. Prepare the Pizza Dough:
- In a large mixing bowl, combine **3 cups of all-purpose flour**, **1 teaspoon salt**, and **1 teaspoon sugar**. Make a well in the center.
- **In a small bowl**, dissolve **1 packet (2 1/4 teaspoons) active dry yeast** in **1 cup warm water (110°F)** with **1 tablespoon olive oil**. Let it sit for 5 minutes until it starts to foam.
- Pour the yeast mixture into the well of flour and mix with a wooden spoon until a dough forms.
- Knead the dough for 5 minutes on a lightly floured surface until smooth and elastic.
- Place the dough in an oiled bowl, cover it with a clean towel, and let it rise in a warm place for 1-2 hours or until doubled in size.

2. Prepare the Pizza Sauce:
- Heat **1 tablespoon of olive oil** in a small saucepan over medium heat. Add **1 clove of minced garlic** and sauté for 1 minute until fragrant.
- Stir in **1 cup of crushed tomatoes, 1 teaspoon dried oregano, 1/2 teaspoon dried basil, a pinch of sugar (if needed), salt**, and **pepper**. Simmer the sauce for 15 minutes on low heat, stirring occasionally. Set aside.

3. Preheat the Oven:
- Preheat your oven to **475°F (245°C)**. If you have a pizza stone, place it in the oven to preheat as well.

4. Roll Out the Pizza Dough:
- On a lightly floured surface, roll the pizza dough out into two round pizzas, each about **12 inches in diameter**.
- Transfer each rolled-out pizza dough to a baking sheet or pizza stone lined with parchment paper or lightly oiled.

5. Assemble the Pizza:
- Spread **1/2 cup of pizza sauce** over each pizza crust, leaving a 1-inch border around the edges.
- **Top with 1/2 cup of shredded mozzarella cheese.**
- Evenly distribute **fresh spinach leaves, sliced tomatoes, sliced red onion, diced bell peppers**, and **black olives** over each pizza.
- Optionally, add **1/4 cup cooked Italian sausage or pepperoni** to one pizza if desired.
- Finish with a light sprinkle of **dried oregano** and **red pepper flakes** (for heat).

6. Bake the Pizza:
- Transfer the pizzas to the preheated oven. Bake for **12-15 minutes**, or until the cheese is melted, bubbly, and the crust is golden brown.

7. Garnish and Serve:
- Once the pizzas are done baking, remove from the oven and top with **fresh arugula or parsley**.
- Slice, serve, and enjoy your warm, cozy homemade pizza night!

VARIATIONS AND ADAPTATIONS
- **Vegan Option:** Use **dairy-free cheese** (e.g. vegan mozzarella or cashew cheese) and top with more seasonal vegetables like **roasted butternut squash, broccoli**, or **spinach**.
- **Gluten-Free Option:** Substitute **gluten-free pizza crust mix** or **cauliflower crust** for a lighter, gluten-free option.

NUTRITIONAL INFORMATION (PER SERVING, 2 SLICES PER PIZZA):

Calories: 550	Cholesterol: 30mg	Fiber: 4g	Calcium:.............. 20% DV
Total Fat: 23g	Sodium: 850mg	Sugars: 5g	Iron: ....15% DV
Saturated Fat: 9g	Carbohydrates: ...68g	Protein: 20g	

CORN DOGS IN THE OVEN

Yield: 6 corn dogs   **Prep Time:** 10 minutes   **Cook Time:** 20-25 minutes

INGREDIENTS

For the Corn Dog Batter:
- 1 cup all-purpose flour
- 1/2 cup cornmeal
- 1 tablespoon sugar
- 1 teaspoon baking powder
- 1/2 teaspoon salt
- 1/4 teaspoon black pepper
- 1/2 teaspoon paprika
- 1/2 cup milk
- 1 large egg
- 1 tablespoon vegetable oil
- 1 teaspoon Dijon mustard

For the Corn Dogs:
- 6 hot dogs
- 6 wooden skewers or lollipop sticks

For Baking:
- **Cooking spray** (for greasing the baking sheet)
- **1 tablespoon melted butter** (optional, for extra crispiness)

STEP-BY-STEP INSTRUCTIONS

1. Preheat the Oven:
- Preheat your oven to **400°F (200°C)**. Line a baking sheet with parchment paper or lightly grease with cooking spray to prevent the corn dogs from sticking.

2. Prepare the Corn Dog Batter:
- In a large mixing bowl, whisk together **1 cup of all-purpose flour, 1/2 cup cornmeal, 1 tablespoon sugar, 1 teaspoon baking powder, 1/2 teaspoon salt, 1/4 teaspoon black pepper**, and **1/2 teaspoon paprika**.
- In a separate bowl, whisk together **1/2 cup milk, 1 large egg, 1 tablespoon vegetable oil**, and **1 teaspoon Dijon mustard** (if using).
- Pour the wet ingredients into the dry ingredients and stir until just combined, forming a thick batter. The batter should be thick enough to coat the hot dogs without dripping off easily.

3. Prepare the Hot Dogs:
- If your hot dogs are not already skewered, carefully insert a **wooden skewer or lollipop stick** into each hot dog, leaving enough of the stick exposed for easy handling.
- Lightly pat the hot dogs dry with a paper towel to help the batter stick better.

4. Coat the Hot Dogs:
- Pour the corn dog batter into a tall glass or a deep bowl (this helps you dip the hot dogs more easily).
- Dip each skewered hot dog into the batter, rolling it to coat evenly and thoroughly. You can use a spoon to help spread the batter around the hot dog if necessary.

5. Bake the Corn Dogs:
- Place the battered hot dogs on the prepared baking sheet, leaving space between each one.
- If desired, brush the tops of the corn dogs with **1 tablespoon melted butter** for a crispier, golden finish.
- Bake in the preheated oven for **20-25 minutes**, or until the batter is golden brown and cooked through. You can rotate the corn dogs halfway through for even baking.

6. Serve:
- Once the corn dogs are golden and crispy, remove them from the oven. Let them cool for a minute before serving.
- Serve with your favorite dipping sauces, such as **ketchup, mustard**, or **honey mustard**.

VARIATIONS AND ADAPTATIONS
- **Vegetarian Option:** Use **vegetarian hot dogs** or **tofu dogs** for a plant-based version.
- **Spicy Corn Dogs:** Add a pinch of **cayenne pepper** or **chili powder** to the batter for a spicy kick.
- **Cheese-Stuffed Corn Dogs:** Insert a **slice of cheese** (cheddar or mozzarella) inside the hot dog before battering it for an extra cheesy bite.
- **Gluten-Free Option:** Use a **gluten-free all-purpose flour** and ensure the cornmeal is also gluten-free.

NUTRITIONAL INFORMATION (PER CORN DOG):

Calories: 270	Cholesterol: 30mg	Fiber: 1g	Calcium: ....4% DV
Total Fat: 14g	Sodium: 620mg	Sugars: 3g	Iron: ....6% DV
Saturated Fat: 2g	Carbohydrates: ...30g	Protein: 7g	

TACO MAC AND CHEESE

Yield: 6 servings   **Prepn Time:** 10 minutes   **Cook Time:** 20-25 minutes

INGREDIENTS

For the Mac and Cheese:
- 8 oz elbow macaroni
- 2 tablespoons unsalted butter
- 2 tablespoons all-purpose flour
- 2 cups whole milk
- 1 1/2 cups shredded cheddar cheese
- 1/2 cup shredded Monterey Jack cheese
- 1/2 teaspoon garlic powder
- 1/2 teaspoon onion powder
- 1/4 teaspoon paprika
- 1/4 teaspoon salt
- 1/4 teaspoon black pepper

For the Taco Meat:
- 1 lb ground beef
- 1 packet taco seasoning
- 1 tablespoon olive oil
- 1/2 cup diced onion
- 1 clove garlic, minced
- 1/2 cup diced tomatoes

Taco Seasoning (optional):
- 1 tablespoon chili powder
- 1 teaspoon cumin
- 1 teaspoon paprika
- 1/2 teaspoon garlic powder
- 1/2 teaspoon onion powder
- 1/4 teaspoon black pepper
- 1/4 teaspoon salt

For Toppings (optional):
- 1/2 cup chopped fresh cilantro
- Sour cream (optional)
- Sliced jalapeños (optional)
- Salsa (optional)
- Shredded lettuce
- Chopped tomatoes

STEP-BY-STEP INSTRUCTIONS

1. Cook the Pasta:
- Bring a large pot of salted water to a boil. Add the **elbow macaroni** and cook according to the package instructions, about 8-10 minutes, until al dente.
- Drain the pasta and set it aside.

2. Prepare the Taco Meat:
- In a large skillet, heat **1 tablespoon olive oil** over medium heat.
- Add the **diced onion** and cook for 2-3 minutes, until softened.
- Add the **minced garlic** and cook for an additional 1 minute until fragrant.
- Add the **ground beef** (or turkey/chicken) to the skillet and cook, breaking it up with a spatula, until browned and fully cooked, about 6-8 minutes.
- Stir in the **taco seasoning** (either store-bought or homemade) and the **diced tomatoes**. Cook for an additional 2-3 minutes, allowing the flavors to combine. Set aside.

3. Make the Cheese Sauce:
- In a large saucepan, melt **2 tablespoons butter** over medium heat.
- Whisk in the **flour** and cook for 1-2 minutes, creating a roux (paste), stirring constantly.
- Slowly pour in the **milk**, whisking continuously to avoid lumps. Bring the mixture to a simmer, and cook for 3-4 minutes until the sauce thickens.
- Stir in the **shredded cheddar cheese** and **Monterey Jack cheese**, continuing to stir until the cheese is melted and the sauce is smooth.
- Add the **garlic powder, onion powder, paprika, salt,** and **black pepper**. Adjust seasoning to taste.

4. Combine:
- Add the cooked pasta to the cheese sauce, stirring to coat evenly.
- Stir in the taco meat mixture, making sure everything is combined and well coated in the cheese sauce.

5. Serve:
- Spoon the **Taco Mac and Cheese** onto serving plates.
- Top with **fresh cilantro, sour cream, sliced jalapeños, salsa,** or **shredded lettuce** as desired.

VARIATIONS AND ADAPTATIONS
- **Vegetarian Version:** Use **black beans** or **pinto beans** as a substitute for meat, along with some sautéed bell peppers and onions for extra flavor.
- **Spicy Taco Mac:** Add **sriracha** or **chopped jalapeños** to the taco meat or cheese sauce for an extra kick.
- **Different Meats:** Swap the **ground beef** for **ground chicken, turkey,** or even **chorizo** for different flavor profiles.
- **Vegan Version:** Use **plant-based ground meat** (or black beans), **vegan butter, vegan cheese,** and **almond milk** for a dairy-free version of this dish.

NUTRITIONAL INFORMATION (PER SERVING): Calories: 540, Total Fat: 28g, Saturated Fat: 12g, Cholesterol: 50mg, Sodium: 700mg, Carbohydrates: 47g, Fiber: 3g, Sugars: 5g, Protein: 26g, Calcium: 30% DV Iron: 15% DV

BBQ MEATBALL SKEWERS

Yield: 4 servings   **Prep Time:** 15 minutes   **Cook Time:** 20-25 minutes

INGREDIENTS

For the Meatballs:

- 1 lb ground beef
- 1/2 cup breadcrumbs
- 1/4 cup grated Parmesan cheese
- 1/4 cup finely chopped parsley
- 1 egg
- 2 cloves garlic, minced
- 1/2 teaspoon onion powder
- 1/2 teaspoon smoked paprika
- 1/4 teaspoon salt
- 1/4 teaspoon black pepper

For the BBQ Sauce:

- 1 cup ketchup
- 2 tablespoons apple cider vinegar
- 2 tablespoons brown sugar
- 1 tablespoon Worcestershire sauce
- 1 tablespoon Dijon mustard
- 1/2 teaspoon garlic powder
- 1/4 teaspoon smoked paprika
- Salt and pepper to taste

For the Skewers:

- Wooden or metal skewers

For Serving (optional):

- Fresh parsley or cilantro for garnish
- Grilled vegetables (zucchini, bell peppers, or onions)

STEP-BY-STEP INSTRUCTIONS

1. Prepare the Meatballs:

- Preheat the oven to **400°F (200°C)**.
- In a large mixing bowl, combine **ground beef, breadcrumbs, grated Parmesan, chopped parsley, egg, minced garlic, onion powder, smoked paprika, salt,** and **black pepper**.
- Mix well until all ingredients are evenly incorporated. You can use your hands or a spoon to mix.
- Shape the mixture into **1-inch meatballs** and place them on a baking sheet lined with parchment paper. This should make about **20-24 meatballs**.

2. Prepare the BBQ Sauce:

- In a small saucepan, combine **ketchup, apple cider vinegar, brown sugar, Worcestershire sauce, Dijon mustard, garlic powder,** and **smoked paprika** (if using).
- Bring to a simmer over medium heat, stirring occasionally. Let the sauce cook for 5-7 minutes until it thickens slightly. Taste and adjust seasoning with salt and pepper as needed.
- Remove the sauce from heat and set aside.

3. Bake the Meatballs:

- Place the meatballs in the preheated oven and bake for **15-20 minutes**, or until they are cooked through and golden brown. The internal temperature should reach **165°F (74°C)** when checked with a meat thermometer.

4. Assemble the Skewers:

- Once the meatballs are done baking, allow them to cool slightly.
- Thread the meatballs onto the skewers, alternating with slices of **grilled vegetables** such as **zucchini, bell peppers,** or **onions** if desired. You can also use other vegetables like **mushrooms** or **cherry tomatoes** for variety.

5. Grill or Broil the Skewers:

- **Grill Method:** Preheat your grill or grill pan over medium heat. Place the skewers on the grill and cook for **3-4 minutes per side**, brushing with the BBQ sauce during the last few minutes of grilling.
- **Broil Method:** Alternatively, you can place the skewers under a broiler on a baking sheet. Broil for **2-3 minutes per side**, basting with BBQ sauce as they cook.

6. Serve:

- Once the skewers are grilled to your liking, remove them from the heat. Brush with additional BBQ sauce, if desired, and garnish with **fresh parsley** or **cilantro**.
- Serve the BBQ meatball skewers with a side of **rice, salad,** or **grilled vegetables** for a complete meal.

VARIATIONS AND ADAPTATIONS

- **Vegetarian Version:** Use **plant-based ground meat** or make meatballs using **lentils** and **quinoa** as a base. Add **chopped vegetables** like **mushrooms** and **zucchini** to the mixture for added texture.
- **Spicy BBQ Meatball Skewers:** Add **chili powder, cayenne pepper,** or **sriracha** to the BBQ sauce for an extra spicy kick.
- **Different Meat Choices:** Swap out the **ground beef** for **ground turkey, chicken,** or even **pork** for different flavor profiles.
- **International Twist:** Experiment with different seasonings and sauces—add **cumin, coriander,** and **lime juice** for a Mexican-inspired version, or **soy sauce** and **ginger** for an Asian twist.

NUTRITIONAL INFORMATION (PER SERVING): Calories: 320, **Total Fat:** 20g, **Saturated Fat:** 8g, **Cholesterol:** 70mg, **Sodium:** 600mg, **Carbohydrates:** 12g, **Fiber:** 2g, **Sugars:** 7g, **Protein:** 28g, **Calcium:** 15% DV, **Iron:** 15% DV

BREAKFAST FOR DINNER PANCAKES

Yield: 4 servings (about 12 pancakes)   **Prep Time:** 10 minutes   **Cooking Time:** 15-20 minutes

INGREDIENTS

For the Pancakes:
- 1 1/2 cups all-purpose flour
- 2 tablespoons sugar
- 2 teaspoons baking powder
- 1/2 teaspoon salt
- 1 1/4 cups milk
- 2 large eggs
- 2 tablespoons butter, melted
- 1 teaspoon vanilla extract

For Toppings:
- **Butter** (for greasing the pan and adding extra on top)
- **Maple syrup** (local, or a natural honey or fruit syrup)
- **Fresh fruit** (seasonal berries, bananas, or apple slices)
- **Whipped cream** (optional, for added indulgence)

STEP-BY-STEP INSTRUCTIONS

1. Prepare the Pancake Batter:
- In a large mixing bowl, whisk together **flour**, **sugar**, **baking powder**, and **salt** until combined.
- In a separate bowl, whisk together **milk**, **eggs**, **melted butter**, and **vanilla extract** until smooth.
- Pour the wet ingredients into the dry ingredients and stir gently to combine. Be careful not to overmix—it's okay if the batter is slightly lumpy. Overmixing can make the pancakes tough.

2. Heat the Pan:
- Place a **large skillet** or **griddle** over medium heat and let it warm up for about 2 minutes. To check if it's ready, drop a small amount of water onto the surface. If it sizzles, the pan is hot.
- Lightly grease the pan with a small amount of **butter** or **cooking spray** to prevent the pancakes from sticking.

3. Cook the Pancakes:
- Using a 1/4 cup measuring cup, pour the batter onto the skillet to form pancakes. You can cook 2-3 pancakes at a time, depending on the size of your pan.
- Cook the pancakes for **2-3 minutes** on the first side, or until small bubbles form on the surface and the edges start to look set.
- Flip the pancakes carefully with a spatula and cook for another **1-2 minutes** until the other side is golden brown.
- Remove the pancakes from the skillet and keep them warm by placing them on a plate and covering with a clean towel or foil. Repeat with the remaining batter.

4. Serve:
- Stack the pancakes on plates and top with **butter**, **maple syrup**, and **seasonal fresh fruit** like **berries**, **banana slices**, or **apple slices**.
- For an extra indulgent touch, add a dollop of **whipped cream** or a sprinkle of **powdered sugar**.

VARIATIONS AND ADAPTATIONS

- **Savory Version:** Add **crispy bacon** or **sausage** as a topping for a savory twist, or fold cooked **spinach** and **cheddar cheese** into the batter for a savory pancake option.
- **Gluten-Free:** Use **gluten-free flour** and check that the baking powder is also gluten-free.
- **Vegan Option:** Use **plant-based milk**, replace the eggs with **flax eggs** (1 tablespoon ground flaxseed mixed with 3 tablespoons water, let sit for 5 minutes), and substitute the butter with **vegan butter** or coconut oil.
- **Flavored Pancakes:** Add **cinnamon**, **nutmeg**, or **lemon zest** to the batter for added flavor.
- **International Twist:** Try adding **masala spices** (turmeric, cumin) for an Indian-inspired pancake or top with a **savory yogurt sauce**.

NUTRITIONAL INFORMATION (PER SERVING)

Calories: 300	Cholesterol: 100mg	Fiber: 2g	Calcium: ....15% DV
Total Fat: 12g	Sodium: 370mg	Sugars: 8g	Iron: ....10% DV
Saturated Fat: 7g	Carbohydrates: ...41g	Protein: 8g	

SWEET AND SOUR CHICKEN

Yield: 4 servings   **Preparation Time:** 15 minutes   **Cooking Time:** 20-25 minutes

INGREDIENTS

For the Chicken:
- 1 lb boneless, skinless chicken breasts
- 1/2 cup all-purpose flour
- 1/2 teaspoon salt
- 1/2 teaspoon black pepper
- 1/2 teaspoon garlic powder
- 1/2 teaspoon onion powder
- 1 large egg
- 2 tablespoons vegetable oil

For the Sweet and Sour Sauce:
- 1/2 cup pineapple juice
- 1/4 cup rice vinegar
- 1/4 cup ketchup
- 3 tablespoons brown sugar
- 2 tablespoons soy sauce
- 1 teaspoon cornstarch
- 1/2 cup diced bell pepper
- 1/2 cup diced onion
- 1/2 cup pineapple chunks

STEP-BY-STEP INSTRUCTIONS

1. Prepare the Chicken:
- Cut the **chicken breasts** into bite-sized cubes.
- In a shallow bowl, whisk together **flour, salt, pepper, garlic powder**, and **onion powder**.
- In another bowl, beat the **egg**.
- Dip each chicken piece first in the egg, then coat in the flour mixture, pressing gently to ensure an even coat.

2. Cook the Chicken:
- Heat **2 tablespoons of vegetable oil** in a large skillet or wok over medium-high heat.
- Once the oil is hot, add the breaded chicken pieces and cook for **4-5 minutes**, flipping halfway through until the chicken is golden brown and fully cooked (internal temperature should reach 165°F).
- Remove the cooked chicken from the skillet and set aside.

3. Make the Sweet and Sour Sauce:
- In the same skillet, add the **pineapple juice, rice vinegar, ketchup, brown sugar**, and **soy sauce**. Stir to combine.
- Bring the sauce to a simmer over medium heat.
- In a small bowl, mix the **cornstarch** with **2 tablespoons of water** to create a slurry, then add it to the sauce to thicken.
- Stir the sauce for 1-2 minutes until it thickens slightly.

4. Combine the Chicken and Vegetables:
- Add the **diced bell pepper, onion**, and **pineapple chunks** to the sauce, stirring to combine.
- Let the vegetables cook in the sauce for about **3-4 minutes** until they soften but still have some crunch.
- Return the cooked chicken to the skillet and stir to coat the chicken evenly in the sauce. Cook for another **2-3 minutes** until everything is heated through.

5. Serve:
- Serve the Sweet and Sour Chicken over steamed **rice** (jasmine or brown rice) or alongside **quinoa** for a healthier option.
- Garnish with sesame seeds or fresh cilantro for added flavor and color, if desired.

VARIATIONS AND ADAPTATIONS

- **Vegetarian Version:** Substitute the chicken with **tofu** or **tempeh**. Press the tofu to remove excess moisture, then cube and bread it in the same way as the chicken. Sauté until crispy, and proceed with the recipe as directed.
- **Different Meats:** Use **pork** or **beef** in place of chicken. For pork, boneless loin or tenderloin works well, while beef can be substituted with flank steak or sirloin.
- **Vegetable Boost:** Add **carrots, zucchini**, or **snap peas** for added nutrition and color. You can also use **sweet potato cubes** for a more filling version.
- **Heat Level:** For a spicier version, add **chili flakes** or **sriracha** to the sauce, adjusting to your desired spice level.

NUTRITIONAL INFORMATION (PER SERVING)

Calories: 380	Cholesterol: 140mg	Fiber: 3g	Calcium: ....4% DV
Total Fat: 0g	Sodium: 900mg	Sugars: 22g	Iron: ....10% DV
Saturated Fat: 1.5g	Carbohydrates: ...38g	Protein: 30g	

VEGGIE-PACKED QUESADILLAS

Yield: 4 servings (2 quesadillas per serving)

Prep Time: 15 minutes

Cooking Time: 10-12 minutes

INGREDIENTS

For the Quesadillas:
- **4 large whole wheat flour tortillas**
- **1 tablespoon olive oil**
- **1 small onion**, finely chopped
- **1 bell pepper**, chopped
- **1 zucchini**, diced
- **1 cup corn kernels**
- **1 cup spinach**, chopped
- **1/2 cup shredded cheddar cheese**
- **1/2 cup shredded mozzarella cheese**
- **1/4 teaspoon cumin**
- **1/4 teaspoon smoked paprika**
- **Salt and pepper**, to taste

For the Serving:
- **Sour cream** (local or plain yogurt)
- **Guacamole**
- **Salsa**

STEP-BY-STEP INSTRUCTIONS

1. Prepare the Vegetables:
- Heat the **olive oil** in a large skillet over medium heat.
- Add the **onion, bell pepper**, and **zucchini** to the skillet and sauté for about **5-6 minutes**, until the vegetables are soft and starting to brown.
- Add the **corn kernels** and cook for another **2-3 minutes** until the corn is heated through.
- Add the **spinach** to the skillet and stir until wilted, about **1-2 minutes**.
- Season with **cumin, smoked paprika, salt**, and **pepper**. Remove from heat and set aside.

2. Assemble the Quesadillas:
- Lay the **tortillas** flat on a clean surface.
- Evenly distribute the **vegetable mixture** onto one half of each tortilla.
- Sprinkle **cheddar cheese** and **mozzarella cheese** over the vegetables. The cheese will help the quesadillas stick together when grilled.
- Fold the other half of the tortilla over the filling, creating a half-moon shape.

3. Cook the Quesadillas:
- Heat a non-stick skillet or griddle over medium heat.
- Lightly grease the pan with a little more **olive oil** or cooking spray.
- Place the quesadillas in the skillet, cooking **1-2 at a time**, depending on the size of your pan.
- Cook for about **3-4 minutes per side**, pressing gently with a spatula to help the quesadillas brown and crisp up. Flip carefully to avoid spilling the filling.
- Once golden and the cheese is melted, remove the quesadilla from the skillet and set aside to rest for a minute before cutting.

4. Serve:
- Slice the quesadillas into wedges and serve with **sour cream, guacamole**, and **salsa** on the side for dipping.

VARIATIONS AND ADAPTATIONS
- **Protein Boost:** Add cooked **chicken breast, ground turkey**, or **black beans** to the filling for extra protein. Season ground turkey or chicken with taco seasoning for a flavorful twist.
- **Spicy Kick:** Add finely chopped **jalapeños** or a drizzle of **sriracha sauce** to the filling or the sides for extra heat.
- **Different Veggies:** Experiment with other seasonal veggies like **sweet potatoes, mushrooms, broccoli**, or **tomatoes**. Roasted sweet potatoes add a sweet flavor that complements the savory veggies.
- **Cheese Options:** Try different cheese combinations like **pepper jack** for a spicier flavor or **feta** for a Mediterranean twist.
- **Dairy-Free:** Use dairy-free cheese (like cashew or coconut-based cheese) and opt for a non-dairy sour cream or yogurt substitute.

NUTRITIONAL INFORMATION (PER SERVING)

Calories: 350	Cholesterol: 20mg	Fiber:.................. 6g	Calcium: ....20% DV
Total Fat: 16g	Sodium: 450mg	Sugars: 6g	Iron: ....10% DV
Saturated Fat: 4g	Carbohydrates: ...40g	Protein: 14g	

CHAPTER 6:
VEGETARIAN DELIGHTS

PRACTICAL TIPS

Cooking vegetarian meals is a wonderful way to embrace fresh, wholesome ingredients while exploring bold flavors and satisfying textures. This chapter is filled with recipes that celebrate vegetables, legumes, grains, and plant-based proteins. Here are some practical tips to help you make the most of these vegetarian delights!

1. Choose Seasonal Ingredients:
♦ Highlight the freshest local produce available for maximum flavor and nutrition. For example, use tomatoes and zucchini in the summer, squash and kale in the fall.

♦ Seasonal vegetables are often more affordable and environmentally friendly.

2. Build Layers of Flavor:
♦ Use aromatics like garlic, onions, ginger, and fresh herbs to enhance the depth of your dishes.

♦ Add spices such as cumin, paprika, turmeric, or chili flakes for an extra kick.

3. Focus on Texture:
♦ Combine soft and crunchy elements in your meals. For example, pair creamy hummus with crispy roasted chickpeas or tender roasted vegetables with a crunchy slaw.

♦ Experiment with roasting, grilling, steaming, and sautéing to bring out unique textures.

4. Prioritize Protein-Rich Ingredients:
♦ Incorporate beans, lentils, tofu, tempeh, or edamame to make meals more filling and nutritionally balanced.

♦ Add nuts, seeds, or quinoa to salads and bowls for an extra protein boost.

5. Experiment with Plant-Based Sauces:
♦ Create rich and creamy sauces using blended cashews, tahini, or avocado.

♦ Use vegetable-based broths to enhance soups and stews without relying on meat stocks.

6. Cook Grains to Perfection:
♦ Use whole grains like farro, bulgur, or barley to add heartiness to your meals.

♦ Rinse grains before cooking and season the cooking water with a pinch of salt for enhanced flavor.

7. Balance Your Plate:
♦ Pair complex carbohydrates, healthy fats, and proteins to create a nutritionally complete dish.

♦ For example, combine a lentil curry with brown rice and a side of roasted vegetables.

8. Recreate Comfort Foods:
♦ Reinvent classics like lasagna, burgers, or tacos with plant-based alternatives. For instance:

◊ Use eggplant or zucchini slices in place of pasta for lasagna.

◊ Opt for black bean or chickpea patties for burgers.

◊ Substitute mushrooms or jackfruit for taco fillings.

♦ 9. Use Fresh Herbs and Citrus:

♦ Garnish meals with fresh herbs like cilantro, parsley, or basil to brighten flavors.

♦ A squeeze of lemon or lime juice can elevate the taste of soups, salads, and curries.

10. Incorporate Dairy or Dairy Alternatives:
♦ Add creamy cheeses like feta, goat cheese, or ricotta to enrich your dishes.

♦ For vegan options, use plant-based cheeses, coconut milk, or almond yogurt.

11. Roast for Intense Flavor:
♦ Roasting vegetables like carrots, sweet potatoes, and Brussels sprouts enhances their natural sweetness.

♦ Toss vegetables in olive oil and seasonings before roasting for the best results.

12. Make Use of Leftovers:
♦ Turn leftover roasted veggies into hearty soups or add them to grain bowls.

♦ Blend extra greens into pesto or sauces to reduce waste and add flavor.

13. Embrace International Flavors:
♦ Explore cuisines that naturally emphasize vegetarian dishes, such as Indian (dal, curries), Mediterranean (falafel, tabbouleh), or Asian (stir-fries, noodle dishes).

♦ Incorporate spices and sauces like garam masala, miso, or harissa to diversify your meals.

14. Batch Cook for Convenience:
♦ Prepare staples like grains, legumes, or vegetable broths in advance to save time on busy nights.

♦ Store chopped vegetables or pre-made sauces in the fridge for quick assembly during the week.

15. Create Eye-Catching Presentations:

- Use colorful vegetables to make meals visually appealing. Think bright bell peppers, purple cabbage, and golden beets.

- Arrange components like grain bowls or platters neatly for a restaurant-style feel.

16. Plan for Protein Pairings:

- Combine incomplete plant proteins like rice and beans or hummus and pita to ensure your meals include all essential amino acids.

17. Taste and Adjust:

- Regularly taste your food as you cook, adjusting seasoning as needed to highlight the natural flavors of the ingredients.

18. Have Fun with Meat Alternatives:

- Try marinated tofu, tempeh, or plant-based meat substitutes to mimic the textures of traditional dishes.

- Experiment with mushrooms or eggplant for their meaty, satisfying texture.

19. Keep it Simple:

- Many vegetarian dishes shine with just a few high-quality ingredients. Focus on simplicity for weeknight dinners.

20. Celebrate Plant-Based Eating:

- View vegetarian cooking as an opportunity to highlight the diversity and versatility of plant-based foods. Celebrate the richness of vegetables, legumes, grains, and herbs in each dish.

CONCLUSION:

This chapter showcases how vegetarian meals can be nourishing, vibrant, and satisfying. With these tips, you'll be able to craft dishes that appeal to vegetarians and non-vegetarians alike. Whether you're roasting vegetables, simmering hearty soups, or assembling fresh salads, enjoy the creativity and coziness that comes with plant-based cooking!

LENTIL CURRY WITH RICE

Yield: 4 servings   **Prep Time:** 10 minutes   **Cook Time:** 30-35 minutes

INGREDIENTS

For the Lentil Curry:
- **1 tablespoon olive oil**
- **1 medium onion**, diced
- **2 cloves garlic**, minced
- **1 tablespoon ginger**, freshly grated
- **1 medium carrot**, diced
- **1 bell pepper**, chopped
- **1 cup dried red lentils**
- **1 can (14.5 oz) diced tomatoes**
- **1 can (14 oz) coconut milk**
- **2 cups vegetable broth**
- **2 teaspoons curry powder**
- **1 teaspoon ground turmeric**
- **1 teaspoon ground cumin**
- **1/2 teaspoon ground coriander**
- **1/2 teaspoon cinnamon**
- **Salt and pepper**, to taste
- **1 tablespoon fresh cilantro**, chopped
- **1 tablespoon lemon juice**

For the Rice:
- **1 cup basmati rice**
- **2 cups water** or **vegetable broth**
- **1 tablespoon olive oil** (optional)
- **Salt**, to taste

STEP-BY-STEP INSTRUCTIONS

1. Prepare the Rice:
- In a medium saucepan, briﬡally, stir in 1 tablespoon olive oil for extra richness.

2. Start the Lentil Curry:
- Heat **1 tablespoon olive oil** in a large pot over medium heat.
- Add the **diced onion**, and sauté for **4-5 minutes** until softened and golden.
- Add the **garlic**, **ginger**, **carrot**, and **bell pepper**. Sauté for an additional **3-4 minutes** until the vegetables begin to soften.

3. Add the Spices:
- Stir in the **curry powder**, **turmeric**, **cumin**, **coriander**, and **cinnamon** (if using), and cook for **1-2 minutes** until the spices are fragrant.

4. Add the Lentils and Liquids:
- Add the **dried lentils**, **diced tomatoes**, **coconut milk**, and **vegetable broth** to the pot. Stir everything together.
- Bring the mixture to a boil, then reduce the heat to low. Cover and simmer for **20-25 minutes**, stirring occasionally, until the lentils are tender and the curry has thickened. Add more broth or water if the curry is too thick.

5. Adjust the Seasoning:
- Once the lentils are cooked through, season the curry with **salt**, **pepper**, and **lemon juice** to taste.
- If you'd like more heat, you can add a pinch of red chili flakes or fresh chopped chili at this stage.

6. Serve:
- Spoon the **lentil curry** over a serving of **basmati rice**.
- Garnish with **fresh cilantro** and serve with optional sides like a dollop of **yogurt**, **naan bread**, or a fresh **green salad**.

VARIATIONS AND ADAPTATIONS

- **Protein Boost:** Add **chicken breast**, **tofu**, or **paneer** for a protein-packed version. For chicken, cook it separately, then add to the curry towards the end.
- **Vegan:** This recipe is naturally vegan if you use a plant-based broth and optional dairy-free toppings like cashew cream or coconut yogurt.
- **Different Vegetables:** You can swap out or add vegetables like **sweet potatoes**, **spinach**, or **cauliflower**. They all pair well with the curry flavors.
- **Spicy Option:** For more heat, include **fresh chilies** or a tablespoon of **sriracha** or **hot sauce** when adding the spices.
- **Herbs:** Try adding **mint** or **basil** for a fresh twist, or even a bit of **fresh parsley** for a milder flavor.

NUTRITIONAL INFORMATION (PER SERVING)

Calories: 380	Sodium: 550mg	Protein: 14g
Total Fat: 12g	Carbohydrates: ...55g	Calcium: ....8% DV
Saturated Fat: 6g	Fiber: 15g	Iron: ....25% DV
Cholesterol: 0mg	Sugars: 7g	

EGGPLANT PARMESAN

Yield: 4 servings　　　　**Prepn Time:** 15 minutes　　　　**Cook Time:** 40 minutes

INGREDIENTS

For the Eggplant:

- **2 medium eggplants**, sliced into 1/2-inch thick rounds
- **1 teaspoon salt** (for draining)
- **1 cup all-purpose flour**
- **2 large eggs**, beaten
- **2 cups seasoned breadcrumbs**
- **1/2 cup grated Parmesan** cheese
- **1 cup shredded mozzarella cheese**
- **Olive oil spray** or **1/4 cup olive oil**

For the Marinara Sauce:

- **1 tablespoon olive oil**
- **1 small onion**, finely chopped
- **2 cloves garlic**, minced
- **1 can (28 oz) crushed tomatoes** (or 4-5 medium tomatoes)
- **1 teaspoon dried basil**
- **1 teaspoon dried oregano**
- **1/2 teaspoon red pepper flakes**
- **Salt and pepper**, to taste
- **1 tablespoon fresh basil**, chopped

STEP-BY-STEP INSTRUCTIONS

1. Prepare the Eggplant:

- Begin by salting the **eggplant slices**. Lay them on a large baking sheet in a single layer, sprinkling both sides with **1 teaspoon salt**. Let them sit for about **30 minutes** to draw out excess moisture.
- After 30 minutes, rinse the salt off the eggplant slices and gently pat them dry with a clean towel or paper towels.

2. Make the Marinara Sauce:

- While the eggplant is draining, heat **1 tablespoon olive oil** in a large skillet over medium heat.
- Add the **chopped onion** and sauté for **5 minutes** until softened.
- Add the **minced garlic** and sauté for another **1 minute** until fragrant.
- Stir in the **crushed tomatoes**, **dried basil**, **oregano**, and **red pepper flakes** (if using). Season with **salt** and **pepper** to taste.
- Bring to a simmer, then reduce the heat and let it cook, uncovered, for **15-20 minutes** while you prepare the eggplant.

3. Bread the Eggplant:

- Preheat your oven to **375°F (190°C)**.
- In one shallow bowl, place the **flour**. In a second bowl, place the **beaten eggs**. In a third bowl, mix the **breadcrumbs** and **Parmesan cheese** together.
- Dredge each **eggplant slice** first in the flour, then dip it in the egg, and finally coat it in the breadcrumb mixture. Press gently to ensure the breadcrumbs adhere well.
- Arrange the breaded slices on a baking sheet lined with parchment paper. Optionally, lightly spray them with **olive oil** for a crispy texture when baked.

4. Bake the Eggplant:

- Place the baking sheet in the preheated oven and bake for **20-25 minutes**, flipping the eggplant slices halfway through until they are golden brown and crispy.

5. Assemble the Eggplant Parmesan:

- Once the eggplant slices are done, reduce the oven temperature to **350°F (175°C)**.
- In a 9x13-inch baking dish, spread a thin layer of the marinara sauce on the bottom.
- Place a layer of **baked eggplant slices** on top of the sauce. Spoon more marinara sauce over the eggplant, followed by a sprinkle of **shredded mozzarella** and a dusting of **grated Parmesan**.
- Repeat the layering process (eggplant, sauce, mozzarella, Parmesan) until all the ingredients are used up, finishing with a layer of mozzarella and Parmesan on top.

6. Bake the Eggplant Parmesan:

- Bake the assembled dish in the oven for **20-25 minutes** until the cheese is melted and bubbly, and the top is golden brown.

7. Serve:

- Let the dish rest for **5-10 minutes** before serving.
- Garnish with **fresh basil** if desired.
- Serve alongside a simple green salad or over a bed of spaghetti for a complete meal.

VARIATIONS AND ADAPTATIONS

- **Protein Options:** You can add **grilled chicken breast** or **turkey meatballs** between the layers of eggplant for extra protein. Alternatively, use **ground beef** or **turkey** in the marinara sauce.
- **Vegan Option:** For a dairy-free version, use **vegan mozzarella cheese** and skip the Parmesan or replace it with a plant-based alternative.

NUTRITIONAL INFORMATION (PER SERVING)

Calories: 350
Total Fat: 20g
Saturated Fat: 7g
Cholesterol: 50mg
Sodium: 700mg
Carbohydrates: ...38g
Fiber: 9g
Sugars: 12g
Protein: 13g
Calcium: ....25% DV
Iron: ....15% DV

SPINACH AND RICOTTA STUFFED SHELLS

Yield: 4 servings   **Prep Time:** 15 minutes   **Cook Time:** 45 minutes

INGREDIENTS

For the Stuffed Shells:
- 12 large pasta shells
- 2 cups ricotta cheese
- 2 cups fresh spinach, chopped
- 1 cup shredded mozzarella cheese
- 1/4 cup grated Parmesan cheese
- 1 large egg (local)
- 1/2 teaspoon dried oregano
- 1/2 teaspoon garlic powder
- Salt and pepper, to taste

For the Marinara Sauce:
- 1 tablespoon olive oil
- 1 small onion, finely chopped
- 2 cloves garlic, minced
- 1 can (28 oz) crushed tomatoes
- 1 teaspoon dried basil
- 1 teaspoon dried oregano
- 1/2 teaspoon red pepper flakes
- Salt and pepper, to taste
- 1 tablespoon fresh basil, chopped

STEP-BY-STEP INSTRUCTIONS

1. Preheat the Oven:
- Preheat your oven to **375°F (190°C)**.

2. Cook the Pasta:
- Bring a large pot of salted water to a boil. Add the **pasta shells** and cook according to package instructions until al dente, about **8-10 minutes**. Drain and set aside to cool slightly.

3. Prepare the Marinara Sauce:
- While the pasta is cooking, heat **1 tablespoon olive oil** in a large skillet over medium heat.
- Add the **chopped onion** and sauté for **5 minutes** until softened.
- Add the **minced garlic** and sauté for another **1 minute** until fragrant.
- Stir in the **crushed tomatoes, dried basil, oregano,** and **red pepper flakes** (if using). Season with **salt** and **pepper** to taste.
- Bring the sauce to a simmer, then reduce the heat and let it cook for **15-20 minutes**, stirring occasionally.

4. Prepare the Spinach and Ricotta Filling:
- In a large mixing bowl, combine the **ricotta cheese, chopped spinach, mozzarella cheese, Parmesan cheese, egg, oregano, garlic powder, salt,** and **pepper**. Stir until everything is well incorporated.

5. Stuff the Shells:
- Once the pasta shells are cool enough to handle, carefully stuff each shell with the ricotta and spinach mixture.
- Place the stuffed shells in a **9x13-inch baking dish**, lining them up in a single layer.

6. Assemble the Dish:
- Pour the prepared **marinara sauce** over the stuffed shells, ensuring they are well covered. You can spoon any extra sauce over the top for added flavor.
- Sprinkle the remaining **mozzarella cheese** on top for a melty, cheesy finish.

7. Bake the Stuffed Shells:
- Cover the baking dish with foil and bake in the preheated oven for **25 minutes**. After 25 minutes, remove the foil and bake for an additional **10-15 minutes** until the cheese is bubbly and golden brown.

8. Serve:
- Let the stuffed shells rest for **5-10 minutes** before serving.
- Garnish with **fresh basil** (optional) and serve with a side of garlic bread or a simple salad for a complete meal.

VARIATIONS AND ADAPTATIONS

- **Meat Version:** For a heartier dish, add cooked **ground beef, sausage,** or **chicken** to the ricotta mixture or layer it in the baking dish along with the shells.
- **Vegetable Options:** You can add **mushrooms, zucchini,** or **roasted bell peppers** to the ricotta filling for added flavor and texture.
- **Vegan Version:** Use **vegan ricotta** and **vegan mozzarella** to make this dish completely plant-based. Omit the egg or use a flax egg as a binder.
- **Gluten-Free Version:** Use **gluten-free pasta shells** to cater to those with gluten sensitivities.

NUTRITIONAL INFORMATION (PER SERVING)

Calories: 380	Cholesterol: 45mg	Fiber: 5g	Calcium: ....25% DV
Total Fat: 20g	Sodium: 500mg	Sugars: 6g	Iron: ....15% DV
Saturated Fat: 8g	Carbohydrates: ...35g	Protein: 18g	

BUTTERNUT SQUASH SOUP

Yield: 4 servings   **Prep Time:** 15 minutes   **Cook Time:** 35-40 minutes

INGREDIENTS

- **1 medium butternut squash** (about 2 lbs), peeled, seeded, and cubed
- **1 tablespoon olive oil**
- **1 medium onion**, diced
- **2 cloves garlic**, minced
- **1 medium carrot**, peeled and diced
- **1 apple**, peeled, cored, and diced
- **4 cups vegetable broth**
- **1/2 teaspoon ground cinnamon**
- **1/4 teaspoon ground nutmeg**
- **Salt and pepper**, to taste
- **1/2 cup coconut milk** or heavy cream
- **Fresh parsley** (optional, for garnish)
- **Crusty bread** (optional, for serving)

STEP-BY-STEP INSTRUCTIONS

1. Prepare the Butternut Squash:
- Peel and cube the **butternut squash**, removing the seeds. If you're short on time, you can use pre-cut butternut squash, which is often available at grocery stores during the fall and winter.

2. Sauté the Vegetables:
- Heat **1 tablespoon of olive oil** in a large pot over medium heat.
- Add the **diced onion** and sauté for about **5 minutes** until softened and translucent.
- Add the **minced garlic**, **diced carrot**, and **diced apple**. Continue to cook for **3-4 minutes**, stirring occasionally.

3. Cook the Squash:
- Add the **cubed butternut squash** to the pot. Stir to combine with the vegetables, and cook for another **5 minutes** to allow the flavors to meld.

4. Add the Broth and Seasonings:
- Pour in the **vegetable broth**, and sprinkle in the **cinnamon, nutmeg, salt**, and **pepper**. Bring the soup to a gentle boil over medium-high heat.
- Once boiling, reduce the heat to low and simmer for **25-30 minutes**, or until the butternut squash is fork-tender.

5. Blend the Soup:
- Once the squash and vegetables are soft, remove the pot from the heat. Use an **immersion blender** directly in the pot to puree the soup until smooth and creamy. If you don't have an immersion blender, you can transfer the soup in batches to a regular blender.
- If you prefer a thinner consistency, you can add a little extra vegetable broth or water to reach your desired texture.

6. Add Creaminess (Optional):
- If you want a richer, creamier soup, stir in **1/2 cup of coconut milk** or **heavy cream** at this stage. This will also add a touch of sweetness and smoothness to the soup.

7. Adjust Seasoning:
- Taste the soup and adjust the seasoning with more **salt**, **pepper**, or **cinnamon**, depending on your preference.

8. Serve:
- Ladle the soup into bowls, and garnish with a sprinkle of **fresh parsley** if desired. Serve with **crusty bread** on the side for dipping, and enjoy the warmth of this comforting dish.

VARIATIONS AND ADAPTATIONS
- **Meat Version:** You can add cooked **chicken**, **bacon**, or **sausage** for a heartier version. Simply cook the meat separately and add it back into the soup just before blending.
- **Roasted Squash Version:** For an added depth of flavor, you can **roast the butternut squash**. Cut the squash in half, remove the seeds, and roast it in the oven at 400°F (200°C) for about **25-30 minutes**, then scoop out the flesh and add it to the pot with the other vegetables.
- **Spicy Twist:** Add a pinch of **cayenne pepper** or **chili flakes** for a spicy kick that balances the sweetness of the squash.
- **Vegan Version:** Use **coconut milk** or a plant-based cream to keep the soup dairy-free. You can also add **toasted pumpkin seeds** as a garnish for crunch.

NUTRITIONAL INFORMATION (PER SERVING)
Calories: 180
Total Fat: 7g
Saturated Fat: 3g
Cholesterol: 0mg
Sodium: 400mg
Carbohydrates: ...31g
Fiber: 7g
Sugars: 10g
Protein: 2g
Calcium: ....6% DV
Iron: ....8% DV

GRILLED PORTOBELLO MUSHROOM BURGERS

Yield: 4 servings   **Prep Time:** 10 minutes   **Cook Time:** 10-15 minutes

INGREDIENTS

- **4 large Portobello mushrooms**
- **2 tablespoons olive oil**
- **2 tablespoons balsamic vinegar**
- **1 teaspoon garlic powder**
- **1/2 teaspoon dried thyme**
- **1/2 teaspoon salt** (or to taste)
- **1/4 teaspoon freshly ground black pepper**

- **4 whole wheat or brioche burger buns**
- **4 slices of cheese** (cheddar, mozzarella)
- **Lettuce leaves**, for serving
- **Tomato slices**, for serving
- **Red onion slices**, for serving
- **Pickles** (optional, for extra crunch)
- **Condiments (ketchup, mustard, or mayonnaise)**, for serving

STEP-BY-STEP INSTRUCTIONS

1. Prepare the Mushrooms:

- Clean the **Portobello mushrooms** by gently wiping them with a damp cloth. Remove the stems and scrape out the gills with a spoon (optional, but helps with texture and flavor absorption).

2. Marinate the Mushrooms:

- In a small bowl, mix **olive oil, balsamic vinegar, garlic powder, dried thyme, salt**, and **pepper**.

- Brush both sides of each mushroom cap with the marinade, ensuring they are well-coated. Let the mushrooms sit for about **5 minutes** to absorb the flavors.

3. Preheat the Grill:

- Preheat the grill or grill pan to medium-high heat. If you're using an outdoor grill, ensure it's clean and lightly oiled to prevent sticking.

4. Grill the Mushrooms:

- Place the marinated mushroom caps on the grill, gill side up. Grill for about **5-7 minutes** on each side, until they are tender and have grill marks. If desired, place a slice of **cheese** on top of the mushrooms during the last minute of grilling to melt.

5. Toast the Buns:

- While the mushrooms are grilling, cut the burger buns in half and toast them lightly on the grill or in a pan until golden brown.

6. Assemble the Burgers:

- Once the mushrooms are grilled, place each one on the bottom half of a toasted bun.

- Top with **lettuce leaves, tomato slices, red onion slices**, and **pickles** (if using).

- Add your preferred condiments (ketchup, mustard, mayo) on the top half of the bun and place it on top of the mushroom.

7. Serve:

- Serve the grilled Portobello mushroom burgers with a side of **crispy fries, salad**, or **chips** for a complete meal. Enjoy the savory, meaty texture of the mushrooms in place of a traditional beef patty.

VARIATIONS AND ADAPTATIONS

- **Vegan Version:** Skip the cheese or use **vegan cheese** for a completely plant-based burger. You can also try **vegan mayo** or **guacamole** instead of traditional condiments.

- **Different Mushrooms:** If Portobello mushrooms are not available, you can substitute with **large cremini mushrooms** or **shiitake mushrooms** for a different texture and flavor.

- **Add Protein:** For an extra protein boost, add a layer of **grilled tofu** or **tempeh** alongside the mushrooms, or even a **bean patty** for additional heartiness.

- **Spicy Twist:** Add **jalapeño slices** or a **spicy aioli** to give your burger a spicy kick.

- **Mediterranean Style:** Replace the balsamic marinade with **olive oil, lemon juice**, and **oregano**, and serve the burgers with **tzatziki sauce, cucumber**, and **feta cheese** for a Greek-inspired twist.

NUTRITIONAL INFORMATION (PER SERVING)

Calories: 290	Cholesterol: 10mg	Carbohydrates: ...28g	Protein: 8g
Total Fat: 15g	(if using cheese)	Fiber: 5g	Calcium: ....10% DV
Saturated Fat: 3g	Sodium: 350mg	Sugars: 5g	(with cheese)
			Iron: 12%DV

CHICKPEA AND SPINACH STEW

Yield: 4 servings   **Prep Time:** 10 minutes   **Cook Time:** 25 minutes

INGREDIENTS

- **2 tablespoons olive oil**
- **1 medium onion**, finely chopped
- **2 cloves garlic**, minced
- **1 can (15 oz) chickpeas**, drained and rinsed
- **4 cups fresh spinach**
- **1 medium carrot**, diced
- **1 zucchini**, diced
- **1 can (14 oz) diced tomatoes**
- **2 cups vegetable broth**
- **1 teaspoon cumin**
- **1/2 teaspoon turmeric**
- **1/2 teaspoon smoked paprika**
- **1/4 teaspoon ground cinnamon**
- **1/2 teaspoon salt** (or to taste)
- **1/4 teaspoon freshly ground black pepper**
- **1 tablespoon lemon juice**
- **Fresh cilantro or parsley**, chopped

STEP-BY-STEP INSTRUCTIONS

1. Prepare the Vegetables:
- Begin by **chopping the onion**, **mincing the garlic**, **dicing the carrot** and **zucchini**, and rinsing the **spinach**. If using fresh chickpeas, cook them beforehand or use canned chickpeas to save time.

2. Sauté the Aromatics:
- Heat the **olive oil** in a large pot over medium heat. Once the oil is hot, add the **chopped onion** and **garlic**. Sauté for 3-4 minutes, until softened and fragrant.

3. Add the Vegetables:
- Add the **diced carrot** and **zucchini** to the pot. Stir occasionally and cook for about **5 minutes**, until the vegetables start to soften.

4. Season the Stew:
- Sprinkle in the **cumin, turmeric, smoked paprika,** and **cinnamon** (if using). Stir well to coat the vegetables with the spices and cook for another **1-2 minutes** to release the flavors.

5. Add the Chickpeas and Tomatoes:
- Stir in the **chickpeas** and **diced tomatoes** (with their juices). Mix everything together and cook for another **2-3 minutes**.

6. Add the Broth:
- Pour in the **vegetable broth** (or chicken broth) and bring the stew to a simmer. Reduce the heat to low and let it cook for **10-12 minutes**, allowing the flavors to meld together and the vegetables to fully soften.

7. Add the Spinach:
- Add the **fresh spinach** to the stew, stirring it in until wilted and tender. This should take about **2-3 minutes**.

8. Finish the Stew:
- Stir in **lemon juice** and season with **salt** and **pepper** to taste. If you prefer a thicker stew, you can mash a portion of the chickpeas with a spoon or potato masher to create a creamier texture.

9. Serve:
- Ladle the stew into bowls and garnish with **chopped cilantro** or **parsley**. Serve warm with **crusty bread** or over **rice** for a complete meal.

VARIATIONS AND ADAPTATIONS

- **Add Protein:** For a more substantial meal, consider adding **shredded rotisserie chicken, turkey,** or **tofu** for extra protein.

- **Different Vegetables:** Feel free to swap the **carrot** and **zucchini** for other seasonal vegetables like **sweet potato, butternut squash,** or **bell peppers**.

- **Spicy Version:** If you prefer a little heat, add **1/2 teaspoon cayenne pepper** or a chopped **jalapeño** to the stew along with the spices.

- **Indian Influence:** Add **curry powder** instead of cumin and turmeric for a more Indian-inspired flavor. You can also stir in a dollop of **plain yogurt** before serving for creaminess.

- **Middle Eastern Twist:** Add **ground coriander** and **cinnamon** to the spice mix and serve the stew with a side of **hummus** and **pita bread**.

NUTRITIONAL INFORMATION (PER SERVING)

Calories: 220	Cholesterol: 0mg	Fiber: 9g	Calcium: ....10% DV
Total Fat: 9g	Sodium: 600mg	Sugars: 6g	Iron: ....15% DV
Saturated Fat: 1g	Carbohydrates: ...28g	Protein: 9g	

ROASTED CAULIFLOWER TACOS

Yield: 4 servings   **Prep Time:** 15 minutes   **Cook Time:** 25 minutes

INGREDIENTS

For the Roasted Cauliflower:
- **1 medium head of cauliflower**, cut into florets
- **2 tablespoons olive oil**
- **1 teaspoon chili powder**
- **1/2 teaspoon cumin**
- **1/2 teaspoon smoked paprika**
- **1/4 teaspoon garlic powder**
- **1/4 teaspoon onion powder**
- **Salt and pepper**, to taste

For the Taco Assembly:
- **8 small corn or flour tortillas**
- **1/2 red onion**, thinly sliced
- **1/2 cup fresh cilantro**, chopped
- **1 avocado**, sliced
- **1/2 cup crumbled queso fresco** or shredded cheese
- **Lime wedges**, for serving
- **Hot sauce or salsa**, to taste

STEP-BY-STEP INSTRUCTIONS

1. Preheat the Oven:
- Preheat the oven to **425°F (220°C)**.

2. Prepare the Cauliflower:
- Cut the **cauliflower** into bite-sized florets. Place the florets in a large bowl.

3. Season the Cauliflower:
- Drizzle the **olive oil** over the cauliflower and sprinkle with **chili powder**, **cumin**, **smoked paprika**, **garlic powder**, and **onion powder**. Toss well to coat evenly. Season with **salt** and **pepper** to taste.

4. Roast the Cauliflower:
- Spread the seasoned cauliflower florets in a single layer on a baking sheet. Roast in the preheated oven for about **20-25 minutes**, flipping halfway through, until the cauliflower is golden and tender with slightly crispy edges.

5. Prepare the Toppings:
- While the cauliflower is roasting, **slice the red onion** thinly and chop the **cilantro**. **Slice the avocado** and set aside.

6. Warm the Tortillas:
- While the cauliflower finishes roasting, warm the **tortillas** in a dry skillet over medium heat for about 1 minute per side, or microwave them for 20-30 seconds until soft and pliable.

7. Assemble the Tacos:
- Once the cauliflower is roasted, remove it from the oven and set aside to cool slightly. Begin assembling the tacos by placing a few spoonfuls of roasted cauliflower in each tortilla.
- Top with **red onion slices**, **chopped cilantro**, and **sliced avocado**. Add a sprinkle of **queso fresco** or shredded cheese, if desired.

8. Serve:
- Serve the tacos with **lime wedges** for squeezing over the top, and drizzle with your favorite **hot sauce** or **salsa** for extra flavor.

VARIATIONS AND ADAPTATIONS

- **Meat Option:** For a heartier taco, you can add grilled chicken, shrimp, or even ground turkey to the roasted cauliflower for a protein-packed option.
- **Vegan/Gluten-Free:** These tacos are naturally vegan and gluten-free when served with corn tortillas. You can also swap the cheese for a dairy-free alternative.
- **Spicy:** Add a few slices of **jalapeño** or **serrano pepper** to the tacos for an extra kick.
- **Different Vegetables:** Swap the cauliflower for other seasonal vegetables such as **sweet potatoes**, **zucchini**, or **butternut squash** for a different flavor profile.
- **Latin Influence:** Top the tacos with a **chipotle crema** (made from blending vegan mayo, chipotle peppers, lime juice, and garlic) for a smoky, creamy addition.

NUTRITIONAL INFORMATION (PER SERVING)

Calories: 290	(if using cheese)	Sugars: 5g	Iron: 10% DV
Total Fat: 18g	Sodium: 320mg	Protein: 6g	
Saturated Fat: 3g	Carbohydrates: 31g	Calcium: 10% DV	
Cholesterol: 10mg	Fiber: 8g	(with cheese)	

VEGAN PAD THAI

Yield: 4 servings | **Prep Time:** 15 minutes | **Cook Time:** 15 minutes

INGREDIENTS

For the Pad Thai Sauce:
- **3 tablespoons tamari** (or soy sauce)
- **1 tablespoon peanut butter**
- **1 tablespoon maple syrup**
- **2 tablespoons lime juice**
- **1 tablespoon rice vinegar**
- **1 teaspoon sriracha**
- **1 teaspoon grated ginger**
- **1 garlic clove**, minced

For the Pad Thai:
- **8 oz rice noodles**
- **1 tablespoon sesame oil** (or vegetable oil)
- **1 medium carrot**, julienned
- **1 bell pepper**, thinly sliced
- **1/2 cup red cabbage**, thinly sliced
- **1/2 cup green onions**, chopped
- **1 cup firm tofu**, cubed
- **1/4 cup roasted peanuts**, chopped (for garnish)
- **1/4 cup fresh cilantro**, chopped
- **1 lime**, cut into wedges

STEP-BY-STEP INSTRUCTIONS

1. Prepare the Rice Noodles:
- Bring a large pot of water to a boil. Add the **rice noodles** and cook according to the package instructions (usually about 4-6 minutes for dried noodles). Drain the noodles and rinse with cold water to stop the cooking process. Set aside.

2. Make the Pad Thai Sauce:
- In a small bowl, whisk together **tamari, peanut butter, maple syrup, lime juice, rice vinegar, sriracha, grated ginger,** and **minced garlic** until smooth. Adjust the seasonings to taste, adding more sweetener or spice if needed. Set the sauce aside.

3. Prepare the Tofu:
- Press the **tofu** to remove excess moisture, then cut it into small cubes. Heat **1 tablespoon sesame oil** in a large skillet or wok over medium heat. Add the tofu cubes and sauté for about 5-7 minutes, until golden brown on all sides. Remove tofu from the pan and set aside.

4. Sauté the Vegetables:
- In the same skillet, add a little more oil if necessary. Add the **carrot, bell pepper,** and **red cabbage**. Stir-fry for about 3-4 minutes, until the vegetables are tender but still crisp.

5. Combine Noodles and Sauce:
- Add the cooked rice noodles to the skillet with the sautéed vegetables. Pour the prepared Pad Thai sauce over the noodles and toss everything together gently to coat the noodles evenly.

6. Add Tofu and Garnish:
- Add the cooked tofu back into the pan and toss it with the noodles and veggies. Continue to cook for 2-3 more minutes to ensure everything is heated through.

7. Serve the Pad Thai:
- Divide the Pad Thai among serving plates. Garnish with **chopped roasted peanuts, fresh cilantro,** and additional **lime wedges** on the side. Serve immediately.

VARIATIONS AND ADAPTATIONS

- **Vegetable Variations:** You can add other seasonal vegetables such as **zucchini, broccoli,** or **snow peas** depending on what's available.

- **Protein Substitution:** If you prefer a different protein, you can substitute the tofu with **tempeh, edamame,** or even **chickpeas** for added texture and protein.

- **Nut-Free Option:** For a nut-free version, use sunflower butter instead of peanut butter in the sauce.

- **Spicier Option:** For an extra kick, increase the **sriracha** or add chopped **fresh chilies** to the dish.

NUTRITIONAL INFORMATION (PER SERVING)

Calories: 350	Cholesterol: 0mg	Fiber: 5g	Calcium: ....8% DV
Total Fat: 16g	Sodium: 700mg	Sugars: 7g	Iron: ....15% DV
Saturated Fat: 2g	Carbohydrates: ...45g	Protein: 15g	

SWEET POTATO GNOCCHI

Yield: 4 servings   **Prep Time:** 15 minutes   **Cook Time:** 30 minutes

INGREDIENTS

For the Gnocchi:
- **2 medium sweet potatoes** (about 2 cups mashed)
- **1 1/2 cups all-purpose flour**
- **1/2 teaspoon salt**
- **1/4 teaspoon ground nutmeg**
- **1/4 teaspoon ground cinnamon**
- **1 egg**

For the Sauce:
- **2 tablespoons olive oil**
- **2 cloves garlic**, minced
- **1/2 cup vegetable broth**
- **1/4 cup coconut milk** (optional)
- **2 tablespoons fresh sage**, chopped
- **Salt and pepper**, to taste

For Garnish:
- **Freshly grated Parmesan** (optional, or nutritional yeast for vegan option)

STEP-BY-STEP INSTRUCTIONS

1. Prepare the Sweet Potatoes:
- Pierce the **sweet potatoes** with a fork and bake them at 400°F (200°C) for 45-60 minutes, or until soft. Alternatively, you can microwave the sweet potatoes for 10 minutes, or boil them in a pot of water for 20-25 minutes until tender.
- Once cooked, let the sweet potatoes cool slightly, then scoop out the flesh and mash it until smooth. You should have about 2 cups of mashed sweet potato.

2. Make the Gnocchi Dough:
- In a large bowl, combine the mashed sweet potato, **1 1/2 cups of flour**, **salt**, **nutmeg**, and **cinnamon** (if using).
- Crack the **egg** into the bowl and mix the ingredients together until you have a smooth dough. If the dough feels sticky, add more flour, a tablespoon at a time, until it holds together but is still soft and pliable.

3. Shape the Gnocchi:
- Lightly flour your work surface and divide the dough into 4 portions.
- Roll each portion into a long rope, about 1/2 inch in diameter. Cut the ropes into 1-inch pieces.
- To shape the gnocchi, use a fork to gently press into each piece, creating the traditional ridges. Alternatively, you can leave them as small, round pieces.
- Set the shaped gnocchi aside on a floured tray.

4. Cook the Gnocchi:
- Bring a large pot of salted water to a boil. Carefully drop the gnocchi into the boiling water in batches. When the gnocchi float to the surface (after about 2-3 minutes), they are done. Use a slotted spoon to remove them from the water and set aside on a plate.

5. Prepare the Sauce:
- In a large skillet, heat **olive oil** over medium heat. Add the **garlic** and sauté for about 1 minute until fragrant.
- Add the **vegetable broth** and **coconut milk** (if using) and bring to a simmer. Let it cook for about 3-4 minutes until slightly reduced.
- Add the **fresh sage** and season with **salt** and **pepper** to taste.

6. Combine Gnocchi and Sauce:
- Add the cooked gnocchi to the skillet and gently toss to coat them in the sauce. Cook for another 2-3 minutes, allowing the gnocchi to absorb the flavors of the sauce.

7. Serve:
- Plate the gnocchi and top with **freshly grated Parmesan** or **nutritional yeast** for a vegan option.
- Serve immediately, garnished with extra sage if desired.

VARIATIONS AND ADAPTATIONS
- **Vegetable Variations:** Add **spinach**, **kale**, or **roasted butternut squash** to the sauce to boost the nutritional value and flavor.
- **Meat Additions:** For a heartier meal, top the gnocchi with **grilled chicken**, **sausage**, or **ground turkey**.
- **Spicy Option:** Add a pinch of **red pepper flakes** to the sauce for a spicy kick.
- **Vegan Option:** To make this recipe fully vegan, use **nutritional yeast** in place of Parmesan, and ensure your vegetable broth is plant-based.

NUTRITIONAL INFORMATION (PER SERVING)

Calories: 350	Cholesterol: 55mg	Fiber: 6g	Calcium: ....4% DV
Total Fat: 10g	Sodium: 350mg	Sugars: 12g	Iron: ....10% DV
Saturated Fat: 1g	Carbohydrates: ...55g	Protein: 6g	

CAPRESE STUFFED ZUCCHINI BOATS

Yield: 4 servings | **Prep Time:** 15 minutes | **Cook Time:** 25 minutes

INGREDIENTS

For the Zucchini Boats:
- 4 medium zucchinis
- 1 tablespoon olive oil
- 1/2 cup cherry tomatoes, halved
- 1/2 cup fresh mozzarella cheese, diced or shredded

- 1/4 cup fresh basil leaves, chopped
- 1 tablespoon balsamic vinegar (optional)
- Salt and pepper, to taste

For the Topping:
- 1/4 cup grated Parmesan cheese (optional)
- Olive oil for drizzling

STEP-BY-STEP INSTRUCTIONS

1. Preheat the Oven:
- Preheat your oven to **375°F (190°C)**. Line a baking sheet with parchment paper for easy cleanup.

2. Prepare the Zucchini Boats:
- Cut the zucchinis in half lengthwise. Using a spoon, scoop out the center of each zucchini half to create a «boat,» leaving about a 1/4-inch thick shell around the edges.

- Place the zucchini boats on the prepared baking sheet, and drizzle with **1 tablespoon of olive oil**. Season with **salt** and **pepper**.

3. Make the Caprese Filling:
- In a medium bowl, combine the **cherry tomatoes**, **mozzarella cheese**, **basil leaves**, and **balsamic vinegar** (if using). Stir to combine.

4. Stuff the Zucchini Boats:
- Spoon the Caprese mixture into each zucchini boat, filling them generously with the tomato, mozzarella, and basil mixture.

5. Bake the Zucchini Boats:
- Place the stuffed zucchini boats in the oven and bake for **20-25 minutes**, or until the zucchini is tender and the cheese is melted and bubbly.

6. Add the Topping:
- If using **Parmesan cheese**, sprinkle it on top of the stuffed zucchini boats during the last 5 minutes of baking. Drizzle with a little more **olive oil** for extra flavor.

7. Serve:
- Remove the zucchini boats from the oven and let them cool slightly. Garnish with additional **fresh basil** before serving.

VARIATIONS AND ADAPTATIONS

- **Protein Additions:** Add **grilled chicken** or **ground turkey** to the Caprese filling for a heartier meal. Simply cook the meat ahead of time and mix it with the tomatoes and mozzarella before stuffing the zucchini.

- **Vegetarian Option:** You can also add **cooked quinoa** or **farro** to the filling for an extra boost of fiber and protein, making it even more filling.

- **Spicy Kick:** For a little heat, add **red pepper flakes** to the filling, or drizzle the boats with some **sriracha sauce** before serving.

- **Flavorful Sauce:** If you prefer a saucier dish, serve the zucchini boats over a bed of **tomato sauce** or drizzle with **pesto** before baking.

NUTRITIONAL INFORMATION (PER SERVING)

Calories: 220	Cholesterol: 25mg	Fiber: 3g	Calcium: ....20% DV
Total Fat: 14g	Sodium: 350mg	Sugars: 7g	Iron: ....6% DV
Saturated Fat: 6g	Carbohydrates: ...14g	Protein: 12g	

CHAPTER 7:
GLOBAL FLAVORS IN A HURRY

PRACTICAL TIPS

This chapter is all about bringing the world's most beloved flavors to your dinner table—quickly and easily! From savory stir-fries to aromatic curries and flavorful pasta dishes, these recipes are designed for busy nights when you want to travel the globe without leaving your kitchen. Use these tips to master global cuisine in no time while keeping the process simple and enjoyable.

1. Stock an International Pantry:
- Keep essential global ingredients on hand, such as soy sauce, sesame oil, curry paste, coconut milk, spices like cumin and paprika, and pantry staples like rice and noodles.
- These versatile items will help you prepare a variety of international dishes quickly.

2. Prep Ahead for Speed:
- Chop vegetables, measure spices, and marinate proteins in advance to streamline your cooking process.
- Use pre-washed and pre-cut produce if you're short on time.

3. Embrace Bold Flavors:
- Don't shy away from spices, herbs, and sauces that define global dishes. Examples include smoked paprika for Spanish dishes, garam masala for Indian cuisine, and za'atar for Middle Eastern recipes.
- Taste as you go and adjust seasoning to suit your preferences.

4. Use Time-Saving Techniques:
- Opt for one-pot or one-pan methods to reduce cleanup, like stir-frying, simmering, or sheet-pan roasting.
- Quick-cooking proteins such as shrimp, chicken breast, or tofu make meals faster without sacrificing flavor.

5. Experiment with Versatile Sauces:
- Create quick sauces to transform simple ingredients into flavorful dishes. Examples include teriyaki glaze, chimichurri, tahini dressing, or yogurt-based tzatziki.
- Store extra sauce for drizzling over grains, salads, or roasted veggies later in the week.

6. Highlight Fresh Herbs:
- Fresh cilantro, parsley, mint, or basil can elevate any dish, adding brightness and a touch of authenticity.
- Sprinkle herbs just before serving to preserve their vibrant flavors.

7. Balance Flavors for Authenticity:
- Global cuisines often balance sweet, sour, salty, and spicy flavors. Add a splash of vinegar, a squeeze of lemon, or a drizzle of honey to create harmony in your dish.
- Experiment with chili flakes or sriracha for heat and coconut milk or yogurt for cooling elements.

8. Choose the Right Cooking Techniques:
- Stir-frying is ideal for Asian dishes, roasting works well for Mediterranean meals, and simmering is perfect for soups and stews from around the world.
- Learn to quickly toast spices in oil to release their aroma, a technique used in Indian and Middle Eastern cuisines.

9. Adapt to Local and Seasonal Ingredients:
- Swap out hard-to-find ingredients for locally available ones. For instance, use spinach instead of bok choy in a stir-fry or substitute sweet potatoes for butternut squash in a curry.
- Seasonal ingredients often taste better and cost less.

10. Leverage Pre-Made Shortcuts:
- Use store-bought curry pastes, marinara sauces, or pre-cooked grains for speedy preparation.
- Frozen vegetables can be a lifesaver when fresh produce isn't available.

11. Explore Global Grains:
- Incorporate international staples like quinoa, couscous, basmati rice, or udon noodles to bring authenticity to your meals.
- Cook grains in vegetable or chicken broth for extra flavor.

12. Add a Personal Touch:
- Feel free to tweak recipes to suit your family's preferences. For example, reduce spice levels for kids or substitute proteins based on dietary needs.
- Garnish dishes with your favorite toppings, such as toasted nuts, crispy onions, or crumbled cheese.

13. Pair the Right Sides:
- Serve naan or pita with curries, crusty bread with European soups, or jasmine rice with stir-fries to round out your meal.
- Complement main dishes with quick salads, like a Greek salad or cucumber-yogurt side.

14. Take Inspiration from Street Food:
- Recreate street food favorites like tacos, spring rolls, or kebabs for a fun, family-friendly dinner.
- Use tortillas, lettuce wraps, or skewers to add an inter-

active element to your meal.

15. Keep it Simple:
- Many global dishes have just a few key ingredients that shine. Focus on those and avoid overcomplicating recipes.

- For example, a Caprese salad relies on fresh tomatoes, mozzarella, basil, and olive oil—simple yet delicious!

16. Repurpose Leftovers Creatively:
- Use leftover roasted vegetables to make a Mediterranean grain bowl or stir them into a Thai curry.

- Wrap leftover proteins in tortillas for quick tacos or fold them into fried rice for a new meal.

17. Cook with Love and Curiosity:
- View each recipe as an opportunity to learn about and appreciate another culture.

- Cooking global dishes brings a sense of adventure and warmth to your home kitchen.

18. Quick Fixes for Busy Nights:
- When short on time, focus on dishes that cook in under 30 minutes, like noodle stir-fries, fried rice, or hearty soups.

- Use rotisserie chicken or canned beans for protein-packed meals with minimal prep.

19. Serve Family-Style:
- Arrange global dishes like curries, paella, or fajitas on a large platter so everyone can serve themselves.

- This approach creates a cozy, communal dining experience.

20. Savor the Experience:
- Take a moment to enjoy the rich aromas and vibrant flavors of your meal.

- Share stories about the cuisine's cultural origins to make dinner more engaging and meaningful.

CONCLUSION:

Chapter 7 is your passport to quick, flavorful dinners inspired by kitchens around the world. By following these tips, you'll bring global flair to your meals without spending hours in the kitchen. Enjoy the diversity of tastes and textures as you explore these easy, delicious recipes!

THAI GREEN CURRY

Yield: 4 servings   Preparation Time: 15 minutes   Cooking Time: 25 minutes

INGREDIENTS

For the Curry:
- **1 tablespoon vegetable oil**
- **1 medium onion,** thinly sliced
- **2 cloves garlic,** minced
- **1 tablespoon fresh ginger,** grated
- **2 tablespoons green curry paste**
- **1 can (14 oz) coconut milk**
- **1 cup vegetable broth** (or chicken broth)
- **2 medium carrots,** sliced
- **1 red bell pepper,** sliced
- **1 zucchini,** sliced
- **1 cup green beans,** trimmed
- **1 tablespoon soy sauce or tamari** for gluten-free option
- **1 tablespoon lime juice**
- **1 tablespoon brown sugar**
- **1/2 cup fresh basil leaves,** chopped
- **1 tablespoon fresh cilantro, chopped**
- **1 tablespoon fish sauce**
- **1 tablespoon sesame oil**

For Serving:
- **2 cups cooked jasmine rice**
- **Lime wedges,** for garnish
- **Fresh cilantro,** for garnish

STEP-BY-STEP INSTRUCTIONS

1. Prepare the Ingredients:
- Slice the onion, carrots, zucchini, and bell pepper. Trim the green beans and set aside.
- Cook jasmine rice according to package instructions, and set aside.

2. Heat the Oil:
- In a large pot or deep skillet, heat 1 tablespoon of vegetable oil over medium heat. Once hot, add the onion and sauté until softened, about 3-4 minutes.

3. Add the Aromatics:
- Add the garlic and ginger to the onions, and sauté for another 1-2 minutes until fragrant.

4. Stir in the Curry Paste:
- Stir in 2 tablespoons of green curry paste and cook for 1 minute, allowing the paste to release its flavors.

5. Add Coconut Milk and Broth:
- Pour in the coconut milk and vegetable broth, stirring to combine. Bring to a simmer.

6. Add Vegetables:
- Add the carrots, bell pepper, zucchini, and green beans to the pot. Simmer for about 10 minutes, or until the vegetables are tender but still slightly crisp.

7. Season the Curry:
- Stir in soy sauce, lime juice, and brown sugar. Add fish sauce (if using), and adjust seasoning with more salt or soy sauce if needed.

8. Finish the Curry:
- Add sesame oil, and stir to combine. Let the curry simmer for another 2-3 minutes to meld the flavors.

9. Serve:
- Spoon the cooked jasmine rice into bowls. Ladle the green curry over the rice, and garnish with fresh basil, cilantro, and a squeeze of lime juice.

VARIATIONS AND ADAPTATIONS

- Protein Options: Add tofu for a vegetarian or vegan version. For non-vegetarian options, you can add chicken breast (cut into thin strips), shrimp, or beef (thinly sliced). Simply sauté the protein with the onions and cook until browned before adding the rest of the ingredients.

- Different Vegetables: Feel free to swap or add seasonal vegetables such as sweet potatoes, eggplant, or baby corn. You can also use broccoli or spinach for a leafy green alternative.

- Spicy Kick: For a spicier dish, increase the amount of green curry paste, or add sliced Thai bird's eye chilies to the curry paste. You can also serve with a drizzle of sriracha.

- Influences from Other Cuisines: Add a touch of lemongrass or curry leaves for a deeper Thai flavor, or use coconut milk and curry powder for a simplified, Indian-inspired version.

NUTRITIONAL INFORMATION (PER SERVING)

Calories: 350	Cholesterol: 0mg	Fiber: 5g	Vitamin A: ....150% DV
Total Fat: 25g	Sodium: 600mg	Sugars: 12g	Vitamin C: ....90% DV
Saturated Fa........ 13g	Carbohydrates: ...30g	Protein: 4g	Calcium: ....4% DV
			Iron: ....15% DV

MEXICAN ENCHILADAS

Yield: 4 servings   **Prep Time:** 15 minutes   **Cook Time:** 30 minutes

INGREDIENTS
For the Enchiladas:
- 12 corn tortillas
- 1 tablespoon vegetable oil
- 2 cups shredded chicken
- 1 medium onion, diced
- 2 cloves garlic, minced
- 1 can (14 oz) enchilada sauce
- 1 cup shredded cheese (cheddar, Monterey Jack)
- 1/2 cup sour cream
- Fresh cilantro, for garnish

For the Enchilada Sauce:
- 2 tablespoons vegetable oil
- 1/4 cup chili powder
- 1 teaspoon cumin
- 1 teaspoon paprika
- 1/2 teaspoon garlic powder
- 1/2 teaspoon onion powder
- 1/2 teaspoon oregano
- 1/4 teaspoon cayenne pepper
- 1 can (14 oz) tomato sauce
- 1 cup water
- Salt to taste

STEP-BY-STEP INSTRUCTIONS

1. Prepare the Enchilada Sauce (if making homemade):
- Heat 2 tablespoons vegetable oil in a saucepan over medium heat. Add the chili powder, cumin, paprika, garlic powder, onion powder, oregano, and cayenne pepper. Stir for about 1 minute, allowing the spices to bloom.
- Add tomato sauce and water to the pan, stirring to combine. Season with salt to taste.
- Bring to a simmer and cook for about 10-12 minutes, allowing the sauce to thicken. Set aside.

2. Prepare the Filling:
- In a skillet, heat 1 tablespoon vegetable oil over medium heat. Add the diced onion and sauté for 3-4 minutes until softened.
- Add the minced garlic and cook for another 1 minute.
- Stir in the shredded chicken and 1/2 cup of the prepared enchilada sauce. Cook for 5 minutes, letting the chicken absorb the flavors. Remove from heat.

3. Warm the Tortillas:
- Heat the corn tortillas in a dry skillet for 30 seconds per side, or wrap them in a damp paper towel and microwave them for 30 seconds to soften. This will help prevent them from cracking when rolled.

4. Assemble the Enchiladas:
- Preheat the oven to 375°F (190°C).
- Spread a thin layer of enchilada sauce on the bottom of a 9x13-inch baking dish.
- Take each tortilla and spoon a few tablespoons of the chicken filling into the center. Roll the tortilla tightly and place it seam-side down in the baking dish.
- Repeat for all 12 tortillas, arranging them snugly in the baking dish.

5. Bake the Enchiladas:
- Pour the remaining enchilada sauce over the rolled tortillas.
- Sprinkle the shredded cheese evenly over the top.
- Cover the baking dish with aluminum foil and bake for 20 minutes.
- After 20 minutes, remove the foil and bake for an additional 5-10 minutes until the cheese is melted and bubbly.

6. Serve:
- Remove the enchiladas from the oven and let them rest for a few minutes.
- Top with a dollop of sour cream and a sprinkle of fresh cilantro for garnish.
- Serve with a side of Mexican rice, black beans, or a simple salad.

VARIATIONS AND ADAPTATIONS
- **Vegetarian Version:** Substitute the chicken with black beans, sweet potatoes, or grilled zucchini for a hearty, vegetable-packed enchilada.
- **Spicy Kick:** Add chopped jalapeños or serrano peppers to the filling or sauce for extra heat.
- **Beef Enchiladas:** Replace the chicken with ground beef or shredded beef. Brown the beef first, then season with taco seasoning or cumin, garlic, and onion for added flavor.
- **Cheese Variations:** Try using queso fresco, Mexican crema, or pepper jack cheese for a twist on the classic.

NUTRITIONAL INFORMATION (PER SERVING)

Calories: 350	Sodium: 900mg	Protein: 22g	Iron: ....15% DV
Total Fat: 18g	Carbohydrates: ...30g	Vitamin A: ....20% DV	
Saturated Fat: 7g	Fiber: 5g	Vitamin C: ....15% DV	
Cholesterol: 40mg	Sugars: 6g	Calcium: ....20% DV	

ITALIAN MARGHERITA FLATBREAD

Yield: 4 servings   **Prep Time:** 10 minutes   **Cook Time:** 15 minutes   **Total Time:** 25 minutes

INGREDIENTS

For the Flatbread:
- **1 package (8 oz) pizza dough**
- **2 tablespoons olive oil**
- **1 garlic clove,** minced
- **1 teaspoon dried oregano**
- **1/2 teaspoon sea salt**

For the Toppings:
- **1/2 cup marinara sauce**
- **8 oz fresh mozzarella cheese,** sliced
- **2 medium tomatoes,** thinly sliced
- **Fresh basil leaves**
- **Olive oil,** for drizzling
- **Freshly cracked black pepper,** to taste

STEP-BY-STEP INSTRUCTIONS

1. Preheat the Oven:
- Preheat your oven to 475°F (245°C). Place a baking sheet or pizza stone in the oven to heat up.

2. Prepare the Flatbread Dough:
- If using store-bought dough, allow it to come to room temperature (about 10 minutes).
- Roll the dough out on a lightly floured surface until it reaches a 10-12 inch circle or rectangle, depending on your preference. If you prefer a thinner crust, roll it out a little more.

3. Add Flavored Oil:
- In a small bowl, combine 2 tablespoons of olive oil, minced garlic, oregano, and sea salt. Brush this mixture evenly over the flatbread dough. This will infuse the crust with delicious flavor.

4. Add the Toppings:
- Spread a thin layer of marinara sauce over the flatbread, leaving a small border around the edges for the crust.
- Arrange the fresh mozzarella slices evenly on top of the sauce.
- Place the tomato slices on top of the mozzarella.

5. Bake the Flatbread:
- Carefully transfer the prepared flatbread to the preheated baking sheet or pizza stone in the oven.
- Bake for about 12-15 minutes, or until the edges of the flatbread are golden and the cheese is melted and bubbly.

6. Garnish and Serve:
- Once the flatbread is out of the oven, top with fresh basil leaves.
- Drizzle with a little more olive oil and season with freshly cracked black pepper to taste.
- Slice and serve hot!

VARIATIONS AND ADAPTATIONS
- **Vegetarian Version:** For added veggies, try adding sliced bell peppers, zucchini ribbons, or red onions along with the tomatoes for extra flavor.
- **Protein Option:** Add grilled chicken or prosciutto for a heartier version of this flatbread.
- **Spicy Kick:** Add a few red pepper flakes on top before baking or drizzle with spicy olive oil for a little heat.
- **Gluten-Free:** Use a gluten-free pizza dough or cauliflower crust for a gluten-free option.

NUTRITIONAL INFORMATION (PER SERVING)

Calories: 330	Cholesterol: 35mg	Fiber: 2g	Vitamin A: ....10% DV
Total Fat: 18g	Sodium: 700mg	Sugars: 5g	Vitamin C: ....25% DV
Saturated Fat: 6g	Carbohydrates: ...33g	Protein: 12g	Calcium:............. 20% DV
			Iron: ....10% DV

INDIAN BUTTER CHICKEN (MURGH MAKHANI)

Yield: 4 servings   **Prep Time:** 10 minutes   **Cook Time:** 30 minutes   **Total Time:** 40 minutes

INGREDIENTS

For the Marinade:
- 1 lb (450g) boneless, skinless chicken thighs
- 1/2 cup plain yogurt
- 1 tablespoon lemon juice
- 2 teaspoons ground turmeric
- 2 teaspoons ground cumin
- 2 teaspoons ground coriander
- 1 teaspoon ground paprika
- 1 teaspoon ground cinnamon
- 1 teaspoon ground ginger
- 2 garlic cloves, minced
- 1 tablespoon grated fresh ginger
- 1/2 teaspoon salt

For the Sauce:
- 2 tablespoons ghee
- 1 tablespoon vegetable oil
- 1 onion, finely chopped
- 2 garlic cloves, minced
- 1 tablespoon grated fresh ginger
- 1/2 cup tomato paste
- 1 cup canned crushed tomatoes
- • 1 cup heavy cream
- 1/4 cup water (adjust as needed)
- 1 teaspoon garam masala
- 1 teaspoon ground cumin
- 1/2 teaspoon ground turmeric
- Salt, to taste
- 1 tablespoon honey
- 1/4 cup fresh cilantro, chopped

STEP-BY-STEP INSTRUCTIONS

1. Marinate the Chicken:
- In a large bowl, combine yogurt, lemon juice, ground spices (turmeric, cumin, coriander, paprika, cinnamon, ginger), minced garlic, grated ginger, and salt. Add the chicken thighs and toss to coat. Cover the bowl and let the chicken marinate in the refrigerator for at least 30 minutes, or up to overnight for deeper flavor.

2. Sear the Chicken:
- Heat 1 tablespoon oil (or ghee) in a large skillet or pan over medium-high heat. Once hot, add the marinated chicken, cooking in batches if necessary. Sear the chicken for 3-4 minutes per side, until browned but not fully cooked through. Remove the chicken and set it aside.

3. Make the Sauce:
- In the same skillet, add 2 tablespoons ghee. Add the chopped onion and sauté for 5 minutes until soft and translucent.
- Add the minced garlic and grated ginger, and cook for another 1 minute until fragrant.
- Stir in the tomato paste and cook for 2 minutes, then add the crushed tomatoes and water. Bring to a simmer and cook for about 5-7 minutes until the sauce thickens slightly.
- Stir in the heavy cream, garam masala, ground cumin, turmeric, and honey. Season with salt to taste. Simmer for another 5 minutes.

4. Add Chicken to the Sauce:
- Return the seared chicken to the pan, and simmer in the sauce for 10-12 minutes, or until the chicken is fully cooked and tender.

5. Garnish and Serve:
- Once the chicken is cooked through, remove the pan from the heat. Garnish with chopped fresh cilantro.
- Serve the butter chicken with basmati rice or naan bread for a complete meal.

VARIATIONS AND ADAPTATIONS

- **Vegetarian Version:** Substitute the chicken with paneer or tofu for a vegetarian version of this dish.
- Different Meat Options: You can use chicken breast, lamb, or shrimp as the protein in place of chicken thighs.
- **Spicy Version:** For those who enjoy a bit of heat, add fresh chili peppers or chili powder to the marinade or sauce.
- **Coconut Cream Substitute:** For a dairy-free version, substitute the heavy cream with coconut cream for a richer, slightly sweet flavor.
- **Vegetable Options:** Add seasonal vegetables like spinach, bell peppers, or cauliflower to the sauce for extra nutrition and flavor.

NUTRITIONAL INFORMATION (PER SERVING)

Calories: 480	Cholesterol: 140mg	Fiber: 2g	Vitamin A: ....25% DV
Total Fat: 36g	Sodium: 560mg	Sugars: 6g	Vitamin C: ....15% DV
Saturated Fat: 16g	Carbohydrates: ...13g	Protein: 33g	Calcium: ....12% DV
			Iron: ....20% DV

CHINESE ORANGE BEEF STIR-FRY

Yield: 4 servings   **Prep Time:** 15 minutes   **Cook Time:** 15 minutes   **Total Time:** 30 minutes

INGREDIENTS

For the Beef Marinade:
- 1 lb (450g) flank steak or sirloin steak, thinly sliced
- 2 tablespoons soy sauce
- 1 tablespoon rice vinegar
- 1 tablespoon cornstarch
- 1 teaspoon sesame oil

For the Orange Sauce:
- 1/2 cup fresh orange juice (about 2 oranges)
- 1 tablespoon orange zest
- 3 tablespoons soy sauce
- 2 tablespoons rice vinegar
- 2 tablespoons honey
- 2 teaspoons ginger, grated
- 1 garlic clove, minced
- 1 teaspoon cornstarch
- 1/4 teaspoon red pepper flakes

For the Stir-Fry:
- 2 tablespoons vegetable oil
- 1 red bell pepper, thinly sliced
- 1/2 medium onion, thinly sliced
- 1 cup broccoli florets
- 1/4 cup green onions, chopped
- Sesame seeds, for garnish (optional)

STEP-BY-STEP INSTRUCTIONS

1. Marinate the Beef:
- In a medium bowl, combine the soy sauce, rice vinegar, cornstarch, and sesame oil. Add the sliced flank steak or sirloin steak to the marinade and toss to coat. Let the beef marinate for about 10-15 minutes to absorb the flavors.

2. Make the Orange Sauce:
- In a small saucepan, whisk together the fresh orange juice, orange zest, soy sauce, rice vinegar, honey, grated ginger, and minced garlic.
- Bring the mixture to a gentle simmer over medium heat. Let it cook for about 2-3 minutes.
- In a separate small bowl, mix the 1 teaspoon of cornstarch with 1 tablespoon of water to make a slurry. Stir this into the sauce, and cook for an additional 2-3 minutes until the sauce thickens.
- If you prefer some heat, add red pepper flakes to the sauce at this point. Remove from heat and set aside.

3. Stir-Fry the Vegetables:
- Heat 1 tablespoon of vegetable oil in a large skillet or wok over medium-high heat. Add the red bell pepper and onion, and stir-fry for 2-3 minutes until they begin to soften but still have a bit of crunch.
- Add the broccoli florets (or alternative vegetables) and cook for an additional 3-4 minutes, until tender-crisp. Remove the vegetables from the skillet and set them aside.

4. Cook the Beef:
- In the same skillet, add 1 tablespoon of vegetable oil over medium-high heat. Add the marinated beef in batches, making sure not to overcrowd the pan. Stir-fry the beef for 2-3 minutes until browned and cooked through, then remove the beef from the skillet.

5. Combine and Coat with Sauce:
- Return the cooked beef and vegetables to the skillet. Pour the orange sauce over the beef and vegetables, tossing everything together to coat evenly. Let everything cook together for an additional 1-2 minutes, allowing the flavors to meld.

6. Garnish and Serve:
- Remove from heat and sprinkle with chopped green onions and sesame seeds (optional) for added flavor and presentation.
- Serve immediately with steamed jasmine rice, brown rice, or noodles.

VARIATIONS AND ADAPTATIONS

- **Vegetarian Version:** Use tofu or tempeh as a substitute for the beef. Press the tofu to remove excess moisture and cut it into cubes before marinating and cooking.
- **Different Protein Options:** You can substitute the beef with chicken breast, pork, or even shrimp. Adjust cooking time as needed based on the protein choice.
- **Vegetable Variations:** Use other seasonal vegetables like snow peas, carrots, or baby corn. If you want more greens, try adding spinach or bok choy.
- **Spicy Orange Sauce:** If you like a spicier dish, add extra chili paste, sriracha, or fresh sliced chilies when preparing the sauce.

NUTRITIONAL INFORMATION (PER SERVING)

Calories: 320	Cholesterol: 60mg	Fiber: 3g	Vitamin A: 30% DV
Total Fat: 14g	Sodium: 700mg	Sugars: 16g	Vitamin C: 70% DV
Saturated Fat: 2g	Carbohydrates: 24g	Protein: 25g	Calcium: 6% DV
			Iron: 20% DV

GREEK CHICKEN SOUVLAKI

Yield: 4 servings **Prep Time**: 15 minutes **Marinating Time**: 30 minutes **Cook Time**: 15 minutes **Total Time**: 1 hour

INGREDIENTS

For the Chicken Marinade:
- 1 ½ pounds chicken breast or thighs, cut into 1-inch cubes
- 3 tablespoons olive oil
- 3 tablespoons lemon juice
- 3 garlic cloves, minced
- 1 teaspoon dried oregano
- 1 teaspoon ground cumin
- ½ teaspoon smoked paprika
- ½ teaspoon salt
- ½ teaspoon black pepper

For Serving:
- 4 pita breads
- 1 cup cherry tomatoes, halved
- 1 cucumber, diced
- ½ red onion, thinly sliced
- 1 cup tzatziki sauce
- 1/4 cup fresh parsley, chopped

STEP-BY-STEP INSTRUCTIONS

1. Prepare the Marinade:
- In a large mixing bowl, whisk together olive oil, lemon juice, garlic, oregano, cumin, smoked paprika, salt, and pepper.
- Add the chicken cubes, ensuring they are evenly coated in the marinade.
- Cover the bowl with plastic wrap and marinate in the refrigerator for at least 30 minutes or overnight for deeper flavor.

2. Skewer and Cook the Chicken:
- If using wooden skewers, soak them in water for 30 minutes to prevent burning.
- Thread the marinated chicken onto the skewers.
- Preheat a grill or grill pan over medium-high heat. Lightly grease with oil to prevent sticking.
- Cook the chicken skewers for 10–12 minutes, turning every few minutes until fully cooked and slightly charred. Internal temperature should reach 165°F (74°C).

3. Warm the Pita Bread:
- While the chicken is cooking, lightly warm the pita bread on the grill or in a skillet for about 30 seconds per side.

4. Assemble the Souvlaki:
- Place a skewer of grilled chicken onto each warmed pita bread.
- Top with cherry tomatoes, cucumber, red onion, and a dollop of tzatziki sauce.
- Sprinkle with chopped parsley for freshness.

VARIATIONS AND ADAPTATIONS
- **Vegetarian Option:** Replace chicken with marinated cubes of halloumi or extra-firm tofu.
- **Meat Alternatives:** Use lamb or pork for a different Greek-style protein.
- **Gluten-Free Option:** Serve the chicken and toppings over a bed of quinoa or rice instead of pita.
- **Add Greens:** Include arugula or spinach for an extra layer of freshness.
- **International Fusion:** Use a garlic tahini sauce instead of tzatziki for a Middle Eastern twist.

NUTRITIONAL INFORMATION (PER SERVING)

Calories: 420	Sodium: 680mg	Protein: 35g	Calcium: ....10% DV
Total Fat: 15g	Carbohydrates: ...35g	Vitamin A: ....8% DV	Iron: ....15% DV
Saturated Fat: 3g	Fiber: 3g	Vitamin C: ....20% DV	
Cholesterol: 95mg	Sugars: 4g		

MOROCCAN SPICED COUSCOUS

Yield: 4 servings   **Prep Time:** 10 minutes   **Cook Time:** 10 minutes   **Total Time:** 20 minutes

INGREDIENTS

For the Couscous:
- **1 cup couscous**
- **1 tablespoon olive oil**
- **1 1/4 cups vegetable broth**
- **1/4 teaspoon ground turmeric**
- **1/2 teaspoon ground cumin**
- **1/2 teaspoon ground cinnamon**
- **1/4 teaspoon ground ginger**
- **Salt**, to taste
- **Freshly ground black pepper,** to taste

For the Vegetables and Garnish:
- **1/2 cup dried apricots,** chopped
- **1/4 cup roasted almonds,** sliced or chopped
- **1/2 cup carrots,** peeled and thinly sliced
- **1/2 cup zucchini,** diced
- **1/4 cup fresh parsley,** chopped
- **1 tablespoon pomegranate seeds**

Optional Protein Additions:
- **1 cup cooked chickpeas or 1/2 lb grilled chicken**

STEP-BY-STEP INSTRUCTIONS

1. Prepare the Couscous:
- In a medium-sized pot, bring vegetable broth (or water) to a boil. Add olive oil, turmeric, cumin, cinnamon, ginger, salt, and pepper. Stir to combine.
- Once the liquid is boiling, add the couscous, and stir briefly. Remove from heat, cover, and let it sit for 5-7 minutes until the couscous absorbs all the liquid.
- Fluff the couscous with a fork to separate the grains and make it light and airy.

2. Prepare the Vegetables:
- While the couscous is cooking, heat a non-stick skillet or frying pan over medium heat and add 1 tablespoon olive oil.
- Add the carrots and zucchini to the pan and sauté for 4-5 minutes until the vegetables are tender but still vibrant in color.
- Stir in the chopped dried apricots and cook for an additional 1-2 minutes to allow the apricots to soften.

3. Combine Couscous and Vegetables:
- Once the couscous is ready, add the sautéed vegetables and apricots to the couscous. Gently stir to combine.
- Add the roasted almonds and fresh parsley. Mix gently to incorporate all the ingredients.

4. Optional Protein Additions:
- If using chickpeas, stir them into the couscous mixture for added protein.
- Alternatively, grilled chicken can be served alongside or on top of the couscous, providing an extra hearty option.

5. Serve and Garnish:
- Spoon the couscous onto plates and garnish with pomegranate seeds and additional fresh parsley, if desired.
- Serve immediately as a warm, satisfying main dish or a side to a larger meal.

VARIATIONS AND ADAPTATIONS
- **Vegetarian Version:** This dish is already vegetarian and vegan-friendly, but to make it heartier, add toasted chickpeas or roasted sweet potatoes as a protein substitute for meat.
- **Meat Variations:** Use lamb or chicken for a more traditional Moroccan twist. Lamb meatballs spiced with cinnamon, cumin, and coriander would be a great accompaniment.
- **Spicy Variation:** Add a pinch of cayenne pepper or chili flakes to the spices for a bit of heat.
- **Citrus Infusion:** Stir in a little lemon zest or orange zest into the couscous for a burst of fresh citrus flavor, especially if you are serving the dish with a rich protein like lamb.

NUTRITIONAL INFORMATION (PER SERVING)

Calories: 280	Cholesterol: 0mg	Fiber: 5g	Protein: 7g
Total Fat: 12g	Sodium: 300mg	Sugars: 13g	Vitamin A:.........120%DV
Saturated Fat: 1g	Carbohydrates: ...41g	(from pricots)	Vitamin C: ....15% DV
			Calcium: ....4% DV
			Iron:.................10% DV

JAPANESE TERIYAKI CHICKEN

Yield: 4 servings   **Prep Time:** 10 minutes   **Cook Time:** 15 minutes   **Total Time:** 25 minutes

INGREDIENTS

For the Teriyaki Chicken:
- **4 boneless,** skinless chicken breasts
- **2 tablespoons olive oil**
- **Salt,** to taste
- **Black pepper, to taste**

For the Teriyaki Sauce:
- **1/4 cup soy sauce** (or tamari)
- **2 tablespoons honey**
- **2 tablespoons rice vinegar** (or apple cider vinegar)
- **2 tablespoons mirin** (optional)
- **1 teaspoon sesame oil**
- **2 cloves garlic,** minced
- **1 teaspoon fresh ginger,** grated
- **1 tablespoon cornstarch** (optional)

For Garnish:
- **1 tablespoon sesame seeds**
- **2 green onions,** sliced

For Serving:
- **Steamed jasmine rice or steamed vegetables**

STEP-BY-STEP INSTRUCTIONS

1. Prepare the Chicken:
- Season the chicken breasts with a pinch of salt and black pepper on both sides.
- Heat 2 tablespoons of olive oil in a large skillet over medium heat. Once the oil is hot, add the chicken breasts and cook for 6-7 minutes per side, or until golden brown and fully cooked through (internal temperature should reach 165°F). Remove the chicken from the pan and set aside to rest.

2. Prepare the Teriyaki Sauce:
- In a small saucepan, combine soy sauce, honey, rice vinegar, mirin, and sesame oil. Stir in minced garlic and grated ginger.
- Bring the sauce mixture to a simmer over medium heat, stirring occasionally. Let it cook for 2-3 minutes to allow the flavors to meld.
- If you prefer a thicker sauce, whisk in 1 tablespoon of cornstarch mixed with 2 tablespoons of water. Continue simmering until the sauce thickens, about 1-2 minutes. Adjust sweetness or tanginess with extra honey or vinegar, if needed.

3. Combine Chicken and Sauce:
- Slice the cooked chicken breasts into thin strips or leave them whole for a more traditional presentation.
- Return the chicken to the skillet with the teriyaki sauce, and cook for an additional 2-3 minutes over low heat, allowing the chicken to soak up the flavors of the sauce.

4. Serve:
- Serve the teriyaki chicken over a bed of steamed jasmine rice or alongside steamed vegetables (such as broccoli, snap peas, or carrots).
- Garnish with a sprinkle of sesame seeds and sliced green onions for extra flavor and visual appeal.

VARIATIONS AND ADAPTATIONS

- **Vegetarian Version:** Replace the chicken with tofu (firm, pressed, and sliced) or tempeh for a plant-based twist. Sauté until golden and crispy, then toss in the teriyaki sauce.
- **Other Meats:** You can use chicken thighs, pork tenderloin, or even beef for a different protein choice.
- **Extra Veggies:** Add baby corn, bell peppers, or mushrooms to the sauce for added texture and flavor.
- **Gluten-Free Version:** Use tamari instead of soy sauce for a gluten-free teriyaki sauce.
- **Spicy Teriyaki:** Add a pinch of red pepper flakes or sriracha to the sauce for a bit of heat.

NUTRITIONAL INFORMATION (PER SERVING)

Calories: 350	Sodium: 1100mg (can be reduced by using low-sodium soy sauce)	Fiber: 1g	Vitamin C: ....4% DV
Total Fat: 14g		Sugars: 13g	Calcium: ....4% DV
Saturated Fat: 2g		Protein: 35g	Iron: ....8% DV
Cholesterol: 70mg	Carbohydrates: ...17g	Vitamin A: ....6% DV	

FRENCH RATATOUILLE

Yield: 4 servings   **Prep Time:** 15 minutes   **Cook Time:** 30 minutes   **Total Time:** 45 minutes

INGREDIENTS
For the Ratatouille:
- **2 tablespoons olive oil**
- **1 medium onion,** diced
- **2 cloves garlic,** minced
- **1 medium eggplant,** diced
- **2 medium zucchinis,** sliced
- **1 red bell pepper,** diced
- **1 yellow bell pepper,** diced
- **2 medium tomatoes,** chopped
- **1 teaspoon dried thyme**
- **1 teaspoon dried oregano**
- **Salt and pepper,** to taste
- **Fresh basil, chopped (for garnish)**

For Serving:
- **Crusty bread or steamed rice** (local, if available)

STEP-BY-STEP INSTRUCTIONS

1. Prepare the Vegetables:
- Begin by washing and chopping the eggplant, zucchinis, bell peppers, and tomatoes into bite-sized pieces. Mince the garlic and dice the onion.

2. Sauté the Onion and Garlic:
- Heat 2 tablespoons of olive oil in a large skillet or sauté pan over medium heat.
- Add the onion and garlic to the pan, and sauté for 3-4 minutes, or until the onion becomes translucent and aromatic.

3. Add the Vegetables:
- Add the eggplant, zucchinis, and bell peppers to the pan, and cook for 8-10 minutes, stirring occasionally, until the vegetables begin to soften.

4. Add Tomatoes and Seasonings:
- Stir in the tomatoes, dried thyme, dried oregano, salt, and pepper. Continue to cook for an additional 5-7 minutes, allowing the vegetables to break down slightly and the flavors to meld together.

5. Simmer:
- Lower the heat to medium-low and let the mixture simmer for 10-15 minutes, stirring occasionally. If the mixture looks too dry, add a small splash of water or vegetable broth.

6. Garnish and Serve:
- Once the vegetables are tender and fully cooked, remove from the heat and garnish with freshly chopped basil.
- Serve the ratatouille alongside crusty bread or steamed rice for a satisfying meal.

VARIATIONS AND ADAPTATIONS
- **Add Protein:** For a heartier dish, you can add chickpeas, lentils, or tofu for a plant-based protein option. Alternatively, add grilled chicken or sausage for a meaty variation.
- **Spicy Twist:** Add a pinch of red pepper flakes or fresh chili for some extra heat, or incorporate a bit of curry powder for a spicier, more exotic flavor.
- **Roasted Ratatouille:** Instead of sautéing, you can roast the vegetables in the oven. Toss the chopped vegetables with olive oil, thyme, and oregano, and roast at 400°F for 25-30 minutes until tender and caramelized.
- **French Influence:** For a more traditional French twist, add a small amount of herbes de Provence or a splash of white wine to deepen the flavor.

NUTRITIONAL INFORMATION (PER SERVING)

Calories: 170	Sodium: 220mg	Protein: 4g	Calcium: ....6% DV
Total Fat: 10g	Carbohydrates: ...20g	Vitamin A: ....12% DV	Iron: ....10% DV
Saturated Fat: 1.5g	Fiber: 7g	Vitamin C: ....60% DV	
Cholesterol:......... 0mg	Sugars: 10g		

KOREAN BEEF BOWLS

Yield: 4 servings **Prep Time:** 10 minutes **Cook Time:** 15 minutes **Total Time:** 25 minutes

INGREDIENTS
For the Beef:
- 1 lb (450g) ground beef
- 2 tablespoons soy sauce
- 1 tablespoon sesame oil
- 2 cloves garlic, minced
- 1 tablespoon fresh ginger, grated (optional)
- 2 tablespoons brown sugar
- 1 tablespoon rice vinegar
- 1 tablespoon gochujang (Korean chili paste)
- 1 teaspoon sesame seeds
- 2 green onions, sliced

For the Rice:
- 2 cups jasmine rice
- 3 cups water or low-sodium broth

For Serving:
- **Cucumber,** thinly sliced
- **Carrots,** shredded
- **Steamed broccoli or sautéed spinach**

STEP-BY-STEP INSTRUCTIONS

1. Cook the Rice:
- Rinse the jasmine rice under cold water until the water runs clear.
- In a medium saucepan, combine the rinsed rice and 3 cups of water or low-sodium broth.
- Bring the mixture to a boil, then reduce the heat to low and cover. Simmer for 15 minutes, or until the rice is tender and the liquid has been absorbed. Fluff with a fork and set aside.

2. PREPARE THE BEEF:
- Heat 1 tablespoon of sesame oil in a large skillet or wok over medium-high heat.
- Add the ground beef and cook for 5-7 minutes, breaking it up with a wooden spoon, until browned and fully cooked.
- Add the minced garlic and grated ginger, and sauté for an additional 1-2 minutes until fragrant.

3. Add the Sauce:
- Stir in the soy sauce, brown sugar, rice vinegar, and gochujang to the cooked beef. Mix well to combine and let the sauce simmer for about 2-3 minutes until it thickens slightly and coats the beef.

4. Assemble the Bowls:
- To serve, spoon a generous portion of the cooked rice into each bowl.
- Top with the Korean-style beef mixture.
- Garnish with sliced green onions, sesame seeds, and a drizzle of sesame oil for extra flavor.
- Add thin slices of cucumber and shredded carrots on the side for a fresh, crunchy contrast. You can also add some steamed broccoli or sautéed spinach for extra vegetables.

VARIATIONS AND ADAPTATIONS
- **Vegetarian Version:** Substitute the ground beef with tofu or tempeh for a plant-based version. Crumble the tofu and sauté it until golden brown before adding the sauce.
- **Chicken or Pork:** Swap the ground beef for ground chicken or ground pork for a different protein. Chicken thighs or pork shoulder can also be used, sliced thinly and cooked in the sauce.
- **Add More Veggies:** Add sautéed mushrooms, bell peppers, or bok choy for more texture and flavor. You can also serve the bowls with pickled radishes for an extra tang.
- **Rice Substitutes:** For a lower-carb version, serve the beef on a bed of cauliflower rice or zoodles (zucchini noodles).

NUTRITIONAL INFORMATION (PER SERVING)

Calories: 450	Sodium: 580mg	Protein: 26g	Calcium: ....8% DV
Total Fat: 22g	Carbohydrates: ...36g	Vitamin A: ....25% DV	Iron: ....15% DV
Saturated Fat: 6g	Fiber: 2g	Vitamin C: ....35% DV	
Cholesterol: 60mg	Sugars: 14g		

CHAPTER 8:
MAKE-AHEAD DINNERS

PRACTICAL TIPS FOR STORING AND REHEATING MAKE-AHEAD DINNERS

As a culinary expert, ensuring that your make-ahead dinners remain fresh, flavorful, and easy to reheat is crucial. Whether you're preparing meals for a busy week or making sure dinner is ready to go at a moment's notice, here are some practical tips for storing and reheating your make-ahead dishes.

1. Proper Storage Techniques

- **Use Airtight Containers:** For best results, store your make-ahead meals in airtight containers to preserve their flavor, texture, and freshness. Glass containers with snap-tight lids or BPA-free plastic containers work well. Make sure to choose containers that are appropriately sized for the amount of food, as excess air can cause your meals to spoil faster.

- **Portion Control:** When prepping meals in advance, portioning them into single servings before storing is a great way to prevent waste. This allows for easy grab-and-go meals and ensures you only reheat the amount you need.

- **Label Everything:** Always label your containers with the date they were made. This will help you keep track of when the food was prepared and ensure you consume it within a safe timeframe. Use masking tape and a permanent marker or invest in some reusable labels.

- **Cool Before Storing:** Allow your food to cool to room temperature before placing it in the refrigerator or freezer. Storing hot food can raise the temperature inside your fridge or freezer, potentially leading to bacterial growth. Always cool your meals quickly and safely to prevent this.

2. Refrigeration vs. Freezing

- **Refrigeration:** Meals stored in the refrigerator will generally last for 3–4 days. For dishes like casseroles, soups, or stews, refrigeration is usually the best option if you plan to eat them within a few days.

- **Freezing:** For meals that you won't be eating in the next few days, freezing is the best option. Most make-ahead dinners can be frozen for 2–3 months without compromising too much on texture or taste. Make sure to use freezer-safe containers or bags, and remove as much air as possible to avoid freezer burn.

- **Tip:** For casseroles and stews, freezing them in individual servings is a convenient way to reheat just what you need. You can also freeze components of the meal separately (e.g., meats, sauces, or grains) and assemble them later for a quicker dinner.

3. Reheating Methods for Optimal Taste and Texture

- **Reheating in the Oven:** Reheating meals in the oven is the best way to preserve the original texture, especially for casseroles, roasted meats, or baked dishes. Preheat the oven to 350°F (175°C), cover your dish with foil to prevent drying out, and reheat for 20–30 minutes, depending on the size of the dish. Remove the foil for the last 10 minutes to allow the top to become golden and crispy.

- **Stovetop Reheating:** For soups, stews, or stir-fries, reheating on the stovetop is ideal. Heat over medium heat, stirring occasionally to ensure even reheating. Add a splash of water, broth, or oil to help loosen up any thickened sauce or to keep the dish moist.

- **Microwave Reheating:** The microwave is the quickest method, but it can sometimes result in uneven heating. To achieve more even results, stir the dish halfway through heating. For foods like pasta, rice, or grains, consider adding a small amount of water to prevent them from drying out. Cover with a microwave-safe lid or plate to trap steam and ensure the food heats evenly.

- **Tip:** If you have large portions, break them down into smaller pieces to heat more evenly.

4. Maintaining Quality

- **Add Fresh Ingredients After Reheating:** Some dishes, like salads or fresh salsas, can lose their texture or flavor when stored and reheated. It's best to add any fresh herbs, greens, or dressings after reheating to maintain their vibrant taste and texture.

- **Be Mindful of Sauces:** When reheating pasta, casseroles, or stir-fries, consider adding a little extra sauce, broth, or oil to rehydrate the dish. This will help prevent the food from drying out and keep the sauce creamy and flavorful.

- **Reheat Only Once:** For food safety and quality, it's important not to repeatedly reheat leftovers. Each reheating process affects both flavor and texture. Only reheat what you plan to eat and store the rest properly.

5. Freezer-Friendly Meal Ideas

- Some dishes freeze and reheat better than others,

but here are a few great make-ahead options:

- Lasagna: Freezes well and can be baked straight from the freezer.
- **Casseroles:** Whether it's a chicken pot pie, baked ziti, or shepherd's pie, these dishes freeze beautifully.
- **Soups and Stews:** Both freeze and reheat very well. Just make sure to cool them properly before freezing.
- **Chili:** A classic freezer-friendly option that tastes even better after a few days.

CONCLUSION:

By following these tips, your make-ahead dinners will be more convenient, flavorful, and ready to serve with minimal effort. Storing and reheating your meals properly will help maintain the quality of your food while saving you time, all while keeping your meals fresh and cozy. Enjoy the convenience of having healthy, homemade dinners waiting for you, and savor the comfort of a warm meal after a busy day!

FREEZER-FRIENDLY LASAGNA

Yield: 8 servings   **Prep Time:** 30 minutes   **Cook Time:** 1 hour

Total Time (including freezing): 1 hour 30 minutes (plus freezing time)

INGREDIENTS
For the Meat Sauce:
- **1 tablespoon olive oil**
- **1 medium onion,** diced
- **3 garlic cloves,** minced
- **1 pound ground beef** (or ground turkey)
- **1 pound ground Italian sausage**
- **1 can (28 oz) crushed tomatoes**
- **1 can (6 oz) tomato paste**
- **1 teaspoon dried basil**
- **1 teaspoon dried oregano**
- **½ teaspoon red pepper flakes** (optional)
- **1 teaspoon salt**
- **½ teaspoon black pepper**

For the Ricotta Mixture:
- **1 container (15 oz) ricotta cheese**
- **1 egg,** beaten
- **½ cup grated Parmesan cheese**
- **2 cups shredded mozzarella cheese** (divided)
- **1 teaspoon dried parsley**

For Assembly:
- **12 lasagna noodles** (no-boil or regular)
- **1 ½ cups shredded mozzarella cheese** (for topping)

STEP-BY-STEP INSTRUCTIONS

1. Prepare the Meat Sauce:
- Heat olive oil in a large skillet over medium heat. Add onions and sauté until softened, about 3–4 minutes.
- Add garlic and cook for 1 minute, stirring frequently.
- Add the ground beef and Italian sausage. Cook until browned, breaking up the meat with a spoon. Drain excess grease if needed.
- Stir in crushed tomatoes, tomato paste, basil, oregano, red pepper flakes, salt, and pepper. Let the sauce simmer for 15–20 minutes, stirring occasionally.

2. Prepare the Ricotta Mixture:
- In a mixing bowl, combine ricotta cheese, beaten egg, Parmesan cheese, 1 cup of mozzarella cheese, and dried parsley. Mix well and set aside.

3. Assemble the Lasagna:
- Preheat your oven to 375°F (190°C) if baking immediately.
- Spread a thin layer of the meat sauce on the bottom of a 9x13-inch baking dish.
- Place 3 lasagna noodles (or more, depending on your dish size) over the sauce.
- Spread 1/3 of the ricotta mixture over the noodles.
- Spoon 1/3 of the meat sauce over the ricotta mixture.
- Repeat the layers (noodles, ricotta, sauce) until all ingredients are used, finishing with a layer of meat sauce.

- Sprinkle the remaining mozzarella cheese on top.

4. Freeze or Bake:
- **Freezer Option:**
  ◇ Cover the assembled lasagna tightly with aluminum foil.
  ◇ Label with the date and store in the freezer for up to 3 months.
- **Baking Option:**
  ◇ Cover the dish with foil and bake for 40 minutes.
  ◇ Remove the foil and bake for an additional 10–15 minutes, or until the cheese is bubbly and golden brown.
  ◇ Let it rest for 10 minutes before slicing.
- **To Bake from Frozen:**
  ◇ Preheat oven to 375°F (190°C).
  ◇ Bake the lasagna (covered) for 90 minutes, then uncover and bake for another 20 minutes, or until fully heated through.

VARIATIONS AND ADAPTATIONS
- **Vegetarian Version:** Replace the meat with sautéed mushrooms, spinach, and zucchini.
- **Cheese Lovers' Delight:** Add an extra layer of ricotta mixture or additional types of cheese, such as provolone or gouda.
- Gluten-Free Option: Use gluten-free lasagna noodles.
- **Mediterranean Twist:** Incorporate layers of roasted eggplant and feta cheese.

NUTRITIONAL INFORMATION (PER SERVING)

Calories: 480	Cholesterol: 110mg	Fiber: 4g	Vitamin A: ....20% DV
Total Fat: 24g	Sodium: 850mg	Sugars: 8g	Vitamin C: ....15% DV
Saturated Fat: 10g	Carbohydrates: ...35g	Protein: 33g	Calcium: ....30% DV
			Iron: ....20% DV

SLOW COOKER PULLED PORK

Yield: 8 servings

Prep Time: 15 minutes

Cook Time: 8–10 hours on low or 4–6 hours on high

Total Time: Up to 10 hours 15 minutes

INGREDIENTS

- **4–5 lbs pork shoulder (or pork butt)**
- **1 medium onion,** thinly sliced
- **3 garlic cloves,** minced
- **1 cup barbecue sauce**
- **½ cup chicken broth** (or water)
- **¼ cup apple cider vinegar**
- **2 tablespoons brown sugar**
- **1 tablespoon smoked paprika**
- **1 teaspoon chili powder**
- **1 teaspoon ground cumin**
- **1 teaspoon salt**
- **½ teaspoon black pepper**
- **1 tablespoon olive oil**

Optional Garnishes and Serving Suggestions:
- **Burger buns or slider rolls**
- **Coleslaw**
- **Pickles**
- **Extra barbecue sauce**

STEP-BY-STEP INSTRUCTIONS

1. Prepare the Pork:
- Pat the pork shoulder dry with paper towels.
- In a small bowl, mix smoked paprika, chili powder, cumin, salt, and pepper.
- Rub the spice mixture all over the pork to coat it evenly.

2. Prepare the Slow Cooker:
- Drizzle olive oil at the bottom of the slow cooker.
- Layer the sliced onion and minced garlic as a base.
- Place the seasoned pork on top of the onions.

3. Add Liquid Ingredients:
- In a medium bowl, mix barbecue sauce, chicken broth, apple cider vinegar, and brown sugar.
- Pour this mixture over the pork.

4. Slow Cook:
- Low and Slow Option: Cook on low for 8–10 hours.
- Faster Option: Cook on high for 4–6 hours.

5. Shred the Pork:
- Once cooked, remove the pork from the slow cooker and place it on a cutting board.
- Use two forks to shred the pork into small pieces. Discard excess fat.

6. Finish the Pulled Pork:
- Return the shredded pork to the slow cooker and mix it with the cooking juices.
- Adjust seasoning if necessary.

7. Serve:
- Serve the pulled pork on burger buns or slider rolls, topped with coleslaw and a drizzle of extra barbecue sauce.
- Pair with sides like potato salad, cornbread, or roasted vegetables for a complete meal.

VARIATIONS AND ADAPTATIONS

- **Carnitas-Style Pulled Pork:** Swap the barbecue sauce for orange juice, lime juice, and a touch of oregano. After shredding, crisp the pork under the broiler for a few minutes.

- **Asian-Inspired Pulled Pork:** Replace barbecue sauce with hoisin sauce, soy sauce, and a dash of sesame oil. Serve in steamed bao buns or over rice.

- **Vegetarian Adaptation:** Use jackfruit instead of pork. Prepare as directed, adjusting cooking time to 2–3 hours on low.

- **Spicy Pulled Pork:** Add cayenne pepper or sriracha to the sauce for extra heat.

NUTRITIONAL INFORMATION (PER SERVING)

Calories: 3 20	Sodium: 600mg	Protein: 32g
Total Fat: 14g	Carbohydrates: ... 18g	Vitamin A: .... 10% DV
Saturated Fat: 5g	Fiber: 1g	Iron: .... 10% DV
Cholesterol: 95mg	Sugars: 12g	

CHICKEN ENCHILADA BAKE

Yield: 6 servings   **Prep Time:** 20 minutes   **Cook Time:** 35 minutes   **Total Time:** 55 minutes

INGREDIENTS

- 2 cups cooked shredded chicken
- 1½ cups enchilada sauce, divided
- 8 small corn tortillas, cut into quarters
- 1½ cups shredded cheddar cheese
- 1 cup shredded Monterey Jack cheese
- 1 medium onion, diced
- 1 cup canned black beans, drained and rinsed
- 1 cup corn kernels (fresh, frozen, or canned)
- 1 small jalapeño, diced (optional)
- 1 teaspoon cumin
- 1 teaspoon chili powder
- ½ teaspoon garlic powder
- 1 tablespoon olive oil
- ½ cup chopped fresh cilantro, for garnish
- 1 medium avocado, sliced, for topping
- ¼ cup sour cream, for serving

STEP-BY-STEP INSTRUCTIONS

1. Preheat the Oven:
- Preheat your oven to 375°F (190°C). Grease a 9x13-inch baking dish with olive oil or non-stick spray.

2. Sauté the Onion:
- Heat olive oil in a skillet over medium heat.
- Add the diced onion and cook until softened, about 3–4 minutes.
- Stir in the cumin, chili powder, and garlic powder, cooking for another minute.

3. Combine the Filling:
- In a large bowl, mix together the sautéed onion, shredded chicken, black beans, corn, and ½ cup of the enchilada sauce.
- Add the optional jalapeño for a spicy kick.

4. Assemble the Bake:
- Spread ½ cup of the enchilada sauce on the bottom of the baking dish.
- Layer a third of the tortilla pieces over the sauce.
- Add a third of the chicken mixture and sprinkle with a third of the cheese.
- Repeat this process twice more, finishing with a layer of cheese on top.

5. Bake the Dish:
- Cover the baking dish with foil and bake in the pre-heated oven for 25 minutes.
- Remove the foil and bake for an additional 10 minutes, or until the cheese is melted and bubbly.

6. Garnish and Serve:
- Let the dish cool slightly before garnishing with fresh cilantro and serving with avocado slices and a dollop of sour cream.

VARIATIONS AND ADAPTATIONS

- **Vegetarian Enchilada Bake:** Replace the chicken with sautéed zucchini, bell peppers, or sweet potatoes.
- **Beef Enchilada Bake:** Substitute shredded chicken with seasoned ground beef or shredded beef.
- **Tex-Mex Twist:** Add diced tomatoes, green chilies, or a layer of queso fresco.
- **Gluten-Free Option:** Ensure the enchilada sauce and tortillas are certified gluten-free.

NUTRITIONAL INFORMATION (PER SERVING)

Calories: 380	Sodium: 820mg	Protein: 25g	Iron: ....12% DV
Total Fat: 20g	Carbohydrates: ...28g	Vitamin A: ....15% DV	Calcium:.............25% DV
Saturated Fat: 9g	Fiber: 6g	Vitamin C: ....10% DV	
Cholesterol: 85mg	Sugars: 3g		

MARINATED GRILLED VEGGIES

Yield: 4 servings

Prep Time: 15 minutes (plus 30 minutes for marinating)

Cook Time: 15 minutes
Total Time: 1 hour

INGREDIENTS

For the Vegetables:

- **2 medium zucchini,** sliced lengthwise into ½-inch strips
- **1 large red bell pepper,** cut into thick strips
- **1 large yellow bell pepper,** cut into thick strips
- **1 medium red onion,** cut into thick wedges
- **1 cup cherry tomatoes** (or grape tomatoes)
- **1 medium eggplant,** sliced into ½-inch rounds
- **For the Marinade:**
- **3 tablespoons olive oil**
- **2 tablespoons balsamic vinegar**
- **2 cloves garlic,** minced
- **1 teaspoon dried oregano**
- **1 teaspoon dried basil**
- **1 teaspoon smoked paprika**
- **½ teaspoon salt**
- **¼ teaspoon freshly ground black pepper**
- **1 tablespoon fresh lemon juice**

For Garnish:

- **2 tablespoons fresh parsley,** chopped
- **2 tablespoons grated Parmesan cheese** (optional)

STEP-BY-STEP INSTRUCTIONS

1. Prepare the Marinade:

- In a small bowl, whisk together olive oil, balsamic vinegar, garlic, oregano, basil, smoked paprika, salt, pepper, and lemon juice.

2. Marinate the Vegetables:

- Place the prepared vegetables (except cherry tomatoes) in a large mixing bowl or resealable plastic bag.
- Pour the marinade over the vegetables, ensuring they are evenly coated.
- Gently toss or massage the bag, then refrigerate for at least 30 minutes to allow the flavors to meld.

3. Preheat the Grill:

- Preheat your grill or grill pan to medium-high heat.
- Lightly oil the grates or pan to prevent sticking.

4. Grill the Vegetables:

- Place the marinated vegetables (including cherry tomatoes) on the grill in a single layer.
- Cook for 3–4 minutes per side, or until grill marks form and the vegetables are tender.
- Remove the vegetables from the grill and transfer to a serving platter.

5. Garnish and Serve:

- Sprinkle the grilled vegetables with fresh parsley and optional grated Parmesan cheese.
- Serve warm as a standalone dish, or pair with rice, quinoa, or a crusty loaf of bread for a complete meal.

VARIATIONS AND ADAPTATIONS

- **Add Protein:** Include marinated tofu, halloumi cheese, or shrimp skewers for added protein.
- **Middle Eastern Twist:** Swap balsamic vinegar for lemon juice and olive oil, and add cumin, coriander, and sumac to the marinade.
- **Winter Veggie Swap:** Use root vegetables like carrots, parsnips, and sweet potatoes for a seasonal twist.
- **Serve as Tacos:** Dice the grilled veggies and serve in warm tortillas with guacamole and salsa.

NUTRITIONAL INFORMATION (PER SERVING)

Calories: 120	Sodium: 210mg	Protein: 2g	Calcium: ....4% DV
Total Fat: 8g	Carbohydrates: ...11g	Vitamin A: ....35% DV	Iron: .... 6% DV
Saturated Fat: 1g	Fiber: 4g	Vitamin C: ....70% DV	
Cholesterol: 0mg	Sugars: 6g		

TURKEY MEATLOAF

Yield: 6 servings   **Prep Time:** 15 minutes   **Cook Time:** 50 minutes   **Total Time:** 1 hour 5 minutes

INGREDIENTS

For the Meatloaf:
- 1 ½ pounds ground turkey
- 1 medium onion, finely diced
- 2 cloves garlic, minced
- 1 cup breadcrumbs
- 1 large egg, beaten
- ¼ cup milk (or unsweetened almond milk)
- 3 tablespoons ketchup
- 2 teaspoons Worcestershire sauce
- 1 teaspoon Dijon mustard
- 1 teaspoon dried thyme
- ½ teaspoon smoked paprika
- ½ teaspoon salt
- ¼ teaspoon freshly ground black pepper

For the Glaze:
- ¼ cup ketchup
- 1 tablespoon brown sugar
- 1 teaspoon Dijon mustard
- ½ teaspoon apple cider vinegar

STEP-BY-STEP INSTRUCTIONS

1. Preheat the Oven:
- Preheat your oven to 375°F (190°C).
- Lightly grease a loaf pan or line it with parchment paper for easy removal.

2. Prepare the Meatloaf Mixture:
- In a large mixing bowl, combine the ground turkey, onion, garlic, breadcrumbs, egg, milk, ketchup, Worcestershire sauce, Dijon mustard, thyme, paprika, salt, and pepper.
- Mix gently with your hands or a spatula until the ingredients are evenly incorporated. Avoid overmixing to keep the meatloaf tender.

3. Shape the Meatloaf:
- Transfer the mixture into the prepared loaf pan and shape it into a loaf, smoothing the top.

4. Make the Glaze:
- In a small bowl, whisk together the ketchup, brown sugar, Dijon mustard, and apple cider vinegar.
- Spread the glaze evenly over the top of the meatloaf.

5. Bake the Meatloaf:
- Place the meatloaf in the preheated oven and bake for 45–50 minutes, or until the internal temperature reaches 165°F (74°C).
- Let the meatloaf rest for 5 minutes before slicing to retain its juices.

VARIATIONS AND ADAPTATIONS
- **Different Proteins:** Substitute turkey with ground chicken, beef, or a blend of pork and beef for variety.
- **Vegetable Boost:** Add shredded zucchini or carrots to the mixture for extra moisture and nutrients.
- **Mediterranean Twist:** Use feta cheese, sun-dried tomatoes, and fresh parsley in the mix, and replace the glaze with tzatziki sauce.
- **Asian-Inspired:** Replace ketchup with hoisin sauce, add minced ginger, and serve with a drizzle of soy sauce.
- **Gluten-Free:** Use gluten-free breadcrumbs or rolled oats instead of traditional breadcrumbs.

NUTRITIONAL INFORMATION (PER SERVING)

Calories: 220	Sodium: 420mg	Protein: 23g	Calcium: ....4% DV
Total Fat: 9g	Carbohydrates: ...12g	Vitamin A: ....4% DV	Iron: ....10% DV
Saturated Fat: 2g	Fiber: 1g	Vitamin C: ....6% DV	
Cholesterol: 95mg	Sugars: 5g		

MEAL PREP BURRITO BOWLS

Yield: 4 servings   **Prep Time:** 20 minutes   **Cook Time:** 25 minutes   **Total Time:** 45 minutes

INGREDIENTS

For the Bowls:
- **1 cup brown rice** (or quinoa)
- **2 cups water**
- **1 teaspoon olive oil**
- **1 pound boneless, skinless chicken breasts**
- **1 tablespoon taco seasoning**
- **1 tablespoon olive oil**
- **1 cup black beans,** drained and rinsed
- **1 cup sweet corn kernels**
- **1 cup diced cherry tomatoes**
- **1 large avocado, sliced**
- **½ cup shredded cheddar cheese (optional)**
- **½ cup fresh cilantro, chopped**

For the Dressing:
- **¼ cup plain Greek yogurt** (or sour cream)
- **2 tablespoons lime juice** (freshly squeezed)
- **1 teaspoon honey**
- **½ teaspoon garlic powder**
- **Salt and pepper to taste**

STEP-BY-STEP INSTRUCTIONS

1. Cook the Rice:
- Rinse the rice under cold water.
- In a medium saucepan, bring 2 cups of water to a boil. Add the brown rice and a pinch of salt. Reduce heat to low, cover, and simmer for 20–25 minutes, or until the rice is tender and the water is absorbed.
- Fluff the rice with a fork and set aside.

2. Prepare the Chicken:
- Rub the chicken breasts with taco seasoning.
- Heat 1 tablespoon olive oil in a skillet over medium-high heat. Add the chicken and cook for 6–8 minutes per side, or until the internal temperature reaches 165°F (74°C).
- Remove the chicken from the skillet, let it rest for 5 minutes, then dice into bite-sized pieces.

3. Assemble the Bowls:
- Divide the cooked rice evenly among four meal prep containers or bowls.
- Top each portion with diced chicken, black beans, corn, cherry tomatoes, and avocado slices.
- Sprinkle with shredded cheese (if using) and chopped cilantro.

4. Make the Dressing:
- In a small bowl, whisk together Greek yogurt, lime juice, honey, garlic powder, salt, and pepper.
- Drizzle the dressing over the bowls just before serving, or pack it separately in small containers for meal prep.

VARIATIONS AND ADAPTATIONS
- **Vegetarian Option:** Substitute chicken with roasted sweet potatoes, grilled tofu, or sautéed mushrooms.
- **Protein Variations:** Use ground beef, turkey, or shrimp instead of chicken.
- **Grain-Free:** Replace rice with cauliflower rice or a bed of leafy greens for a low-carb option.
- International Twist: Incorporate hummus and roasted red peppers for a Mediterranean flair, or add kimchi and sesame seeds for a Korean-inspired bowl.

STORAGE TIPS
- **Refrigeration:** Store bowls in airtight containers for up to 4 days.
- **Freezing:** Skip the avocado and cheese when freezing; add them fresh after reheating.

NUTRITIONAL INFORMATION (PER SERVING)

Calories: 430	Sodium: 620mg	Protein: 34g	Calcium: ....12% DV
Total Fat: 16g	Carbohydrates: ...44g	Vitamin A: ....15% DV	Iron: ....15% DV
Saturated Fat: 4g	Fiber:.................. 9g	Vitamin C: ....25% DV	
Cholesterol: 80mg	Sugars: 5g		

OVERNIGHT BEEF STEW

Yield: 6 servings   Prep Time: 15 minutes   Cook Time: 8–10 hours (overnight cooking)   Total Time: 8–10 hours (overnight cooking)

INGREDIENTS

For the Stew:

- **2 pounds beef chuck roast**, cut into 1-inch cubes
- **2 tablespoons olive oil**
- **1 large onion**, chopped
- **3 cloves garlic**, minced
- **4 large carrots**, peeled and sliced
- **3 medium potatoes**, peeled and cubed
- **2 cups beef broth**
- **1 cup dry red wine** (optional)
- **1 can (14.5 ounces) diced tomatoes**, with juices
- **2 teaspoons dried thyme**
- **1 teaspoon dried rosemary**
- **1 bay leaf**
- Salt and pepper, to taste
- **1 tablespoon Worcestershire sauce**
- **1 tablespoon cornstarch** (optional)
- **Fresh parsley, chopped** (for garnish)

STEP-BY-STEP INSTRUCTIONS

1. Brown the Beef (Optional, but Recommended):

- In a large skillet, heat 2 tablespoons olive oil over medium-high heat.
- Add the beef cubes in batches, browning them on all sides (about 5 minutes per batch). Remove the beef and set aside.
- This step adds flavor to the stew, but if you're short on time, you can skip it and add the beef directly to the slow cooker.

2. Prepare the Vegetables:

- Chop the onion and garlic, and slice the carrots and potatoes.
- Add the vegetables to your slow cooker.

3. Assemble the Stew:

- Add the browned beef (or raw beef) to the slow cooker with the vegetables.
- Pour in the beef broth, red wine (if using), diced tomatoes, and Worcestershire sauce.
- Sprinkle in the dried thyme, rosemary, bay leaf, salt, and pepper. Stir to combine.

4. Slow Cook the Stew:

- Cover the slow cooker and set it on low heat for 8–10 hours, or until the beef is tender and the vegetables are fully cooked.
- If you prefer a thicker stew, after the cooking time, mix 1 tablespoon of cornstarch with 2 tablespoons of cold water to make a slurry. Stir the slurry into the stew and cook on high for an additional 30 minutes to thicken.

5. Serve and Garnish:

- Before serving, discard the bay leaf.
- Ladle the stew into bowls and garnish with freshly chopped parsley.
- Serve with warm crusty bread or over a bed of mashed potatoes for a comforting meal.

VARIATIONS AND ADAPTATIONS

- **Vegetarian Option:** Replace the beef with mushrooms (such as cremini or portobello) for a hearty, plant-based alternative. Use vegetable broth instead of beef broth.
- **Different Meat:** Swap the beef for lamb or pork shoulder for a different flavor profile. Both meats work well in long, slow braises.
- **Spices and Heat:** Add paprika or a dash of cayenne pepper for a smoky or spicy twist. You can also add bay leaves or cumin for a more complex flavor.
- **Root Vegetables:** For added variety, incorporate other seasonal root vegetables like parsnips, turnips, or celery root into the stew.

STORAGE TIPS

- **Refrigeration:** Store leftovers in an airtight container in the fridge for up to 4 days.
- **Freezing:** This stew freezes well. Let it cool completely before transferring to a freezer-safe container. Freeze for up to 3 months. To reheat, thaw overnight in the refrigerator and heat on the stovetop over low heat.

NUTRITIONAL INFORMATION (PER SERVING)

Calories: 330	Cholesterol: 75mg	Fiber: 4g	Vitamin A: ....90% DV
Total Fat: 16g	Sodium: 580mg	Sugars: 6g	Vitamin C: ....25% DV
Saturated Fat: 5g	Carbohydrates: ...20g	Protein: 30g	Calcium: ....5% DV
			Iron: ....20% DV

CASSEROLE-STYLE SHEPHERD'S PIE

Yield: 6 servings   Preparation Time: 20 minutes   Cooking Time: 40 minutes   Total Time: 1 hour

INGREDIENTS

For the Meat Filling:
- 1 pound ground lamb
- 1 medium onion, chopped
- 2 cloves garlic, minced
- 2 medium carrots, peeled and diced
- 1 cup peas (fresh or frozen)
- 2 tablespoons olive oil
- 2 tablespoons tomato paste
- 1 tablespoon Worcestershire sauce
- 1 cup beef or vegetable broth
- 1 teaspoon dried thyme
- 1 teaspoon dried rosemary
- 1/2 teaspoon paprika
- Salt and pepper, to taste

For the Mashed Potato Topping:
- 4 large potatoes
- 1/2 cup milk
- 4 tablespoons butter
- Salt and pepper, to taste
- 1/2 cup grated cheddar cheese

STEP-BY-STEP INSTRUCTIONS

1. Prepare the Mashed Potatoes:
- Place the peeled and cubed potatoes into a large pot and cover them with water.
- Bring to a boil over high heat, then reduce to a simmer and cook for about 15 minutes or until the potatoes are tender when pierced with a fork.
- Drain the potatoes and return them to the pot.
- Mash the potatoes with a potato masher or use a hand mixer for smoother consistency.
- Stir in 1/2 cup milk, 4 tablespoons butter, and season with salt and pepper.
- If using, fold in grated cheddar cheese for extra creaminess and flavor. Set the mashed potatoes aside.

2. Prepare the Meat Filling:
- In a large skillet, heat 2 tablespoons olive oil over medium heat.
- Add the chopped onion and minced garlic, and sauté until softened, about 3-4 minutes.
- Add the ground lamb to the skillet and cook until browned, breaking it up with a spoon as it cooks (about 5-7 minutes).
- Stir in tomato paste, Worcestershire sauce, dried thyme, dried rosemary, and paprika. Cook for another 2-3 minutes to combine the flavors.
- Add the broth and stir. Bring to a simmer and cook for 5 minutes or until the mixture thickens.
- Stir in the diced carrots and peas, cooking for another 5-7 minutes until the vegetables are tender. Season with salt and pepper to taste.
- Remove the skillet from the heat.

3. Assemble the Shepherd's Pie:
- Preheat your oven to 375°F (190°C).
- Transfer the meat mixture into a greased 9x9-inch baking dish or a similarly sized casserole dish.
- Spoon the mashed potatoes on top of the meat mixture, spreading them evenly to cover the entire surface.
- If you like a golden top, use a fork to make decorative lines on the mashed potatoes or dot with a little extra butter.
- Place the casserole dish in the preheated oven and bake for 20-25 minutes or until the top is golden and the filling is bubbling around the edges.

4. Serve:
- Remove the casserole from the oven and let it cool for a few minutes before serving.
- Slice and serve the Shepherd's Pie with a side salad or crusty bread for a complete meal.

VARIATIONS AND ADAPTATIONS
- **Different Meat:** If you prefer, substitute ground beef or turkey for the lamb. Ground chicken or vegetarian crumbles can also be used for a lighter version.
- **Vegetarian Option:** Replace the ground lamb with a mix of lentils or mushrooms for a hearty, plant-based filling.
- **Vegetable Variations:** Add seasonal veggies such as parsnips, turnips, sweet potatoes, or squash for a unique flavor. You can also add green beans or corn for variety.

NUTRITIONAL INFORMATION (PER SERVING)

Calories: 450	Cholesterol: 70mg	Fiber: 5g	Vitamin C: ....25% DV
Total Fat: 22g	Sodium: 600mg	Sugars: 8g	Calcium: ....10% DV
Saturated Fat: 9g	Carbohydrates: ...35g	Protein: 25g	Iron: ....20% DV
		Vitamin A: ....80% DV	

STUFFED PEPPERS RECIPE

Yield: 4 servings   **Prep Time:** 20 minutes   **Cook Time:** 40 minutes   **Total Time:** 1 hour

INGREDIENTS

For the Stuffed Peppers:

- 4 large bell peppers
- 1 pound ground turkey
- 1 cup cooked rice (preferably brown rice)
- 1 small onion, finely chopped
- 2 cloves garlic, minced
- 1 cup diced tomatoes
- 1/2 cup black beans, drained and rinsed (optional)
- 1 tablespoon olive oil
- 1 teaspoon ground cumin
- 1 teaspoon smoked paprika
- 1/2 teaspoon dried oregano
- Salt and pepper, to taste
- 1/2 cup shredded cheese
- Fresh parsley or cilantro, chopped for garnish

STEP-BY-STEP INSTRUCTIONS

1. Prepare the Peppers:

- Preheat your oven to 375°F (190°C).
- Cut the tops off the bell peppers and remove the seeds and membranes. If the peppers don't stand up on their own, carefully trim a small slice off the bottom to level them.
- Place the peppers in a baking dish, cut side up, and set aside.

2. Cook the Filling:

- Heat 1 tablespoon olive oil in a large skillet over medium heat.
- Add the chopped onion and minced garlic to the pan and sauté for 3–4 minutes until softened and fragrant.
- Add the ground turkey (or ground beef or chicken) to the skillet. Cook, breaking it up with a spoon, until browned and fully cooked, about 5–7 minutes.
- Stir in the diced tomatoes, cooked rice, black beans (if using), and spices: cumin, smoked paprika, oregano, and a pinch of salt and pepper. Cook for another 2–3 minutes, allowing the flavors to meld.
- Taste and adjust seasoning, adding more salt, pepper, or spices if desired. Remove the skillet from the heat.

3. Stuff the Peppers:

- Carefully spoon the prepared filling into each bell pepper, packing the mixture gently but firmly.
- If using cheese, sprinkle 1/2 cup shredded cheese on top of each stuffed pepper.
- Cover the baking dish with foil.

4. Bake the Stuffed Peppers:

- Place the baking dish in the preheated oven and bake for 30 minutes.
- After 30 minutes, remove the foil and continue baking for another 10 minutes or until the peppers are tender and the cheese is melted and bubbly (if using cheese).

5. Serve:

- Remove the stuffed peppers from the oven and let them cool for a few minutes before serving.
- Garnish with fresh parsley or cilantro for a burst of color and flavor.
- Serve with a side salad or crusty bread for a complete meal.
- Storage Tips
- Refrigeration: Store leftovers in an airtight container in the fridge for up to 3–4 days.
- Freezing: Allow the stuffed peppers to cool completely before wrapping them tightly in foil and freezing for up to 3 months. To reheat, bake at 350°F (175°C) for 20–25 minutes, or until heated through.

VARIATIONS AND ADAPTATIONS

- **Vegetarian Option:** Replace the ground turkey with lentils or chopped mushrooms for a plant-based filling. Add more vegetables like zucchini, spinach, or corn for added texture and flavor.
- **Spicy Kick:** Add diced jalapeños or chipotle peppers to the filling mixture for extra heat. You can also top the peppers with a spicy salsa or hot sauce before serving.
- **Different Meat:** Swap out the ground turkey for ground beef, chicken, or even pork for a different flavor profile.
- **Rice Variations:** Use quinoa or farro instead of rice for a gluten-free option or a more nutrient-dense grain.
- **Cheese Variations:** Use a different type of cheese like goat cheese, feta, or parmesan for different textures and flavors.

NUTRITIONAL INFORMATION (PER SERVING)

Calories: 350	Cholesterol: 70mg	Fiber: 7g	Vitamin A: ....45% DV
Total Fat: 14g	Sodium: 600mg	Sugars: 8g	Vitamin C: 160%DV
Saturated Fat: 5g	Carbohydrates: ...33g	Protein: 26g	Calcium: ....15% DV
			Iron: ....20% DV

DIY PIZZA DOUGH AND TOPPINGS RECIPE

Yield: 2 medium pizzas (4 servings)

Prep Time: 15 minutes (for dough) + 1 hour resting time

Cook Time: 15–20 minutes (per pizza)

Total Time: 1 hour 30 minutes

INGREDIENTS

For the Pizza Dough:
- **2 1/4 teaspoons active dry yeast** (or 1 packet)
- **1 teaspoon honey** (or sugar)
- **3/4 cup warm water** (105–110°F)
- **2 tablespoons olive oil**
- **2 1/2 cups all-purpose flour**
- **1 teaspoon salt**
- **1/2 teaspoon garlic powder**

For the Pizza Sauce:
- **1/2 cup tomato sauce**
- **1 tablespoon olive oil**
- **1 garlic clove, minced**
- **1/2 teaspoon dried oregano**
- **1/4 teaspoon crushed red pepper flakes**
- **Salt and pepper, to taste**

For the Toppings:
- **1 cup shredded mozzarella cheese**
- **1/2 cup sliced fresh mushrooms**
- **1/2 cup red bell pepper, thinly sliced**
- **1/4 cup black olives, sliced**
- **1/2 small red onion, thinly sliced**
- **Fresh basil leaves, for garnish**

Other toppings (optional): Fresh tomatoes, pepperoni, sausage, spinach, arugula, or any preferred vegetables

STEP-BY-STEP INSTRUCTIONS

1. Prepare the Dough:
- **Activate the yeast:** In a small bowl, combine 1/2 cup warm water with 1 teaspoon honey. Sprinkle the yeast over the water and let it sit for 5–10 minutes, until it becomes frothy.
- **Mix the dough:** In a large mixing bowl, combine 2 1/2 cups flour, 1 teaspoon salt, and 1/2 teaspoon garlic powder (if using). Add the yeast mixture and 2 tablespoons olive oil. Stir until a dough begins to form.
- **Knead the dough:** Transfer the dough to a lightly floured surface and knead for 5–7 minutes until smooth and elastic. If the dough is too sticky, add a little more flour, a tablespoon at a time.
- **Let the dough rise:** Place the dough in a lightly oiled bowl and cover with a clean towel or plastic wrap. Let it rise in a warm place for 1 hour, or until it doubles in size.

2. Prepare the Pizza Sauce:
- **Cook the sauce:** In a small saucepan, heat 1 tablespoon olive oil over medium heat. Add the minced garlic and cook for 1–2 minutes, until fragrant.
- **Season the sauce:** Stir in 1/2 cup tomato sauce, oregano, red pepper flakes, and salt and pepper. Let the sauce simmer on low heat for about 5–7 minutes, then remove from heat.

3. Assemble the Pizzas:
- **Preheat the oven:** While the dough is rising, preheat your oven to 475°F (245°C) and place a pizza stone or baking sheet in the oven to heat.
- **Shape the dough:** After the dough has risen, punch it down and divide it into two equal portions. Roll each portion into a ball and let them rest for 5 minutes.
- **Roll out the dough:** On a floured surface, roll out each dough ball into a circle about 12 inches in diameter. If you prefer a thicker crust, roll the dough a little thicker.
- **Add sauce and toppings:** Transfer the dough to a parchment paper or pizza peel for easy handling. Spread half of the pizza sauce over each pizza. Top with shredded mozzarella, mushrooms, bell peppers, onions, and black olives (or any other preferred toppings).

4. Bake the Pizzas:
- **Bake the pizzas:** Carefully slide the pizza onto the preheated pizza stone or baking sheet. Bake each pizza for 12–15 minutes, until the crust is golden and the cheese is bubbling and slightly browned.
- **Garnish and serve:** Remove the pizza from the oven and garnish with fresh basil leaves. Let it cool for a few minutes before slicing.

VARIATIONS AND ADAPTATIONS
- **Vegetarian Version:** Add seasonal vegetables like zucchini, spinach, or eggplant. For a Mediterranean twist, top with feta cheese, artichokes, and black olives.
- **Meat Lovers Version:** Add pepperoni, Italian sausage, or chicken breast as protein options.
- **Gluten-Free Version:** Substitute the all-purpose flour with a gluten-free flour blend and ensure the yeast is certified gluten-free.

NUTRITIONAL INFORMATION (PER SERVING)

Calories: 310
Total Fat: 14g
Saturated Fat: 6g

Cholesterol: 25mg
Sodium: 600mg
Carbohydrates: ...35g

Fiber: 3g
Sugars: 5g
Protein: 14g

Vitamin A: ....10% DV
Vitamin C: ....35% DV
Calcium: ....15% DV
Iron: ....12% DV

CHAPTER 9:
DELICIOUS DESSERTS

PRACTICAL TIPS

- **Use Room Temperature Ingredients:** When making desserts like cakes, mousses, or custards, always ensure your butter, eggs, and cream cheese are at room temperature. This ensures a smoother texture and better incorporation when mixing. Cold ingredients can cause lumps or affect the final texture.

- **Precision in Measuring:** Accurate measurements are crucial in baking and dessert preparation. Even slight variations in the amount of sugar, flour, or leavening agents can alter the texture and flavor. Use a digital scale for precise measurements, especially when working with dry ingredients like flour or cocoa powder.

- **Fresh, Seasonal Ingredients:** Whenever possible, use fresh, in-season fruits and ingredients. Seasonal produce will elevate the flavor profile of your dessert. For example, berries in the summer or apples and pears in the fall can make a significant difference in pies, tarts, and compotes.

- **Proper Mixing Techniques:** Overmixing batters, especially in cakes and cookies, can lead to dense and tough textures. Mix your ingredients just until combined. For whipped creams, be mindful not to overwhip, as it can turn into butter.

- **Chill Before Serving:** Many desserts, especially creamy ones like cheesecakes, mousses, or parfaits, require chilling before serving. This helps them set, enhances their flavor, and ensures a firm, smooth consistency. Be sure to follow the chill times in your recipes to achieve the best results.

- **Balancing Sweetness:** Many dessert recipes call for sugar, but it's important to balance sweetness with acidity or bitterness. A touch of lemon or a pinch of salt can enhance sweetness and bring out more complex flavors, especially in chocolate or fruit-based desserts.

- **Garnishing for Appeal:** Garnishing not only makes your desserts look visually appealing but can also enhance flavor. Use fresh herbs like mint, citrus zest, or a dusting of cocoa powder. Edible flowers or a drizzle of caramel or chocolate can elevate the overall presentation.

- **Use a Timer:** Many desserts, especially baked goods, require precise baking times. Overbaking can lead to dry, tough textures, while underbaking can cause your dessert to be too runny or unstable. Set a timer and keep an eye on the color and texture to ensure the perfect outcome.

- **Experiment with Flavors:** Don't be afraid to play with flavors. Try adding spices like cinnamon, nutmeg, or cardamom to baked goods or desserts. Vanilla can be substituted with almond extract for a different twist. Flavored syrups, citrus zest, or even a splash of liqueur can make your dessert uniquely yours.

- **Perfecting the Texture:** Texture is key in desserts. For creamy desserts like puddings, mousses, and custards, a smooth texture is vital. Use a fine-mesh sieve to remove any lumps or egg membranes. For crisp textures, like cookies or pies, ensure your dough or batter is well-chilled before baking.

- **Serving Temperature:** The temperature at which you serve your dessert matters. Some desserts, like ice cream or sorbet, are best served straight from the freezer, while others, like pies or cakes, benefit from a slight warming or cooling period before serving.

- **Avoiding Cracks in Custards and Cheesecakes:** To prevent cracks in delicate custards or cheesecakes, bake them at a low temperature and allow them to cool gradually in the oven with the door slightly ajar. A water bath can also help maintain moisture and even heat distribution.

CONCLUSION:

- By following these practical tips, you can elevate the quality of your desserts, ensuring that they are not only delicious but also a visual and textural delight. Focus on using fresh ingredients, the right techniques, and attention to detail to create desserts that are both comforting and impressive for any occasion.

CLASSIC CHOCOLATE MOUSSE

Yield: 6 servings   **Prep time:** 15 minutes   **Chilling time:** 2 hours   **Total time:** 2 hours 15 minutes

INGREDIENTS:
- **6 oz dark chocolate** (at least 70% cocoa)
- **1 cup heavy cream**
- **2 tbsp powdered sugar** (optional, depending on desired sweetness)
- **2 large egg yolks**
- **1 tsp vanilla extract**
- **Pinch of salt**

INSTRUCTIONS:

1. Melt the chocolate:
- Place the dark chocolate in a heatproof bowl over a pot of simmering water (double boiler method) and gently stir until fully melted. Alternatively, you can melt the chocolate in the microwave in 20-second bursts, stirring in between, until smooth. Let the melted chocolate cool to room temperature.

2. Whip the cream:
- In a separate bowl, use an electric mixer to whip the heavy cream (and powdered sugar if using) until soft peaks form. Be careful not to over-whip, as it can turn into butter. Set aside.

3. Prepare the egg mixture:
- In a heatproof bowl, whisk the egg yolks with a pinch of salt. Place the bowl over a pot of simmering water (like the double boiler method) and whisk continuously until the yolks are warm to the touch and slightly thickened, about 2-3 minutes. Remove from heat.

4. Combine the melted chocolate and egg yolks:
- Gradually add the melted chocolate to the egg yolk mixture while whisking continuously to combine. This ensures a smooth, homogeneous mixture.

5. Fold in the whipped cream:
- Gently fold the whipped cream into the chocolate-egg mixture using a spatula. Be careful not to deflate the whipped cream. The mousse should be light and airy.

6. Chill the mousse:
- Spoon the mousse into serving glasses or bowls and refrigerate for at least 2 hours, or until set. This allows the flavors to meld and the mousse to firm up to a silky texture.

7. Serve:
- Once chilled and set, garnish with shaved chocolate, berries, or a dollop of whipped cream if desired. Serve immediately or store in the fridge until ready to enjoy.

VARIATIONS & ADAPTATIONS:
- **Vegan Option:** Use dairy-free chocolate and coconut cream or another plant-based cream alternative.

- **Flavored Chocolate Mousse:** Add a tablespoon of orange liqueur (such as Grand Marnier) to the melted chocolate for a citrusy twist, or infuse the cream with mint leaves for a fresh flavor.

- **Spicy Chocolate Mousse:** For a bold twist, add a pinch of cinnamon or cayenne pepper to the melted chocolate to introduce a warm, spicy kick.

- **Chocolate Mousse with Coffee:** Mix a tablespoon of instant espresso powder into the melted chocolate to give it a mocha flavor.

NUTRITIONAL INFORMATION (PER SERVING):

Calories: 280kcal	Protein: 3g	Fiber: 3g
Carbohydrates: ...20g	Fat: 22g	Sugar: 17g

QUICK BERRY PARFAITS

Yield: 4 servings   **Prep time:** 10 minutes   **Cook time:** None   **Total time:** 10 minutes

INGREDIENTS:

- **1 ½ cups mixed fresh berries**
- **1 ½ cups plain Greek yogurt**
- **2 tbsp honey**
- **1 tsp vanilla extract**
- **¾ cup granola (**choose a variety with local, seasonal nuts or seeds if possible)
- **Fresh mint leaves (optional)**

INSTRUCTIONS:

1. Prepare the berries:

- Wash and pat the berries dry. Slice the strawberries, if using, to ensure all berries are roughly the same size for even layering.

2. Prepare the yogurt:

- In a small bowl, stir together the Greek yogurt, honey (or maple syrup), and vanilla extract until well combined. This will create a sweetened, flavored yogurt base for the parfaits.

3. Layer the parfaits:

- In 4 individual glasses or bowls, begin by spooning a layer of the yogurt mixture into the bottom of each container.
- Add a layer of the mixed berries on top of the yogurt.
- Spoon a layer of granola over the berries. Repeat the process (yogurt, berries, granola) to create a layered effect. Finish with a few more berries and a sprinkle of granola on top.

4. Garnish and serve:

- Garnish each parfait with a fresh mint leaf for a touch of color and extra freshness.
- Serve immediately, or refrigerate for up to an hour before serving to allow the flavors to meld.

VARIATIONS & ADAPTATIONS:

- **Tropical Parfait:** Substitute the berries with tropical fruits like mango, pineapple, and papaya for a refreshing change.
- **Vegan Option:** Use coconut or almond milk yogurt and maple syrup for a fully plant-based parfait.
- **Granola Substitutes:** Swap out granola for crushed nuts (almonds, pecans, or walnuts) or homemade oat clusters for a crunchier texture.
- **Flavored Yogurt Parfait:** Use flavored yogurts, such as lemon, coconut, or berry-flavored varieties, to infuse additional flavors.

NUTRITIONAL INFORMATION (PER SERVING):

Calories: 240kcal	Protein: 10g	Fiber: 4g
Carbohydrates: ...33g	Fat: 7g	Sugar: 15g

LEMON CHEESECAKE BARS

Yield: 12 servings   **Prep time:** 20 minutes   **Cook time:** 30 minutes   **Total time:** 50 minutes

INGREDIENTS:

For the crust:
- 1 ½ cups graham cracker crumbs
- ¼ cup granulated sugar
- ¼ cup unsalted butter, melted
- Pinch of salt

For the cheesecake filling:
- 2 (8 oz) packages cream cheese, softened
- ½ cup granulated sugar
- 2 large eggs
- 1 cup sour cream
- 2 tbsp fresh lemon juice
- 1 tbsp lemon zest
- 1 tsp vanilla extract

INSTRUCTIONS:

1. Prepare the crust:
- Preheat the oven to 325°F (165°C).
- In a medium bowl, combine the graham cracker crumbs, sugar, melted butter, and a pinch of salt. Stir until the crumbs are evenly coated.
- Press the mixture into the bottom of a greased 9x9-inch baking pan, forming an even layer. Use the back of a spoon to pack the crumbs tightly.
- Bake the crust in the preheated oven for 8-10 minutes, or until golden brown. Remove from the oven and let it cool while you prepare the filling.

2. Prepare the cheesecake filling:
- In a large mixing bowl, beat the softened cream cheese with an electric mixer until smooth and creamy, about 2 minutes.
- Add the sugar and continue to beat until fully combined.
- Add the eggs one at a time, beating well after each addition.
- Stir in the sour cream, lemon juice, lemon zest, and vanilla extract until the mixture is smooth and fully incorporated.

3. Assemble and bake:
- Pour the cheesecake filling over the cooled crust in the baking pan. Spread it into an even layer with a spatula.
- Bake in the preheated oven for 25-30 minutes, or until the center is set and a slight jiggle remains when you shake the pan gently.
- Allow the bars to cool completely in the pan, then refrigerate for at least 2 hours or overnight for the best texture.

4. Serve and garnish:
- Once the bars have chilled, cut into 12 squares.
- Optionally, garnish with extra lemon zest or fresh whipped cream before serving.

VARIATIONS & ADAPTATIONS:

- **Berry Topping:** Top with fresh seasonal berries like blueberries, strawberries, or raspberries for a pop of color and flavor.
- **Gluten-Free Option:** Use gluten-free graham crackers or almond meal for the crust.
- **Flavored Cheesecake Bars:** Experiment with different citrus fruits like lime or orange juice and zest for a twist on the traditional lemon flavor.
- **Vegan Option:** Use dairy-free cream cheese and substitute eggs with flax eggs (1 tbsp flaxseed meal + 3 tbsp water per egg).

NUTRITIONAL INFORMATION (PER SERVING):

Calories: ....265kcal   Protein: ....5g   Fiber: 1g
Carbohydrates: ...32g   Fat: ....15g   Sugar: 19g

NO-BAKE PEANUT BUTTER PIE

Yield: 8 servings   **Prep time:** 15 minutes   **Chill time:** 3-4 hours   **Total time:** 4 hours

INGREDIENTS:

For the crust:
- 1 ½ cups graham cracker crumbs
- ¼ cup granulated sugar
- ⅓ cup unsalted butter, melted
- Pinch of salt

For the filling:
- 1 cup creamy peanut butter
- 8 oz cream cheese, softened
- 1 cup powdered sugar
- 1 cup heavy whipping cream
- 1 tsp vanilla extract

For the topping:
- ½ cup heavy whipping cream
- 2 tbsp powdered sugar
- 1 tbsp peanut butter, for drizzling
- Chocolate shavings or mini chocolate chips

INSTRUCTIONS:

1. Prepare the crust:
- In a medium bowl, combine the graham cracker crumbs, granulated sugar, melted butter, and a pinch of salt. Stir until the crumbs are evenly coated with butter.
- Press the mixture into the bottom of a 9-inch pie dish, creating an even, compact crust.
- Place the crust in the refrigerator to chill while you prepare the filling.

2. Prepare the filling:
- In a large mixing bowl, beat the softened cream cheese and peanut butter together with an electric mixer until smooth and creamy.
- Add the powdered sugar and beat until fully incorporated, making sure the mixture is smooth and lump-free.
- In a separate mixing bowl, whip the heavy whipping cream and vanilla extract until stiff peaks form.
- Gently fold the whipped cream into the peanut butter mixture, being careful not to deflate the cream. Mix until well combined.

3. Assemble the pie:
- Remove the crust from the refrigerator.
- Pour the peanut butter filling into the prepared crust, spreading it out evenly with a spatula.
- Refrigerate the pie for at least 3-4 hours or until it is fully set and firm.

4. Make the topping:
- In a medium bowl, whip the remaining ½ cup of heavy whipping cream and powdered sugar until soft peaks form.
- Transfer the whipped cream to a piping bag or simply spread it on top of the chilled pie with a spatula.
- Drizzle the 1 tbsp of peanut butter over the whipped cream topping, using a spoon to create a decorative swirl.
- Garnish with chocolate shavings or mini chocolate chips for added texture and flavor, if desired.

5. Serve:
- Once the pie has chilled and the topping is set, slice into 8 servings.
- Serve chilled and enjoy this creamy, indulgent treat!

VARIATIONS & ADAPTATIONS:
- **Chocolate Peanut Butter Pie:** Add a layer of melted chocolate on top of the crust before adding the peanut butter filling for a richer chocolate-peanut butter flavor.
- **Vegan Option:** Use dairy-free cream cheese, coconut cream (instead of heavy cream), and a graham cracker crust made without butter.
- **Gluten-Free Option:** Use gluten-free graham crackers for the crust or substitute with ground almonds or a pre-made gluten-free pie crust.
- **Nut-Free:** Replace the peanut butter with sunbutter (made from sunflower seeds) for a nut-free version.
- **Flavor Twist:** Add a teaspoon of cinnamon or a pinch of salt to the filling for extra depth.

NUTRITIONAL INFORMATION (PER SERVING):

Calories: ....370kcal   Protein: ....7g   Fiber: 2g
Carbohydrates: ...32g   Fat: ....26g   Sugar: 18g

CARAMELIZED BANANA SPLITS

Yield: 4 servings   **Prep time:** 10 minutes   **Cook time:** 10 minutes   **Total time:** 20 minutes

INGREDIENTS:
- **4 ripe bananas**
- **1/4 cup unsalted butter**
- **1/4 cup brown sugar** (packed)
- **1/4 tsp ground cinnamon**
- **1/2 tsp vanilla extract**
- **Pinch of sea salt**
- **Vanilla ice cream**
- **Chopped toasted nuts**
- **Chocolate syrup (optional)**
- **Whipped cream** (optional)

INSTRUCTIONS:
Prepare the bananas:
- Peel the bananas and slice them lengthwise into halves. If you prefer smaller portions, you can cut them into thirds as well.

Caramelize the bananas:
- In a large skillet, melt the butter over medium heat.
- Add the brown sugar, cinnamon, and a pinch of sea salt. Stir to combine and cook until the sugar dissolves and the mixture is bubbling.
- Gently place the banana halves into the skillet, cut side down. Cook for about 2-3 minutes, allowing the bananas to caramelize. Once they have a golden brown color, carefully flip them over and cook for another 1-2 minutes on the other side.

Assemble the splits:
- Place each banana half onto a serving dish, forming a split with two halves.
- Scoop vanilla ice cream (or your favorite flavor) onto the center of each banana.

Top and serve:
- Drizzle the caramel sauce from the skillet over the bananas and ice cream.
- Optionally, add chopped toasted nuts for a crunchy texture, a drizzle of chocolate syrup, or a dollop of whipped cream for extra indulgence.

Enjoy!

VARIATIONS & ADAPTATIONS:
- **Fruit variations:** Try caramelizing other fruits, such as peaches or pineapples, for a different twist.
- **Non-dairy ice cream:** Use non-dairy or plant-based ice cream for a dairy-free version.
- **Additional toppings:** For a more decadent dessert, add a sprinkle of shredded coconut or a drizzle of caramel sauce.

NUTRITIONAL INFORMATION (PER SERVING):

Calories: 350-400 kcal	Protein: 3g	Fiber: 4g
Carbohydrates: ...45g	Fat: 20g	Sugar: W30g

CHOCOLATE CHIP COOKIE SKILLET

Yield: 6 servings   **Prep time:** 10 minutes   **Cook time:** 20-25 minutes   **Total time:** 30-35 minutes

INGREDIENTS:
- 1 1/2 cups all-purpose flour
- 1/2 tsp baking soda
- 1/4 tsp salt
- 1/2 cup unsalted butter, softened
- 1/2 cup granulated sugar
- 1/2 cup packed brown sugar
- 1 tsp vanilla extract
- 1 large egg
- 1 1/4 cups semisweet chocolate chips
- 1/4 cup chopped nuts
- Vanilla ice cream for topping (optional)

INSTRUCTIONS:

Preheat oven:
- Preheat your oven to 350°F (175°C). Grease a 10-inch cast-iron skillet or a similar oven-safe skillet with a small amount of butter or cooking spray.

Mix dry ingredients:
- In a small bowl, whisk together the flour, baking soda, and salt. Set aside.

Cream butter and sugars:
- In a large bowl, use a hand mixer or stand mixer to cream the softened butter, granulated sugar, and brown sugar together on medium speed until light and fluffy, about 2-3 minutes.
- Add the egg and vanilla extract, mixing until combined.

Combine wet and dry ingredients:
- Gradually add the dry ingredients to the wet mixture, mixing on low speed until just combined.
- Fold in the chocolate chips and chopped nuts (if using).

Bake the cookie skillet:
- Pour the cookie dough into the prepared skillet, spreading it evenly.
- Bake in the preheated oven for 20-25 minutes, or until the edges are golden brown and the center is slightly set. The cookie will continue to firm up as it cools, so be careful not to overbake.

Serve and enjoy:
- Allow the skillet to cool for a few minutes before serving.
- Optionally, top each serving with a scoop of vanilla ice cream for an extra indulgent treat.

VARIATIONS & ADAPTATIONS:
- **Different mix-ins:** You can customize this recipe by adding white chocolate chips, peanut butter chips, or dried fruits like cranberries.
- **Gluten-free version:** Replace the all-purpose flour with a gluten-free flour blend.
- **Dairy-free:** Use dairy-free butter and chocolate chips to make this recipe suitable for dairy-free diets.

NUTRITIONAL INFORMATION (PER SERVING, WITHOUT ICE CREAM):

Calories: 290kcal	Protein: 2g	Fiber: 1g
Carbohydrates: ...35g	Fat: 16g	Sugar: 24g

STRAWBERRY SHORTCAKE TRIFLES

Yield: 6 servings   **Prep time:** 15 minutes   **Cook time:** 10 minutes (for homemade sponge cake, optional)   **Total time:** 25 minutes (without sponge cake)

INGREDIENTS:

- **2 cups fresh strawberries,** hulled and sliced
- **2 tbsp granulated sugar**
- **1 cup heavy whipping cream**
- **2 tbsp powdered sugar**
- **1 tsp vanilla extract**
- **1 store-bought sponge cake or pound cake,** cut into cubes
- **2 tbsp honey** (optional, for drizzling)
- **Fresh mint leaves** (optional, for garnish)

Optional Homemade Sponge Cake (if using instead of store-bought):

- **1/2 cup all-purpose flour**
- **1/2 tsp baking powder**
- **1/4 tsp salt**
- **1/4 cup unsalted butter,** softened
- **1/4 cup granulated sugar**
- **2 large eggs**
- **1 tsp vanilla extract**

INSTRUCTIONS:

1. Prepare the strawberries:

- In a medium bowl, combine the sliced strawberries with the granulated sugar. Toss to coat evenly and let them sit for about 10 minutes to release their juices.

2. Make whipped cream:

- In a separate bowl, beat the heavy cream, powdered sugar, and vanilla extract with a hand mixer or stand mixer until soft peaks form. Be careful not to over-whip.

3. Make the sponge cake (if homemade):

- Preheat your oven to 350°F (175°C).

- In a medium bowl, whisk together the flour, baking powder, and salt.

- In a separate large bowl, beat together the softened butter and sugar until light and fluffy. Add the eggs, one at a time, mixing well after each addition. Stir in the vanilla extract.

- Gradually add the dry ingredients to the wet mixture, stirring until combined.

- Pour the batter into a greased 8-inch square baking dish and bake for 10-12 minutes or until a toothpick

inserted into the center comes out clean.

- Allow the cake to cool slightly before cutting it into small cubes.

4. Assemble the trifles:

- In individual serving glasses or bowls, layer the components starting with a spoonful of cake cubes, followed by a spoonful of sweetened strawberries, and then a generous dollop of whipped cream.

- Repeat the layers until the glasses are filled.

- Drizzle with honey (optional) and garnish with a few mint leaves for a fresh touch.

5. Serve and enjoy:

- Serve immediately or refrigerate for up to 2 hours before serving. This dish is best enjoyed chilled.

VARIATIONS & ADAPTATIONS:

- **Berries:** Use a combination of fresh berries, such as raspberries, blueberries, or blackberries, for a mixed berry shortcake trifle.

- **Cake options:** If you prefer, you can use angel food cake, ladyfingers, or even biscuit pieces for different textures.

- **Dairy-free version:** Substitute coconut cream for the whipped cream and use a dairy-free cake if needed.

NUTRITIONAL INFORMATION (PER SERVING, USING HOMEMADE SPONGE CAKE):

Calories: ....270kcal   Protein: ....3g   Fiber: 2g
Carbohydrates: ...36g   Fat: ....14g   Sugar: 21g

COCONUT RICE PUDDING

Yield: 4 servings   **Prep time:** 5 minutes   **Cook time:** 30 minutes   **Total time:** 35 minutes

INGREDIENTS:
- **1 cup Arborio rice (or short-grain rice)**
- **2 cups coconut milk** (full-fat, canned; or homemade coconut milk)
- **1 cup whole milk**
- **1/4 cup granulated sugar**
- **1/4 tsp salt**
- **1 tsp vanilla extract**
- **1/2 tsp ground cinnamon** (optional)
- **1/4 tsp ground nutmeg** (optional)
- **Fresh fruit** (such as berries or mango) **for topping (optional)**
- **Toasted coconut flakes for garnish** (optional)

INSTRUCTIONS:

1. Cook the rice:
- In a medium saucepan, combine the Arborio rice, coconut milk, and whole milk. Stir gently and bring the mixture to a simmer over medium heat.
- Once it reaches a simmer, reduce the heat to low and cook, uncovered, for about 25-30 minutes. Stir occasionally to prevent the rice from sticking to the bottom of the pot.
- The rice should absorb the liquid and become creamy as it cooks.

2. Add sweetness and flavor:
- Once the rice has cooked and the mixture is thickened, stir in the granulated sugar, salt, vanilla extract, cinnamon, and nutmeg (if using). Continue to cook for an additional 2-3 minutes, stirring constantly to ensure the sugar dissolves fully and the flavors meld together.

3. Check the consistency:
- If you prefer a thicker rice pudding, continue cooking until it reaches your desired consistency. If it gets too thick, you can add a bit more milk (regular or coconut) to loosen it up.
- Taste and adjust the sweetness or spices if necessary.

4. Serve and garnish:
- Spoon the warm coconut rice pudding into serving bowls or cups.
- Top with fresh fruit, such as berries or slices of mango, for a burst of flavor.
- Optionally, sprinkle with toasted coconut flakes for added texture and flavor.

5. Serve warm or chilled:
- Serve immediately for a warm, comforting dessert or refrigerate for 1-2 hours for a chilled, refreshing treat.

VARIATIONS & ADAPTATIONS:
- **Vegan/ Dairy-free:** Use only coconut milk and a plant-based milk (like almond or oat milk), and opt for maple syrup instead of granulated sugar.
- **Flavor variations:** Add a splash of almond extract or a dash of orange zest for a unique twist. You could also include a tablespoon of cocoa powder to make chocolate coconut rice pudding.
- **Tropical twist:** Top with toasted pineapple, shredded coconut, or macadamia nuts for a tropical-inspired dessert.
- **Spices:** Try adding cardamom or cloves for a spiced variation.

NUTRITIONAL INFORMATION (PER SERVING):

Calories: ....230kcal   Protein: ....4g   Fiber: 1g
Carbohydrates: ...35g   Fat: ....8g   Sugar: 18g

APPLE CRISP IN A MUG

Yield: 1 serving   **Prep time:** 5 minutes   **Cook time:** 2-3 minutes   **Total time:** 7 minutes

INGREDIENTS:
- 1 **medium apple**
- 1 **tbsp butter** (local, or a dairy-free substitute like coconut oil)
- 1 **tbsp brown sugar**
- **1/4 tsp ground cinnamon (optional)**
- **Pinch of salt**
- **2 tbsp rolled oats**
- **1 tbsp all-purpose flour**
- **1 tbsp chopped nuts**
- **Vanilla ice cream or whipped cream for topping**

INSTRUCTIONS:

1. Prepare the apple:
- Peel, core, and chop the apple into small bite-sized pieces. You can leave the skin on for added texture and fiber.

2. Cook the apple:
- In a microwave-safe mug, add the chopped apple, butter, brown sugar (or maple syrup), cinnamon, and a pinch of salt. Stir to combine.
- Microwave the mug on high for about 1-2 minutes, or until the apple is tender and begins to soften. Stir halfway through to ensure even cooking.

3. Make the crisp topping:
- In a small bowl, mix together the oats, flour, and chopped nuts (if using).
- Sprinkle the oat mixture over the cooked apple in the mug. Press down gently to compact the topping.

4. Cook the crisp:
- Microwave the mug for an additional 30-60 seconds, or until the topping is golden and slightly crisped.

5. Serve:
- Allow the apple crisp to cool slightly, then top with a scoop of vanilla ice cream or a dollop of whipped cream for extra indulgence, if desired.

VARIATIONS & ADAPTATIONS:
- **Gluten-free:** Use a gluten-free flour blend or omit the flour entirely for a lighter crisp topping.
- **Vegan:** Use a plant-based butter substitute like coconut oil, and top with dairy-free whipped cream or coconut milk-based ice cream.
- **Spiced apple crisp:** Add a pinch of ground ginger or nutmeg for a deeper, more complex flavor.
- **Fruit variations:** Swap apples for other seasonal fruits like pears, peaches, or berries for a different twist.
- **Toppings:** Add shredded coconut or chia seeds for added texture, or drizzle with honey for more sweetness.

NUTRITIONAL INFORMATION (PER SERVING):

Calories: 280kcal	Protein: 2g	Fiber: 4g
Carbohydrates: ...37g	Fat: 14g	Sugar: 20g

EASY TIRAMISU

Yield: 6 servings   **Prep time:** 20 minutes   **Chilling time:** 4 hours   **Total time:** 4 hours 20 minutes

INGREDIENTS:

- **1 cup heavy cream**
- **8 oz mascarpone cheese**
- **1/2 cup powdered sugar**
- **1 tsp vanilla extract**
- **1 cup strong brewed coffee,** cooled
- **2 tbsp coffee liqueur (optional)**
- **24 ladyfinger cookies**
- **Unsweetened cocoa powder for dusting**
- **Dark chocolate shavings (optional, for garnish)**

INSTRUCTIONS:

1. Prepare the whipped cream:
- In a large mixing bowl, use an electric mixer to beat the heavy cream until stiff peaks form. This will take about 3-5 minutes. Set aside.

2. Mix the mascarpone cream:
- In a separate bowl, whisk together the mascarpone cheese, powdered sugar, and vanilla extract until smooth and creamy. You may use a hand mixer or whisk for this.

3. Fold the whipped cream into the mascarpone:
- Gently fold the whipped cream into the mascarpone mixture, being careful not to deflate the whipped cream. The result should be a smooth, fluffy cream mixture.

4. Prepare the coffee mixture:
- In a shallow dish, combine the cooled coffee and coffee liqueur (if using). Stir to combine. This will be used to soak the ladyfingers.

5. Assemble the tiramisu:
- Dip each ladyfinger briefly into the coffee mixture, making sure not to soak them too long as they can become soggy. Arrange a layer of dipped ladyfingers at the bottom of a 9x9-inch dish or individual serving glasses.
- Spread a layer of the mascarpone mixture over the ladyfingers, smoothing it out evenly.

- Repeat the layers with the remaining ladyfingers and mascarpone cream, ending with a final layer of mascarpone cream.

6. Chill:
- Cover the tiramisu and refrigerate for at least 4 hours, preferably overnight, to allow the flavors to meld and the dessert to set properly.

7. Serve:
- Just before serving, dust the top of the tiramisu with unsweetened cocoa powder. Optionally, garnish with dark chocolate shavings for a little extra flair.

VARIATIONS & ADAPTATIONS:

- **Gluten-Free:** Use gluten-free ladyfingers or an alternative like gluten-free sponge cake.
- **Dairy-Free:** Substitute the mascarpone with a non-dairy cream cheese and use coconut cream instead of heavy cream.
- **Flavor variations:** Add a splash of vanilla extract to the coffee mixture or infuse the whipped cream with orange zest for a citrus twist. You can also substitute coffee liqueur with a flavored liqueur like amaretto for a different flavor profile.
- **Fruit Tiramisu:** For a seasonal twist, layer in fresh berries such as strawberries or raspberries between the ladyfingers and mascarpone mixture. The sweetness of the fruit complements the creamy richness of the tiramisu.

NUTRITIONAL INFORMATION (PER SERVING):

Calories: ....350kcal   Protein: ....4g   Fiber: 1g
Carbohydrates: ...35g   Fat: ....24g   Sugar: 26g

CHAPTER 10: REFRESHING DRINKS

PRACTICAL TIPS

1. Balance Flavors:

- **Sweetness vs. Tartness:** Always strike a balance between sweet and sour elements in your drinks. For example, if you're making a lemonade or a fruit punch, adjust the sweetness with natural sweeteners like honey, agave, or stevia, but ensure the tartness from citrus or berries shines through for depth of flavor.

- **Herbal and Spice Notes:** Adding herbs like mint, basil, or rosemary can elevate your drink's flavor profile. Fresh herbs can offer an aromatic quality, while spices like ginger, cinnamon, or cardamom can add warmth and complexity.

2. Use Seasonal Ingredients:

- Take advantage of the freshness and peak flavors of seasonal fruits and herbs. Summer berries, peaches, watermelon, and citrus fruits add vibrancy and natural sweetness to your drinks. Similarly, fresh herbs such as mint, basil, and lavender can enhance your beverages.

- Using in-season produce not only ensures that your drinks taste amazing, but it also supports local farmers and reduces the environmental impact of out-of-season imports.

3. Consider the Base Liquid:

- The base of your drink sets the tone for its flavor. Water, coconut water, tea, and fruit juice are all excellent choices depending on the desired outcome.

- Water Infusions (e.g., cucumber-mint, strawberry-basil) are an excellent choice for those looking for light, hydrating beverages without added sugar.

- Herbal Teas like chamomile or green tea can add an additional layer of flavor and health benefits. Green tea is rich in antioxidants, while chamomile can have a calming effect.

- Fruit Juices (e.g., orange, cranberry, pineapple) provide a natural sweetness and complexity, but ensure you're using freshly squeezed juice or 100% pure juice without added sugars for a healthier option.

4. Texture Matters:

- **Ice Cubes:** For iced drinks, crushed ice creates a smoother texture, while large ice cubes melt slower, keeping your drink from getting watered down too quickly.

- **Frozen Fruit Ice Cubes:** Freeze fruits like berries, lime wedges, or mint leaves in ice cubes for a colorful and flavorful addition to your drinks. These can serve as both an aesthetic touch and a natural flavor infusion.

- **Smoothie-like Beverages:** For creamy beverages like smoothies, use frozen fruits like bananas, mangoes, or berries to achieve a thick, smooth consistency without needing ice that might dilute the flavor.

5. Presentation is Key:

- **Glassware:** Choose glassware that suits the drink. A tall, clear glass showcases layered beverages like iced tea or fruit punch, while mason jars or stemless glasses are perfect for casual outdoor gatherings.

- **Garnishes:** A garnish can elevate the drink's appearance and flavor. For example, fresh herbs, citrus slices, or edible flowers can add an appealing visual element to your drink. Even a simple lime wedge or sprig of mint can enhance the look and aroma.

- **Straws and Stirring:** Use colorful straws for a festive touch or opt for reusable straws for an eco-friendly option. Stirring can also be a great way to mix flavors evenly in layered drinks like iced coffee or sangria.

6. Customize for Health Benefits:

- Refreshing drinks can also double as wellness boosters. Infuse your beverages with ingredients that support digestion, hydration, and immunity. For instance, ginger can help with digestion, and cucumber is incredibly hydrating.

- Add adaptogens like ashwagandha or holy basil to your beverages for stress relief or immune support.

- If you're making mocktails or non-alcoholic beverages, consider incorporating superfoods like chia seeds or spirulina for an extra health boost.

7. Adjust Sweetness Levels:

- Experiment with natural sweeteners such as honey, agave, or maple syrup. These can often enhance flavors better than refined sugars while keeping the drink natural and refreshing.

- If you prefer a sugar-free alternative, try using stevia or monk fruit as a sweetener. Additionally, using naturally sweet fruits like pineapple or berries can reduce the need for added sugars altogether.

8. Chill and Serve:

- **Chilling Drinks:** If you're making a cold beverage, chill your ingredients ahead of time or let the drink cool completely in the fridge before serving. For drinks like lemonade or iced teas, refrigerating the syrup or infusions before mixing can help maintain a crisp and refreshing temperature.

- ◆ **Serving Immediately:** Serve refreshing beverages as soon as they're made to preserve the flavors and texture. Beverages like smoothies are best enjoyed fresh as they can separate and lose their smooth texture if left standing too long.

9. Experiment with Flavor Combinations:

- ◆ Don't be afraid to experiment with different fruits, herbs, and spices to create unique flavor profiles. For example, combining pineapple with mint, or watermelon with a hint of lime, creates a refreshing twist. You can also explore the contrasts of tart and sweet by pairing citrus with berries or herbs like basil with strawberries.

10. Use Natural Garnishes and Infusions:

- ◆ For a more sophisticated touch, infuse your water, tea, or sparkling beverages with fruits, herbs, or even spices. Infusing water with cucumber and mint or berries and rosemary can add refreshing flavors over time without the need for additional sugar or artificial flavors.

- ◆ Herbal infusions are also perfect for creating flavorful syrups or sweeteners. Lavender, chamomile, and rosemary can add unique and aromatic qualities to any drink.

CLASSIC LEMONADE WITH A TWIST

Yield: 4 servings   **Prep time:** 10 minutes   **Total time:** 10 minutes

INGREDIENTS:

For the classic lemonade:

- **4 large lemons ,** juiced
- **1/2 cup granulated sugar** (or honey, maple syrup for a healthier option)
- **4 cups cold water (filtered if possible)**
- **Ice cubes** (as needed)

For the twist (Choose one or more options below):

- **1/4 cup fresh mint leaves,** muddled
- **1/2 cup fresh strawberries,** blended
- **1 tablespoon grated ginger (for a spicy kick)**
- **1/4 cup cucumber slices, muddled**
- **2 tablespoons lavender syrup** (for a floral note)
- **1/2 cup fresh basil leaves,** muddled

INSTRUCTIONS:

Prepare the base lemonade:

- Start by juicing the lemons. You should get about 1/2 cup of lemon juice from the 4 lemons.
- In a small saucepan, combine 1 cup of water with the sugar (or your choice of sweetener). Heat over medium heat, stirring occasionally, until the sugar is fully dissolved. Remove from heat and let it cool to room temperature.

Mix the lemonade:

- In a large pitcher, combine the freshly squeezed lemon juice, sugar syrup (cooled), and the remaining 3 cups of cold water. Stir well until everything is evenly mixed.

Add the twist:

- Choose one or more of the twists listed above to customize your lemonade:

  ◊ **Mint lemonade:** Muddle fresh mint leaves at the bottom of your pitcher before adding the lemonade mix.

  ◊ **Strawberry lemonade:** Blend fresh strawberries until smooth and stir them into the lemonade for a sweet, fruity flavor.

  ◊ **Ginger lemonade:** Grate fresh ginger and stir it into the lemonade for a zesty, spicy note.

  ◊ **Cucumber lemonade:** Muddle cucumber slices and mix them into the lemonade for a refreshing and cool twist.

  ◊ **Lavender lemonade:** Stir in lavender syrup for a calming floral flavor.

  ◊ **Basil lemonade:** Muddle basil leaves for a fresh, aromatic taste.

Serve:

- Add ice cubes to your lemonade and serve chilled. Garnish with extra mint, lemon slices, or berries for an extra touch of flavor and decoration.

VARIATIONS/ADAPTATIONS:

- **Alcoholic twist:** Add a splash of gin or vodka for an adult version of the lemonade.
- **Sweetener options:** Use honey, agave, or stevia for a natural sweetener alternative.
- **Fruit variations:** Try using other fruits like raspberries, blackberries, or blueberries to switch up the flavor.

NUTRITIONAL INFORMATION (PER SERVING, ASSUMING 4 SERVINGS TOTAL):

Calories: ....60 kcal (with sugar)   Sugars: ....15g   Protein: 0g
Carbohydrates: ...16g   Fat: ....0g   Sodium: 10mg

SPARKLING BERRY SANGRIA (NON-ALCOHOLIC)

Yield: 6 servings   **Prep time:** 10 minutes   **Total time:** 10 minutes

INGREDIENTS:

For the Sangria:
- **2 cups mixed fresh berries** (local and seasonal if possible, such as strawberries, blueberries, raspberries, or blackberries)
- **1 medium orange, thinly sliced**
- **1 lemon,** thinly sliced
- **1 green apple,** thinly sliced (seasonal)
- **3 cups sparkling water** (or sparkling apple cider for added sweetness)
- **2 tablespoons honey or agave syrup** (adjust based on your sweetness preference)
- **1/4 cup pomegranate juice** (for extra depth of flavor)
- **1/4 cup lemon juice** (freshly squeezed)

For garnish (optional):
- **Extra fresh berries** (such as blueberries or raspberries)
- **Fresh mint leaves**
- **Orange slices or lemon wedges**

INSTRUCTIONS:

Prepare the fruit:
- Wash and slice the berries, orange, lemon, and apple. Make sure to remove any seeds from the lemon and orange slices.

Mix the sangria:
- In a large pitcher, combine the mixed berries, orange slices, lemon slices, and apple slices. Gently muddle the fruit with a muddler or the back of a spoon to release some of the juices, enhancing the flavor of the sangria.

Add liquids:
- Pour in the sparkling water (or sparkling apple cider if you prefer a sweeter taste) and pomegranate juice. Add the freshly squeezed lemon juice and stir everything together.

Sweeten to taste:
- Stir in honey or agave syrup to sweeten the sangria, adjusting based on your preference. If you like it sweeter, add more honey or syrup. If you prefer it tangier, add more lemon juice.

Chill:
- Place the sangria in the refrigerator to chill for at least 30 minutes. This allows the flavors to meld together and ensures a refreshing drink.

Serve:
- When ready to serve, pour the sangria into glasses filled with ice. Garnish with extra fresh berries, mint leaves, and additional orange slices or lemon wedges for a festive touch.

VARIATIONS/ADAPTATIONS:

- **Berry varieties:** Feel free to mix and match different berries according to the season. Blackberries, cranberries, and even cherries work beautifully in this sangria.
- **Fruit additions:** Add seasonal fruits like peaches, pineapple, or grapes to vary the flavors.
- **Herbal twist:** Add a sprig of rosemary or basil to the sangria for an herbaceous note.
- **Sweetness level:** For a healthier option, you can substitute honey or agave syrup with stevia or a natural sweetener of your choice.

NUTRITIONAL INFORMATION (PER SERVING, ASSUMING 6 SERVINGS TOTAL):

Calories: ....45 kcal   Sugars: ....10g   Protein: 0g
Carbohydrates: ...11g   Fat: ....0g   Sodium: 10mg

Adjusting sweetness: You can also use fruit juices like apple, orange, or even cranberry juice to replace the pomegranate juice or add more sweetness.

MINT ICED GREEN TEA

Yield: 4 servings   **Prep time:** 5 minutes   **Total time:** 15 minutes
(plus chilling time)

INGREDIENTS:

For the tea:

- **4 cups water**
- **4 green tea bags** (or 4 teaspoons loose-leaf green tea)
- **10 fresh mint leaves** (local and seasonal, if available)

- **1-2 tablespoons honey or agave syrup** (adjust based on sweetness preference)
- **1 lemon** (optional, for added citrus flavor)

For garnish:

- **Extra fresh mint leaves**
- **Lemon slices** (optional)
- **Ice cubes**

INSTRUCTIONS:

Boil the water:

- Begin by bringing 4 cups of water to a boil in a kettle or saucepan. Once the water reaches a boil, remove it from the heat.

Brew the tea:

- Add the green tea bags or loose-leaf green tea (in a tea infuser) to the hot water. Stir in the fresh mint leaves. Allow the tea to steep for about 3-5 minutes, depending on how strong you like your tea. For a milder flavor, steep for 3 minutes; for a stronger brew, let it steep for 5 minutes.

Sweeten the tea:

- While the tea is still warm, stir in 1-2 tablespoons of honey or agave syrup to sweeten it. Adjust the sweetness based on your preference. If you like a more natural flavor, try adding a bit more mint or a squeeze of fresh lemon juice instead.

Cool the tea:

- Once the tea has steeped and is sweetened to your liking, remove the tea bags or tea infuser. Allow the tea to cool for a few minutes at room temperature, then place the tea in the refrigerator to chill for at least 1 hour. If you're in a hurry, you can speed up the process by placing it in the freezer for 15-20 minutes (but be careful not to let it freeze).

Serve:

- Once chilled, pour the mint iced green tea into glasses filled with ice cubes. Garnish with additional fresh mint leaves and lemon slices for a refreshing touch.

Enjoy:

- Serve immediately and enjoy a cool, revitalizing drink on a warm evening or during a busy day.

VARIATIONS/ADAPTATIONS:

- **Citrus twist:** Add slices of orange, lime, or a few drops of lemon juice to the tea for a citrusy burst.

- **Fruit infusion:** For a fruitier twist, try adding sliced strawberries, peaches, or cucumber for a more refreshing, lightly flavored iced tea.

- **Herb variations:** If you're craving different herbal notes, substitute the mint with other herbs like basil or lemon balm for a unique twist on iced tea.

- **Green tea alternatives:** If you don't have green tea or want to try a different variety, swap it for white tea, oolong tea, or even black tea for a different flavor profile.

NUTRITIONAL INFORMATION (PER SERVING, ASSUMING 4 SERVINGS TOTAL):

Calories: ....20 kcal   Sugars: ....5g   Protein: 0g
Carbohydrates: ...5g   Fat: ....0g   Sodium: 0mg

WARM SPICED APPLE CIDER

Yield: 4 servings   **Prep time:** 5 minutes   **Cook time:** 10 minutes   **Total time:** 15 minutes

INGREDIENTS:
For the cider:
- **4 cups fresh apple cider** (preferably from a local farmer's market or seasonal supply)
- **1 cinnamon stick**
- **4 whole cloves**
- **2-3 whole star anise** (optional, for extra flavor)

- **1-2 tablespoons maple syrup or honey** (optional, depending on sweetness preference)
- **1 orange, thinly sliced**
- **1 tablespoon fresh ginger, sliced thinly**

For garnish:
- **Orange slices** (optional)
- **Additional cinnamon sticks** (optional)

INSTRUCTIONS:
Combine the ingredients:
- In a medium-sized saucepan, pour in the 4 cups of fresh apple cider. Add the cinnamon stick, whole cloves, star anise (if using), and the sliced ginger (optional). Stir in the maple syrup or honey, depending on your sweetness preference.

Simmer the cider:
- Place the saucepan over medium heat. Allow the cider to come to a simmer, stirring occasionally. Once it begins to simmer, lower the heat and let it simmer for 8-10 minutes to allow the spices and flavors to infuse into the cider. If you want a stronger spice flavor, let it simmer for a little longer, but make sure it doesn't boil over.

Add the orange:
- Add the thinly sliced orange to the simmering cider. Continue to simmer for another 2-3 minutes to let the citrus flavor meld with the cider. The orange will add a bright, zesty note to balance the spices.

Strain and serve:
- After the cider has simmered, remove it from the heat. Strain the cider to remove the spices, and pour it into mugs. If desired, garnish with additional orange slices and a cinnamon stick for extra flavor and presentation.

Enjoy:
- Serve immediately while hot for a cozy, comforting drink perfect for chilly nights or a busy evening.

VARIATIONS/ADAPTATIONS:
- **Spicy kick:** Add a pinch of cayenne pepper or a few crushed black peppercorns to the cider for an extra warm, spicy kick.

- **Non-sweetened version:** Skip the maple syrup or honey if you prefer a less sweet beverage. The natural sweetness of the apple cider should still shine through.

- **Citrus twist:** Experiment by adding other citrus fruits like lemon or even a few pieces of fresh pineapple for a tropical twist.

- **Alcoholic version:** For an adult twist, add a shot of rum or bourbon after the cider has been heated, just before serving.

NUTRITIONAL INFORMATION (PER SERVING):

Calories: ....130kcal   Sugars: ....28g   Fat: ....0g   Sodium: 10mg
Carbohydrates: ...32g   (if sweetened with maple syrup or honey)   Protein: ....0g   Fiber: 1g

FRESH MANGO SMOOTHIE

Yield: 2 servings **Prep time:** 5 minutes **Cook time:** 0 minutes **Total time:** 5 minutes

INGREDIENTS:

For the smoothie:
- **2 ripe mangoes** (local and seasonal if available)
- **1/2 cup Greek yogurt** (or non-dairy yogurt for a dairy-free version)
- **1/2 cup coconut milk** (or any milk of choice)
- **1 tablespoon honey or maple syrup** (optional, depending on sweetness preference)
- **1/2 teaspoon vanilla extract** (optional, for extra flavor)
- **Ice cubes** (optional, for a thicker and colder texture)

For garnish:
- **Fresh mint leaves** (optional, for garnish)
- **A sprinkle of chia seeds** (optional, for extra texture and nutrition)

INSTRUCTIONS:

Prepare the mangoes:
- Peel the mangoes and remove the pit. Cut the flesh into small chunks. If using frozen mangoes, you can skip this step.

Blend the ingredients:
- In a blender, add the mango chunks, Greek yogurt, coconut milk, honey (or maple syrup), and vanilla extract. Add ice cubes if you prefer a thicker, colder smoothie.

Blend until smooth:
- Blend on high for 30 seconds to 1 minute, or until the mixture is completely smooth. If the smoothie is too thick, you can add a bit more coconut milk or water to achieve your desired consistency.

Taste and adjust:
- Taste the smoothie and adjust the sweetness if needed by adding more honey or maple syrup.

Serve:
- Pour the smoothie into glasses and garnish with fresh mint leaves and a sprinkle of chia seeds for extra texture and nutrition (optional).

Enjoy:
- Serve immediately and enjoy this refreshing, tropical treat!

VARIATIONS/ADAPTATIONS:

- **Tropical twist:** Add a handful of pineapple or a few slices of banana for extra tropical flavors.

- **Green smoothie:** Add a handful of spinach or kale for a green smoothie boost without compromising the taste of the mango.

- **Protein boost:** Add a scoop of protein powder (whey, plant-based, or collagen) for added protein, making this smoothie a more filling meal.

- **Dairy-free version:** Use non-dairy yogurt, such as almond, coconut, or cashew yogurt, and substitute coconut milk or almond milk for a dairy-free option.

NUTRITIONAL INFORMATION (PER SERVING):

Calories: 180kcal
Carbohydrates: ...40g

Sugars: ....35g (natural sugars from mangoes and yogurt)

Fat: 6g
Protein: 4g

Sodium: 30mg
Fiber: 3g

COLD BREW COFFEE WITH VANILLA CREAM

Yield: 2 servings   **Prep time:** 5 minutes   **Steeping time:** 12-24 hours (for cold brew)   **Total time:** 12-24 hours (mostly inactive)

INGREDIENTS:
For the cold brew coffee:
- **1 cup coarsely ground coffee** (local roasts or freshly ground if possible)
- **4 cups cold or room-temperature water**

For the vanilla cream:
- **1/2 cup heavy cream** (or coconut cream for dairy-free option)
- **1 tablespoon powdered sugar** (or maple syrup for a natural sweetener)
- **1 teaspoon vanilla extract** (preferably organic or homemade)

Optional garnish:
- **Ice cubes**
- **Ground cinnamon or nutmeg** (for a seasonal touch)
- **Whipped cream** (optional, for extra indulgence)

INSTRUCTIONS:
Prepare the cold brew coffee:
- In a large jar or pitcher, combine the coarsely ground coffee with the cold or room-temperature water.
- Stir well to ensure the coffee grounds are fully saturated.
- Cover the jar or pitcher and let it steep in the refrigerator for 12-24 hours. The longer the steeping time, the stronger the flavor.

Strain the coffee:
- After the steeping time, strain the coffee through a fine mesh strainer, cheesecloth, or a dedicated cold brew coffee filter to remove the coffee grounds. Transfer the cold brew to a clean jar or pitcher for storage.

Make the vanilla cream:
- In a small mixing bowl, combine the heavy cream, powdered sugar (or maple syrup), and vanilla extract.
- Using a hand mixer or whisk, beat the cream until it reaches soft peaks. Be careful not to overwhip, as it could turn into butter.
- Alternatively, you can use a blender to mix the ingredients and create a more velvety texture.

Assemble the drink:
- Fill two glasses with ice cubes if desired.
- Pour the cold brew coffee into each glass, filling about two-thirds of the way.
- Gently spoon a dollop of the vanilla cream on top of each drink. You can swirl it in for a marbled effect or leave it floating on top for a layered look.

Garnish and serve:
- Optionally, garnish with a sprinkle of ground cinnamon or nutmeg for a warm, seasonal touch.
- Serve immediately and enjoy your refreshing, indulgent cold brew coffee with vanilla cream!

VARIATIONS/ADAPTATIONS:
- **Dairy-Free Version:** Use coconut cream or almond cream instead of heavy cream to make it dairy-free. Maple syrup can also be used as a sweetener for a more natural flavor.
- **Spiced Cold Brew:** Add a cinnamon stick or a few cardamom pods to the cold brew steeping process for extra spice. This creates a more complex, spiced flavor perfect for cooler months.
- **Iced Mocha:** For a chocolatey twist, add a tablespoon of unsweetened cocoa powder or chocolate syrup to the cold brew before serving. Top with whipped cream for an indulgent treat.
- **Sweetener Options:** You can use a variety of natural sweeteners like agave nectar, honey, or stevia, depending on your dietary preferences.

NUTRITIONAL INFORMATION (PER SERVING):

Calories: ....100kcal (using heavy cream and powdered sugar)	Carbohydrates: 8g Sugars: ....7g (from cream and sweetener)	Fat: ....8g Protein: ....1g Sodium: ....10mg Fiber: 0g

PINEAPPLE COCONUT MOCKTAIL

Yield: 2 servings   **Prep time:** 5 minutes   **Total time:** 5 minutes

This Pineapple Coconut Mocktail is a refreshing, tropical drink that's perfect for busy nights when you want something quick, easy, and delicious. With its sweet and tangy pineapple flavor paired with smooth coconut, it's a great non-alcoholic option that evokes a cozy, beachy vibe.

INGREDIENTS:
For the mocktail:
- **1 cup fresh pineapple juice** (preferably freshly squeezed or cold-pressed, seasonal if available)
- **1/2 cup coconut milk** (full-fat or light depending on your preference)
- **1 tablespoon lime juice** (freshly squeezed, for a burst of tang)
- **1 teaspoon honey or maple syrup** (optional, depending on sweetness preference)
- **1/2 teaspoon vanilla extract** (for depth of flavor)
- **Crushed ice (or ice cubes)**

For garnish (optional):
- **Pineapple wedges or slices**
- **Mint leaves**
- **Toasted coconut flakes**

INSTRUCTIONS:
Prepare the ingredients:
- If you're using fresh pineapple, blend or juice it to make fresh pineapple juice. If using store-bought juice, ensure it's 100% pure pineapple juice with no added sugar.
- Squeeze fresh lime juice into a small bowl, ensuring no seeds make their way into the drink.

Mix the mocktail:
- In a shaker or large mixing cup, combine the pineapple juice, coconut milk, lime juice, honey or maple syrup (if using), and vanilla extract.
- Stir or shake the ingredients together until well combined.

Serve:
- Fill two glasses with crushed ice or regular ice cubes.
- Pour the mocktail mixture over the ice, dividing it evenly between the two glasses.

Garnish and enjoy:
- Garnish each glass with a pineapple wedge or slice and a sprig of fresh mint for a touch of freshness.
- Optionally, sprinkle some toasted coconut flakes on top to add a delightful crunch and an extra hint of coconut flavor.

Serve immediately:
- Enjoy this tropical mocktail right away for a refreshing and indulgent drink that's perfect for warm evenings or when you just need to unwind.

VARIATIONS/ADAPTATIONS:
- **Dairy-Free Option:** For a completely dairy-free drink, use light coconut milk or coconut cream instead of regular coconut milk. You can also use almond milk or oat milk for a different twist.
- **Add More Tropical Flavors:** You can add other tropical fruit juices such as mango or passion fruit for a more complex flavor. Simply replace a portion of the pineapple juice with the juice of your choice.
- **Sparkling Version:** For a fizzy twist, top the mocktail with sparkling water or club soda. This will give it a fun effervescence that's perfect for parties or celebrations.
- **Sweetener Options:** If you prefer a natural sweetener, try using agave syrup, stevia, or a few drops of monk fruit extract instead of honey or maple syrup. You can adjust the sweetness to your taste.

NUTRITIONAL INFORMATION (PER SERVING):

Calories: ....100-120 kcal (depending on the amount of sweetener used)

Carbohydrates: ...22g
Sugars: ....20g (natural sugars from pineapple)

Fat: ....5g (from coconut milk)
Protein: 1g

Sodium: 20mg
Fiber: 1g

STRAWBERRY BASIL INFUSED WATER

Yield: 4 servings   **Prep time:** 5 minutes   **Total time:** 1-2 hours (to allow flavors to infuse)

A refreshing and aromatic beverage, this Strawberry Basil Infused Water is perfect for busy nights when you want a quick and easy drink to stay hydrated without any added sugars or artificial flavors. The combination of fresh strawberries and fragrant basil leaves provides a natural, flavorful twist to simple water.

INGREDIENTS:
For the infused water:
- **1 cup fresh strawberries** (preferably local and in season)
- **4-5 fresh basil leaves** (locally sourced if available)
- **4 cups cold water** (filtered or tap water)
- **1-2 teaspoons honey or agave syrup** (optional, depending on sweetness preference)
- **Ice cubes** (optional, for serving)

INSTRUCTIONS:
Prepare the strawberries:
- Rinse the strawberries thoroughly under cold water.
- Slice the strawberries into thin rounds or halves to help release their juices during infusion.

Prepare the basil:
- Gently rinse the fresh basil leaves.
- Lightly bruise the basil leaves by clapping them between your hands or gently rolling them with a rolling pin. This will help release the essential oils and flavors.

Combine ingredients:
- In a large pitcher, add the sliced strawberries and bruised basil leaves.
- Pour in the 4 cups of cold water, ensuring the fruit and herbs are submerged.

Infuse:
- Stir the mixture gently to combine and help the flavors start to mingle.
- Place the pitcher in the fridge and let the ingredients infuse for at least 1 hour, but ideally 2-3 hours for more intense flavor.

Serve:
- When ready to serve, fill glasses with ice cubes (optional), pour the infused water over the ice, and enjoy.

- Optional: Add a touch of honey or agave syrup if you prefer a sweeter drink.

Garnish and enjoy:
- For an extra touch of elegance, garnish the glasses with a few fresh basil leaves or strawberry slices before serving.

VARIATIONS/ADAPTATIONS:
- **Berry Infusion:** Add a handful of other berries like blueberries, raspberries, or blackberries to create a mixed berry-infused water. This variation works well in the summer when fresh berries are in season.
- **Citrus Twist:** Add slices of lemon, lime, or orange to the infusion for a zesty twist. This would pair nicely with the sweetness of the strawberries and the earthiness of the basil.
- **Herb Variations:** If you don't have basil, try swapping it for other fresh herbs like mint, rosemary, or thyme. Mint, in particular, would pair beautifully with strawberries.
- **Chilled Sparkling Water:** For a fizzy version, replace regular water with sparkling water to give the drink a refreshing effervescence.
- **Sugar-Free:** Skip the sweetener entirely for a naturally flavored, sugar-free infusion. The strawberries provide enough sweetness on their own when allowed to infuse.

NUTRITIONAL INFORMATION (PER SERVING):

Calories: ....5-10 kcal (depending on the amount of sweetener used)

Carbohydrates: ...2g
Sugars: ....2g (from strawberries)
Fat: 0g

Protein: 0g
Sodium: 0mg
Fiber: 0g

HOT CHOCOLATE WITH WHIPPED TOPPING

Yield: 2 servings   **Prep time:** 5 minutes   **Cook time:** 5 minutes

This Hot Chocolate with Whipped Topping is the perfect comforting beverage for cold evenings or busy nights when you need a quick, warming treat. Rich, creamy, and indulgent, it's a sweet way to unwind. You can prepare it in just a few minutes using simple ingredients, including locally sourced milk and seasonal chocolate.

INGREDIENTS:

For the hot chocolate:
- **2 cups whole milk**
- **2 tablespoons unsweetened cocoa powder**
- **2 tablespoons dark brown sugar** (or honey for a more natural sweetener)
- **1 teaspoon vanilla extract**
- **A pinch of salt**
- **1/4 cup semi-sweet chocolate chips** (or chopped dark chocolate for a richer flavor)

For the whipped topping:
- **1/2 cup heavy cream** (fresh, local if possible)
- **1 tablespoon powdered sugar**
- **1/2 teaspoon vanilla extract**

Optional toppings:
- **A sprinkle of cinnamon or nutmeg**
- **Mini marshmallows**
- **Shaved chocolate or chocolate shavings**

INSTRUCTIONS:

Prepare the whipped topping:
- In a medium bowl, combine the heavy cream, powdered sugar, and vanilla extract.
- Using a hand mixer or whisk, beat the cream until soft peaks form. Be careful not to overwhip it. Once done, set the whipped topping aside in the fridge to keep it cool while you prepare the hot chocolate.

Make the hot chocolate:
- In a medium saucepan, heat the milk over medium heat until it begins to steam. Do not let it boil.
- Add the cocoa powder, sugar, salt, and vanilla extract to the milk. Stir constantly with a whisk to ensure the cocoa powder dissolves completely.
- Once the cocoa mixture is smooth, add the chocolate chips (or chopped dark chocolate). Stir until the chocolate has fully melted into the milk and the mixture is rich and creamy.
- Taste and adjust sweetness, adding a little more sugar or honey if desired.

Serve the hot chocolate:
- Pour the hot chocolate into two mugs, leaving space for the whipped topping.
- Spoon a generous amount of whipped cream onto the top of each mug.

Garnish and enjoy:
- **Optional:** Sprinkle a dash of cinnamon or nutmeg on top, or add mini marshmallows and shaved chocolate for extra indulgence.
- Serve immediately while warm and enjoy!

VARIATIONS/ADAPTATIONS:

- **Spiced Hot Chocolate:** Add a pinch of cinnamon, nutmeg, or even chili powder to the hot chocolate for a spiced variation. This is especially cozy in the colder months and pairs wonderfully with the creamy whipped topping.
- **Vegan Version:** Substitute the whole milk with almond milk, oat milk, or any plant-based milk. Use coconut cream or a dairy-free whipped cream alternative for the topping.
- **Peppermint Twist:** Add 1/2 teaspoon of peppermint extract to the hot chocolate mixture for a minty flavor. Garnish with crushed peppermint candies for a festive touch.
- **Mexican Hot Chocolate:** Add a bit of ground cinnamon and a small pinch of chili powder to the cocoa mixture for a rich, warming, spiced flavor. This variation is popular for colder months and gives your drink a unique flair.

NUTRITIONAL INFORMATION (PER SERVING):

Calories: ....250 kcal (without optional toppings)	Carbohydrates: ...30g Sugars: ....25g Fat: 12g	Saturated Fat: .....7g Cholesterol:.........40mg Protein: 6g	Sodium: ....70mg Fiber: ....2g (from the cocoa powder)

Note: Nutritional values may vary depending on the specific ingredients used (e.g., sweetener type, milk choice).

ICED LAVENDER LATTE

Yield: 1 serving   **Prep time:** 5 minutes   **Cook time:** 5 minutes (for brewing coffee)

INGREDIENTS:

For the Lavender Syrup:
- **1/4 cup water**
- **1/4 cup granulated sugar** (or honey for a more natural sweetener)
- **1 tablespoon dried lavender buds**

For the Iced Latte:
- **1 shot of espresso** (or 1/2 cup strong brewed coffee)
- **1/2 cup milk** (whole milk or your choice of plant-based milk such as almond, oat, or soy)
- **1-2 tablespoons homemade lavender syrup** (adjust to your taste)
- **Ice cubes** (preferably crushed for a smoother texture)

INSTRUCTIONS:

Step 1: Prepare the Lavender Syrup
- In a small saucepan, combine the water, sugar (or honey), and dried lavender buds.
- Bring to a simmer over medium heat, stirring occasionally until the sugar is dissolved.
- Once the syrup begins to simmer, reduce the heat and allow it to steep for 3-4 minutes. Stir occasionally to ensure the lavender flavor infuses into the syrup.
- Remove from heat and let it cool. Strain the syrup to remove the lavender buds and store the syrup in a small bottle or jar. You can refrigerate any leftover syrup for up to 2 weeks.

Step 2: Brew the Espresso or Coffee
- Brew a shot of espresso using an espresso machine, or brew a strong cup of coffee using a French press or drip coffee maker. Aim for about 1/2 cup of strong coffee to mimic the intensity of espresso.

Step 3: Assemble the Iced Latte
- Fill a glass with ice cubes (crushed ice works best for a smoother consistency).
- Pour the brewed espresso (or strong coffee) over the ice.
- Add the milk of your choice to the glass. You can use whole milk, almond milk, oat milk, or soy milk—whichever you prefer for creaminess.
- Stir in 1-2 tablespoons of lavender syrup (adjust according to your sweetness preference).
- Stir well to combine and chill the ingredients together.

Step 4: Serve and Enjoy
- Optional: Garnish your iced lavender latte with a sprig of lavender or a few dried lavender buds for a decorative touch.
- Serve immediately and enjoy your refreshing and aromatic iced lavender latte.

VARIATIONS/ADAPTATIONS:
- **Vegan Version:** Use your choice of plant-based milk (almond, oat, soy, or coconut) for a dairy-free alternative.
- **Sugar-Free Version:** For a sugar-free option, substitute the granulated sugar with a sugar substitute such as stevia, monk fruit sweetener, or erythritol. You can also leave the syrup out completely and just brew a lightly flavored lavender tea to use as the base.
- **Flavored Latte:** You can customize the latte further by adding a dash of vanilla extract or cinnamon for extra flavor.
- **Cold Brew Option:** Instead of espresso or brewed coffee, use cold brew coffee for a smoother, less acidic flavor.

NUTRITIONAL INFORMATION (PER SERVING):

Calories: ....150 kcal (using whole milk and 2 tablespoons lavender syrup)	Carbohydrates: ...35g Sugars: ....30g (depending on syrup sweetness)	Fat: ....5g Saturated Fat: .....3g Cholesterol: 20mg	Protein: ....4g Sodium: ....50mg Fiber: 0g

(Nutritional values may vary depending on the specific ingredients used, such as the type of milk and sweetener.)

Made in United States
Orlando, FL
21 December 2024

56343138R00072